THE COMMON WIND

THE COMMON WIND

Afro-American Currents in the
Age of the Haitian Revolution

Julius S. Scott

Foreword by Marcus Rediker

VERSO
London • New York

This paperback edition first published by Verso 2020
First published by Verso 2018
© Julius S. Scott 2018, 2020
Foreword © Marcus Rediker 2018, 2020

3 5 7 9 10 8 6 4 2

Verso
UK: 6 Meard Street, London W1F 0EG
US: 20 Jay Street, Suite 1010, Brooklyn, NY 11201
versobooks.com

Verso is the imprint of New Left Books

ISBN-13: 978-1-78873-248-2
ISBN-13: 978-1-78873-249-9 (UK EBK)
ISBN-13: 978-1-78873-250-5 (US EBK)

British Library Cataloguing in Publication Data
A catalogue record for this book is available from the British Library

Library of Congress Cataloging-in-Publication Data
A catalog record for this book is available from the Library of Congress

Typeset in Minion Pro by MJ & N Gavan, Truro, Cornwall
Printed and bound by CPI Group (UK) Ltd, Croydon, CR0 4YY

To my parents and to the
memory of my grandparents

Contents

Foreword

Marcus Rediker

> TOUSSAINT, the most unhappy man of men!
> Whether the whistling Rustic tend his plough
> Within thy hearing, or thy head be now
> Pillowed in some deep dungeon's earless den;—
> O miserable Chieftain! where and when
> Wilt thou find patience? Yet die not; do thou
> Wear rather in thy bonds a cheerful brow:
> Though fallen thyself, never to rise again,
> Live, and take comfort. Thou hast left behind
> Powers that will work for thee; air, earth, and skies;
> There's not a breathing of the common wind
> That will forget thee; thou hast great allies;
> Thy friends are exultations, agonies,
> And love, and man's unconquerable mind.

This book takes its title from a sonnet William Wordsworth wrote in 1802: "To Toussaint L'Ouverture," the great leader of the Haitian Revolution, who would soon die of pneumonia as a prisoner of Napoleon in Fort de Joux in eastern France.

Julius S. Scott shows us the collective human power behind Wordsworth's words. He focuses on "the breathing of the common wind," asking who inhaled the history of Toussaint and the revolution and who whispered it all out again as subversive stories, to circulate with velocity and force around the Atlantic. Scott gives substance to Wordsworth's beautiful abstraction by showing "unconquerable minds" at work—a motley crew of sailors, runaway slaves, free people of color, maroons, deserted soldiers, market women, escaped convicts, and smugglers. These people, in motion, became the vectors through which news and experience circulated in, around, and through the Haitian Revolution. Scott gives us a breathtaking social and intellectual history of revolution from below.

It would not be exactly right to call *The Common Wind* an "underground classic." Its status as a classic is not in doubt, but the landed metaphor would be wrong: the book is about what happened, not underground, but rather *below decks*, at sea, and on the docks, on ships and in canoes, and on the waterfronts of rough-and-tumble port cities in the era of the Haitian Revolution. It would, however, be right to say that the book and its reputation parallel the world of sailors and other mobile workers who are its central subject: both have had a fugitive existence—hard to find and known about largely through word-of-mouth stories. For decades historians have spoken at conferences in hushed, admiring, conspiratorial tones about Scott's work—"have you heard …?" From its inception as a doctoral dissertation in 1986, through its endless citation by scholars in a variety of fields down to the present, *The Common Wind* has long occupied an unusual place in the world of scholarship.

I vividly recall the moment I first heard. Julius S. Scott's friend and mentor at Duke University, Peter Wood, had come in 1985 to Georgetown University, where I taught at the time, to give a lecture. Afterward, as we crossed "Red Square" and discussed questions that arose about his talk, Wood mentioned that he had a Ph.D. student who was studying the movement by sea of the ideas and news of the Haitian Revolution during and after the 1790s, the decade in which the Atlantic was in flames, from Port-au-Prince to Belfast to Paris and London.

My first words to Wood were, "how on earth can someone study *that*?" Bear in mind, I had recently completed a dissertation on eighteenth-century Atlantic sailors, so if anyone could have been expected to know how Scott did it, it might have been me. Even so, I was stunned by Wood's description of the project—and more than curious to learn more. Wood put us in touch, Scott and I began to correspond, and a year or so later, after its submission and defense, I read "The Common Wind." I was convinced then, and I am convinced now, that it is one of the most creative historical studies I have ever read.

Scott takes on an issue that long vexed slaveowners around the Atlantic—what one of them in 1791 called the "unknown mode of conveying intelligence amongst Negroes." Intelligence is precisely the right word, for the knowledge that circulated on "the common wind" was strategic in its applications, linking news of English abolitionism, Spanish reformism, and French revolutionism to local struggles across the Caribbean. Mobile people used webs of commerce and their own autonomous mobility to form subversive networks, of which the ruling classes of the day were keenly aware even if latter-day historians, until Scott, were not.

Scott thus creates a new way to see one of history's biggest themes, what Eric Hobsbawm famously called "the age of revolution." He shifts our view in two directions: we see the flaming epoch from below and from the seaside. By emphasizing the men and women who connected by sea Paris, Sevilla, and London to Port-au-Prince, Santiago de Cuba, and Kingston, and who then in small vessels connected ports, plantations, islands, and colonies to each other, Scott creates a new, highly imaginative transnational geography of struggle. Instances of resistance from below in various, hitherto disconnected parts of the world now appear as constituent parts of a broad human movement. The forces—and the makers—of revolution are illuminated as never before.

The book is populated by long-forgotten figures who once upon a time inspired stories of their own. A Cap Français runaway called himself "Sans-Peur" ("Without Fear")—truly a name with a message, both for his fellow enemies of slavery and for anyone who might try to hunt him down. Nameless African market women in Saint-Domingue called each other "sailor," expressing through their greetings a form of solidarity that stretched back to the seventeenth-century buccaneers. John Anderson, known as "Old Blue," was a Jamaican sailor who escaped his owner with a huge iron collar around his neck. He eluded recapture along the waterfront for fourteen years, during which time his reputation was "as long and distinctive as his graying beard" (74). The richness of the book's narrative is extraordinary.

A key to Scott's work is the port city, where mobile peoples from around the world came together to work. Brought into cooperative laboring relationships by transnational capital to move the commodities of the world, these workers translated their cooperation into projects of their own. Scott shows how the capitalist mode of production actually worked in port cities, not only generating massive wealth through trade, but also producing oppositional movements from below. As the miserable Lord Balcarres, governor of Jamaica, explained in 1800, "turbulent people of all nations" made up the lower class of Kingston. Characterized by "a general levelling spirit throughout" they were primed for insurrection—ready to torch the town and leave it in ashes (70). Scott shows how the waterfront became a "cauldron of insurrection" (114) and how transnational "cycles of unrest" erupted in many port cities during the 1730s, the 1760s, and the 1790s. The last of these exploded into an Atlantic-wide revolution.

Scott was doing transnational and Atlantic history long before that approach and that field had become cutting-edge forces in historical writing. To say that he was ahead of his time would be an understatement. Many of the sentences he penned more than thirty years ago read as if they were written yesterday. "Sweeping across linguistic, geographic, and imperial boundaries, the tempest created by mobile people in … slave societies would prove a major turning point in the history of the Americas" (xv). Such conclusions are based on deep archival research carried out in Spain, Britain, Jamaica, and the United States, and on published primary sources from and about Cuba, Saint Domingue, and other parts of the Caribbean. They tell a startling new story in the proud annals of "history from below."

Scott has drawn creatively on a rich body of radical scholarship in conceptualizing the book. From Christopher Hill's *The World Turned Upside Down: Radical Ideas in the English Revolution* (1972), Scott takes the notion of the "masterless," originally used to describe the footloose, often expropriated men and women of the seventeenth century, to create something entirely new, "the masterless Caribbean," the men and women who occupied and moved around and between the highly "mastered" spaces of the plantation system. From C. L. R. James's *Mariners, Renegades, and Castaways: Herman Melville and the World We Live In* (1953), Scott takes the motley, floating subjects who connected the world in the early modern era and who later came to life in Melville's sea novels. Scott also draws on the work of Georges Lefebvre, the great historian of the French Revolution who coined the phrase "history from below" in the 1930s and who showed, in his classic work *The Great Fear of 1789: Rural Panic in Revolutionary France* (1932), how rumor drove a great social and political upheaval. Rumors of emancipation, spread by masterless motley crews, became a material force across the Caribbean and around the Atlantic during the 1790s.

The Common Wind is one of those rare works that conveys not only new evidence and new arguments, though there are plenty of both, but an entirely new vision of a historical period, in this case the age of revolution, one of the most profound moments in world history. The Haitian Revolution, Wordsworth would be happy to know, "dies not." Julius S. Scott follows in the wake of the undefeated people he studies by telling us a new story—of exultation and agony, of love and revolution. He has given us a gift for the ages.

Preface

In the summer of 1792, just three days before the third anniversary of the storming of the Bastille in Paris, three volunteer army battalions waited anxiously at the French port of La Rochelle to ship out to the French Caribbean. Eager, loyal to the French republic, and firmly committed to the ideals of the revolution which continued to unfold around them, these soldiers nevertheless possessed only a vague notion of the complex situation which awaited them in the colonies.

Once the French Revolution began in 1789, inhabitants of France's possessions overseas perceived the sweeping governmental and social changes in the mother country to represent an opportunity to advance their own interests. Planters and merchants pursued greater freedom from the control of colonial ministers, free people of color sought to rid the colonies of caste inequality, but the slaves, who made up the vast majority of the population in all the French territories in America, mounted the most fundamental challenge to metropolitan authority. Inspired by the ideas of "liberty, equality, and fraternity," sporadic uprisings of slaves occurred in the French islands as early as the fall of 1789. While white colonists managed to contain these early disturbances, in August 1791 a massive rebellion of slaves erupted in Saint-Domingue (present-day Haiti), France's richest and most important Caribbean slave colony. Even as these young troops massed at La Rochelle, French forces continued to fight in vain to subdue the revolution of slaves in Saint-Domingue, which had now lasted almost a full year. The volunteers faced a difficult task:

to re-establish order in Saint-Domingue in the name of the French National Assembly.

Before departing, the young recruits underwent an inspection by one General La Salle, himself ready to leave for Saint-Domingue as part of the same detachment. Two of these newly raised units had, after careful democratic deliberation, adopted slogans describing their mission and their commitment, as did many of the battalions raised in the days of the French Revolution. They emblazoned the precious words across their caps and sewed them upon the colorful banners which they held aloft. La Salle examined the slogans with special interest. The flag of one of the battalions read on one side "Virtue in action," and "I am vigilant for the country" on the other, watchwords which La Salle found acceptable. But the slogan chosen by the Loire battalion caught the general's discerning eye: "Live Free or Die."

Concerned that the soldiers may not understand the delicate nature of their errand, the general assembled the troops and explained to them the danger which such words posed "in a land where all property is based on the enslavement of Negroes, who, if they adopted this slogan themselves, would be driven to massacre their masters and the army which is crossing the sea to bring peace and law to the colony." While commending their strong commitment to the ideal of freedom, La Salle advised the troops to find a new and less provocative way to express that commitment. Faced with the unpleasant prospect of leaving their "richly embroidered" banner behind, members of the battalion reluctantly followed the general's suggestion and covered over their stirring slogan with strips of cloth inscribed with two hastily chosen new credos of very different meaning: "The Nation, the Law, the King" and "The French Constitution." In addition, those sporting "Live Free or Die" on their caps promised that they would "suppress" this slogan. To the further dismay of the troops, the general forced other changes on them. Instead of planting a traditional and symbolic "liberty tree" upon their arrival in Saint-Domingue, the battalions would now plant "a tree of Peace," which would also bear the inscription "The Nation, the Law, the King." Writing ahead to the current governor-general in Saint-Domingue, La Salle concluded that all that remained was to "counteract the influence of the ill-disposed" and keep the soldiers' misguided revolutionary ardor cool during the long transatlantic voyage.[1]

As La Salle recognized, recent developments in the Americas, especially the revolution in Saint-Domingue, had demonstrated convincingly the explosive power of the ideas and rituals of the Age of Revolution in societies based on slavery. For three years, French officials like La Salle had attempted to keep revolutionary slogans and practices from making their way across the Atlantic to circulate in the French islands and inspire slaves and free people of color, but their efforts had failed. Apparently determined to "live free or die," black rebels in the French colony had initiated an insurrection which, despite the opposition of thousands of troops like those who boarded the ships with General La Salle in July 1792, would succeed in winning the liberation of the slaves and culminate in the New World's second independent nation in 1804.

Officials in the British, Spanish, North American, and other territories where African slavery existed shared La Salle's problem. Just as the news and ideas of the French Revolution proved too volatile to contain, accounts of the black rebellion in Saint-Domingue spread rapidly and uncontrollably throughout the hemisphere. Through trade, both legal and illicit, and the mobility of all types of people from sailors to runaway slaves, extensive regional contact among the American colonies occurred before 1790. By the last decade of the eighteenth century, residents of the Caribbean islands and the northern and southern continents alike had grown to depend upon the movement of ships, commodities, people, and information.

Prior to, during, and following the Haitian Revolution, regional networks of communication carried news of special interest to Afro-Americans all over the Caribbean and beyond. Before the outbreak in Saint-Domingue, British and Spanish officials were already battling rampant rumors forecasting the end of slavery. Such reports gathered intensity in the 1790s. While planters viewed with alarm the growing prospect of an autonomous black territory, fearing that a successful

---

1   General La Salle to Governor-General Desparbés, 11 July 1792, reprinted in A. Corre, *Les papiers du Général A.-N. de la Salle (Saint-Domingue 1792–93)* (Quimper, 1897), pp. 26–7.

violent black uprising might tempt their own slaves to revolt, the happenings in Saint-Domingue provided exciting news for slaves and free
coloreds, increasing their interest in regional affairs and stimulating
them to organize conspiracies of their own. By the end of the decade,
rulers in slave societies from Virginia to Venezuela moved to short-
circuit the network of black rebellion by building obstacles to effective
colony-to-colony communication.

While General La Salle understood in 1792 the potential impact
of the revolutionary currents in the Atlantic world on the minds and
aspirations of Caribbean slaves, neither he nor his charges could have
anticipated the extent to which the winds of revolution would blow
in the other direction. Sweeping across linguistic, geographic, and
imperial boundaries, the tempest created by the black revolutionaries of Saint-Domingue and communicated by mobile people in other
slave societies would prove a major turning point in the history of the
Americas.

Acknowledgements

There are many, many people to thank. I couldn't possibly thank them all. I thank first of all the people who helped me in graduate school at Duke University. Peter Wood showed us a whole new way of thinking about ourselves and about intellectual history. He taught me to understand enslaved people as thinking people, and this book is a tribute to him. John Jay TePaske, who taught colonial Latin American history, convinced me to go to Seville. Raymond Gavins taught me how to be a citizen in the profession. I learned much from Larry Goodwyn and Bill Chafe.

I am grateful to the fellows and staff of the Carter G. Woodson Institute at the University of Virginia and to the late Armstead L. Robinson, head of the Institute at the time, who deserves special thanks. In addition, several people have helped me over the years and have supported the enterprise of *The Common Wind*: Laurent Dubois, Ada Ferrer, Neville Hall, Tera Hunter, Robin Kelley, Jane Landers, Peter Linebaugh, Marcus Rediker, Elisha Renne, Larry Rowley, Rebecca Scott, James Sidbury, Matthew Smith, Rachel Toor, and Stephen Ward.

Thanks as well go to the staff of the many archives and libraries I visited: The Archivo General de Indias (Seville), the Public Record Office (London, now called The National Archives), the Jamaica Archives (Spanish Town), the National Library of Jamaica (Kingston), the Institute of Commonwealth Studies (London), the John Carter Brown Library (Providence, Rhode Island), the Historical Society of Pennsylvania (Philadelphia), the American Antiquarian Society

(Worcester, Massachusetts), the Bibliothèque des Frères (Port-au-Prince, Haiti), and the Bibliothèque de Saint-Louis-de-Gonzague. Special thanks go to the Department of Afroamerican and African Studies community at the University of Michigan. Finally, I would like to thank Ben Mabie and Duncan Ranslem of Verso Books for their careful and kind assistance.

Abbreviations

AAS	American Antiquarian Society, Worcester, Massachusetts
ADM	Admiralty Records, Public Record Office, London
AGI	Archivo General de Indias, Sevilla
C.O.	Colonial Office Records, Public Record Office, London
CVSP	Palmer and McRae, eds., *Calendar of Virginia State Papers*
FLB	Letterpress Books, Stephen Fuller Papers, Duke University Library
HSP	Historical Society of Pennsylvania, Philadelphia
JA	Jamaica Archives, Spanish Town
JHCVA	Records of the Jamaica High Court of Vice-Admiralty, Jamaica Archives
leg.	*legajo*; a bundle of documents in Spanish archives
Minutes of WIPM	Minutes of the West India Planters and Merchants, West India Committee Archives, Institute of Commonwealth Studies, London
NLJ	National Library of Jamaica (Institute of Jamaica), Kingston
PRO	Public Record Office, London
RSD	*Revolutions de Saint-Domingue* Collection, John Carter Brown Library, Providence, Rhode Island
W.O.	War Office Records, Public Record Office, London

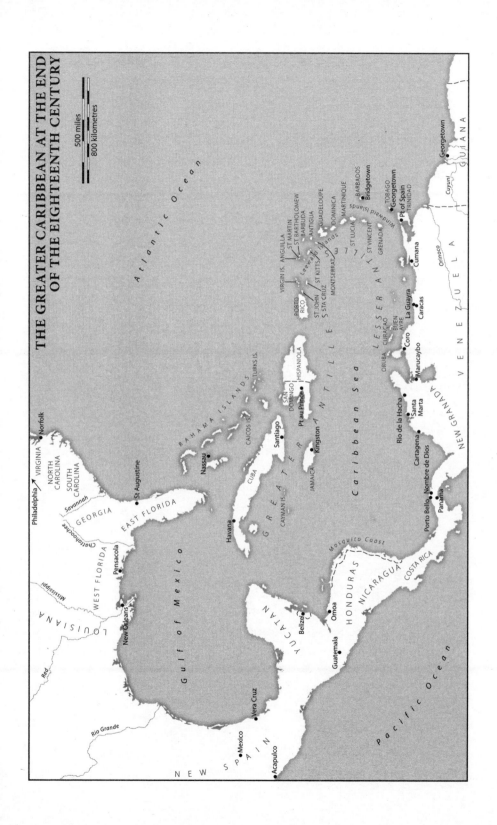

THE GREATER CARIBBEAN AT THE END
OF THE EIGHTEENTH CENTURY

500 miles
800 kilometres

Atlantic Ocean

GUIANA
Georgetown
Cuyuni

BARBADOS
Georgetown
TOBAGO
Pt of Spain
TRINIDAD
Bridgetown

ST MARTIN
ANGUILLA
ST BARTHOLOMEW
BARBUDA
ANTIGUA
GUADELOUPE
DOMINICA
MARTINIQUE
ST LUCIA
ST VINCENT
GRENADA

Windward Islands

VIRGIN IS.
PORTO RICO
ST JOHN
ST KITTS
STA CRUZ
MONTSERRAT

Leeward Islands

LESSER ANTILLES

Cumana
ORUBA
CURAÇAO
BUEN AYRE
La Guaya
Caracas
Coro
Maracaybo

VENEZUELA

Orinoco

NEW GRANADA

Rio de la Hacha
Santa Marta
Cartagena
Nombre de Dios
Porto Bello
Panama

Caribbean Sea

HISPANIOLA
SAN DOMINGO
Pt au Prince

TURKS IS.
CAICOS IS.

BAHAMA ISLANDS

Nassau

Santiago

CUBA

Kingston
JAMAICA
CAYMAN IS.

GREATER ANTILLES

Havana

St Augustine
EAST FLORIDA

GEORGIA
Savannah
SOUTH CAROLINA
NORTH CAROLINA
VIRGINIA
Norfolk
Philadelphia

WEST FLORIDA
Pensacola
Chattahoochee
Mississippi
LOUISIANA
New Orleans
Red

Gulf of Mexico

Mosquito Coast
HONDURAS
NICARAGUA
COSTA RICA

YUCATAN
Belize
Omoa
Guatemala

Vera Cruz

Rio Grande

NEW SPAIN
Mexico
Acapulco

Pacific Ocean

1.

"Pandora's Box"

The Masterless Caribbean at the
End of the Eighteenth Century

Late in the seventeenth century, the European colonizing nations briefly put aside their differences and began a concerted effort to rid the Caribbean of the buccaneers, pirates, and other fugitives who had taken refuge in the region. This move to dislodge the "masterless" people of the West Indies signaled the transformation of the islands from havens for freebooters and renegades into settler colonies based on plantations and slave labor. The same offensive that had given large planters the upper hand in Barbados in the 1670s had gained irreversible momentum throughout the Caribbean by the middle decades of the eighteenth century. The steady rise in sugar prices on the world market after about 1740 favored the expansion of plantation monoculture into areas where cattle and pigs had grazed, and where hide hunters, logwood cutters, runaway slaves, and other Caribbean dissidents had found shelter.

Barely a half century after an earthquake in 1692 destroyed Port Royal, Jamaica, a longstanding outpost for pirates from all over the region, the Caribbean had already become a vastly different place from what it had been during the heyday of the buccaneers. Not only had their old haunts disappeared; older images of "enchanted" islands liberated from the hierarchies of the Old World were difficult to sustain as plantations hungrily gobbled up what was once frontier land. As planters gained control over the land, so they tightened their control of labor. The trade in African slaves steadily increased as the century progressed, and the common scene of slave ships unloading their human cargoes turned on its head in the most graphic of ways earlier dreams of a "masterless" existence. By century's end, the fluid pre-plantation economy and society had long since given way to an ominous landscape of imperial soldiers and warships, plantations and sugar mills, masters and slaves.[1]

Even during such a period of advance and consolidation, however, planters and merchants encountered pockets of resistance to their drive for absolute authority. In fact, employers on both sides of the Atlantic, though flushed with economic prosperity, still worried about the many ways which individuals and groups found to protect and extend masterless existences. In both the Old World and the New, these concerns centered upon the persistent problem of the "seething mobility" of substantial sectors of the laboring classes. In eighteenth-century England, according to E. P. Thompson, masters of labor complained about bothersome aspects of the developing "free" labor market—about "the indiscipline of working people, their lack of economic dependency and their social insubordination"—which resulted from labor's mobility.[2] Planters echoed similar concerns in the Caribbean region, where buccaneers and pirates, the old scourges of the planters and traders, had been effectively suppressed, but where a colorful assortment of saucy and insubordinate characters continued to move about and resist authority. Masters and employers in industrializing Old World economies based on "free" labor felt only mildly threatened by such mobility. In the plantation-based societies of the Caribbean, however, where the unfreedom of the vast majority of the labor force was written into law and sanctioned by force

---

1   For descriptions of this transformation, see Clarence H. Haring, *The Buccaneers in the West Indies in the XVII Century* (London, 1910), pp. 200–31; Richard Pares, *Merchants and Planters* (Cambridge, 1960), pp. 14–20; and Christopher Hill, "Radical Pirates?" in Margaret Jacob and James Jacob, eds., *The Origins of Anglo-American Radicalism* (London, Boston, and Sydney, 1984), pp. 20–8. Hill describes vividly the role of "masterless men" in England in the mid-seventeenth century in *The World Turned Upside Down: Radical Ideas during the English Revolution* (London, 1972), pp. 32–45.

2   E. P. Thompson, "Patrician Society, Plebeian Culture," *Journal of Social History* 7 (Summer 1974), p. 383.

and where "free" workers were the anomaly rather than the rule, the persistence of labor mobility called forth an anguished response from the ruling class. For the same reasons, the prospect of a masterless, mobile existence outside the plantation orbit held an especially seductive appeal for disenchanted people casting about for new options. In England, masters begrudged a certain amount of uncontrolled movement among their workers. In the Caribbean, masters resorted to a profusion of local laws and international treaties to keep this mobility within the narrowest of possible limits.

Though the planters' efforts to curtail freedom over the course of the eighteenth century placed severe restrictions on mobility, these measures never succeeded completely in keeping people from pursuing alternatives to life under the plantation system. At the close of the eighteenth century, as at its beginning, people of many descriptions defied the odds and attempted to escape their masters. Slaves deserted plantations in large numbers; urban workers ducked their owners; seamen jumped ship to avoid floggings and the press gang; militiamen and regular troops grumbled, ignored orders, and deserted their watch; "higglers" left workplaces to peddle their wares in the black market; and smugglers and shady foreigners moved about on mysterious missions from island to island. Furthermore, the very commercial growth which planters and merchants welcomed opened new avenues of mobility. Cities grew and matured, attracting runaway slaves and sheltering a teeming underground with surprising regional connections. Expanding commercial links sanctioned the comings and goings of ships of all sizes and nations. Island ports required pilot boats with experienced navigators to guide the incoming merchantmen to safe anchorages, and they needed a network of coastal vessels and skilled sailors to support their busy markets. This web of commerce brought the region's islands into closer and closer contact as the century progressed, providing channels of communication as well as tempting routes of escape.

On the eve of Caribbean revolution, most English, French, and Spanish planters and traders in the region rode the crest of a long wave of prosperity. Nevertheless, they continued to grope, much as they had at the end of the last century, for common solutions to the problem of controlling runaways, deserters, and vagabonds in the region. As long as masterless men and women found ways to move about and evade the authorities, they reasoned, these people embodied submerged traditions of popular resistance which could burst into the open at any time. Examining the rich world which these mobile fugitives inhabited—the complex (and largely invisible) underground which the "mariners, renegades, and castaways" of the Caribbean created to protect themselves in the face of planter consolidation—is crucial to understanding how news, ideas, and social excitement traveled in the electric political environment of the late eighteenth century.[3]

All of the West Indies felt the effects of the sugar boom of the mid-eighteenth century, particularly the Greater Antilles— Jamaica, Cuba, and Hispaniola, the larger islands of the northwestern Caribbean. In the century after 1670, though at different speeds and by different historical processes, the expansion of sugar cultivation transformed these three islands from sparsely populated frontier out-posts to plantation societies based on captive African labor.

British growth centered in Jamaica. After 1740 the planter class had managed to contain the intense factionalism and black rebelliousness of the previous decade enough to attract white settlers, drawn in large part from the stagnating islands to the east. They began to clear and cultivate new lands in the north and west of the island, and to purchase hundreds of thousands of Africans to work the new plantations. By 1766, Jamaica had bolted well past the other British possessions in the West Indies in its importance both as a commercial entrepôt and as a staple-producing economy. Some 200,000 people, half the population of Britain's sugar colonies, resided there, and its busy ports controlled half the British trade in the region. Despite setbacks encountered during the period of the American Revolution, the rapid extension of sugar monoculture in Jamaica continued through the 1780s.[4]

---

3 The phrase is borrowed from C. L. R. James, *Mariners, Renegades, and Castaways: The Story of Herman Melville and the World We Live In* (New York, 1951).

4 Richard B. Sheridan, *Sugar and Slavery: An Economic History of the British West Indies 1623–1775* (Baltimore, 1973), pp. 216–23; Frances Armytage, *The Free Port System in the British West Indies: A Study in Commercial Policy, 1766–1822*

As sugar came to dominate the economy of Jamaica, the demographic balance between black and white Jamaicans shifted decisively in favor of the African population. Slave imports into the island rose steadily throughout the eighteenth century, surpassing 120,000 for the twenty-year period between 1741 and 1760, totaling nearly 150,000 in the subsequent two decades, and increasing at an even faster rate after 1781. As early as 1730, nine of every ten Jamaicans were black slaves, and by the eve of the American Revolution almost ninety-four percent of the population of the island was of African ancestry.[5]

Cuba's move toward massive investment in the sugar industry, as well as its demographic absorption into Afro-America, occurred both later and more abruptly than in Jamaica. Crucial to the expansion of sugar in this Spanish colony was the British occupation of Havana in 1762. Over a period of eleven months, the British introduced some 10,000 slaves into the island, breathing life into the sugar industry which Cuban planters sustained after the British departure. The Cuban share in the African slave trade, while still miniscule relative to its more thoroughly developed neighbors, increased markedly after 1763. Almost 31,000 Africans were imported between 1763 and 1789, and by 1792 data from the island's second official census revealed that the white population of Cuba had slipped below the numbers of non-whites for the first time in the history of the island.[6]

(London, New York, and Toronto, 1953), p. 4; George Metcalf, *Royal Government and Political Conflict in Jamaica. 1729–1783* (London, 1965), pp. 33–197; Robert V. Wells, *The Population of the British Colonies in America before 1776: A Survey of Census Data* (Princeton, 1975), p. 196.

5 Richard S. Dunn, *Sugar and Slaves: The Rise of the Planter Class in the English West Indies, 1624–1713* (Chapel Hill, 1972), p. 155; Wells, *Population of the British Colonies*, p. 196.

6 Manuel Moreno Fraginals, *The Sugarmill: The Socioeconomic Complex of Sugar in Cuba 1760–1860*, trans. Cedric Belfrage (New York and London, 1976), pp. 15–30; Ramiro Guerra y Sánchez, *Sugar and Society in the Caribbean: An Economic History of Cuban Agriculture* (New Haven and London, 1964), pp. 44–50; Hubert H. S. Aimes, *A History of Slavery in Cuba, 1511 to 1868* (New York and London, 1907), p. 269: Nicolas Sánchez-Albornoz, *The Population of Latin America: A History*, trans. W. A. S. Richardson (Berkeley, Los Angeles, and London, 1974), pp. 139–40.

But nowhere was society transformed more quickly or completely than in the French colony of Saint-Domingue. The progress
of sugar in Jamaica and Cuba paled next to the economic explosion
in this mountainous strip of land comprising the western third of
the island of Hispaniola. Even as French fortunes waxed and finally
waned in the intense imperial competition leading up to the Seven
Years' War, the sudden emergence of Saint-Domingue was astonishing. Still a buccaneering outpost upon its cession to France in 1697,
by 1739 Saint-Domingue was the world's richest and most profitable
slave colony. Already the number of sugar mills had reached 450, up
from just thirty-five at the turn of the century, and there were more
enslaved Africans—over 117,000—working in Saint-Domingue than
in Jamaica or in any other Caribbean island. Three years later Saint-
Domingue produced more sugar than all the British sugar islands
combined. During the American Revolution, French planters took
advantage of famine and economic dislocation in the British territories to carve out an even bigger slice of the world sugar market. The
increased volume of the slave trade to Saint-Domingue reflects the
new boom of the 1770s. In 1771, traders brought slightly more than
10,000 new Africans to Saint-Domingue; five years later, the number
had more than doubled. The expansion of the French colony continued
through the 1780s. In the ten years preceding the French Revolution,
Saint-Domingue's booming economy was primarily responsible for
tripling the volume of the French slave trade over the previous decade,
and official figures showed annual African imports to rival consist-
ently the size of the colony's entire white population year after year,
reaching a dizzying total of 30,000 at least as early as 1785. By 1789,
Saint-Domingue was the world's largest producer of sugar and coffee;
its plantations produced twice as much as all other French colonies
combined; and French ships entering and leaving its ports accounted
for more than a third of the metropole's foreign trade.[7]

---

7   For economic expansion, see Lawrence Henry Gipson, *The British Empire
before the American Revolution*, 15 vols. (New York, 1966–70), II, 252n.; Noel
Deerr, *The History of Sugar*, 2 vols. (London, 1949–50), I, pp. 239–240; and C. L. R.
James, *The Black Jacobins: Toussaint L'Ouverture and the San Domingo Revolution*,
2nd ed., rev. (New York, 1963), pp. 45–6. For figures on population and the slave

While the decisive economic expansion after 1700 sounded the death knell, both in image and reality, of the masterless Caribbean of an earlier time, it also produced new strata of disaffected individuals who continued to strive to place themselves outside the plantation orbit and survive. In addition, forms of resistance already endemic to the region continued to thrive and spread. The practice of Africans fleeing their enslavers, for example, was already a tradition of long standing at the turn of the eighteenth century. As sugar production expanded and regional demography tilted dramatically in favor of Africans, the problem of controlling runaway slaves became one of the paramount concerns of Caribbean planters, colonial officials, and other whites. Workers fleeing plantations and attempting to set up communities of their own provided both concrete alternatives to the plantation regime and a powerful metaphor informing other forms of mobility and resistance in the region.

Africans in Jamaica achieved notable success in their efforts to become independent. The rugged "cockpit country" in the northwest of the island and the Blue Mountains in the east harbored refugees from slavery from the earliest years of Spanish control; these groups of outlying runaway slaves constituted the region's first "maroons." As slave imports soared after 1700, Africans followed the well-worn paths of their forebears, leaving plantations for expanding maroon communities in the parishes of Trelawny, St. James, St. Elizabeth, and St. George. As these communities grew, so did their contacts with the plantations, for maroons and slaves carried on a clandestine trade in ammunition and provisions, and maroons staged periodic raids. During the 1730s, a period of slave unrest throughout the Caribbean, the related problems of slave desertion and the hostile activities of communities

trade, see Philip D. Curtin, *The Atlantic Slave Trade: A Census* (Madison, Milwaukee, and London, 1969), pp. 78–9; Jean Tarrade, *Le commerce colonial de la France à la fin de l'Ancien régime: l'évolution du régime de l'Exclusif de 1763 à 1789*, 2 tomes (Paris, 1972), II, pp. 759–60; Charles Bréard, *Notes sur Saint-Domingue, tirées des papiers d'un armateur du Havre. 1780–1802* (Rouen, 1893), p. 4; Perry Viles, "The Slaving Interest in the Atlantic Ports, 1763–1792," *French Historical Studies* 7 (Fall 1972), p. 530; *Mémoire envoyé le 18 juin 1790, au Comité des Rapports de l'Assemblée Nationale, par M. de la Luzerne* (Paris, 1790), p. 70, in the collection entitled *Révolutions de Saint-Domingue*, John Carter Brown Library, Brown University (hereinafter RSD).

of runaways became particularly acute, driving the planter class into open warfare with the maroons. A decade of conflict finally forced the government to recognize by treaty the semi-independent status of several maroon towns in 1739. By these treaties, the British government agreed to allow these maroon towns to exist under limited self-government, but at the same time enlisted their aid in policing the island. In return for official recognition, the maroons promised to discourage, apprehend, and return future runaways. Designed to drive a wedge between the maroon towns and nearby plantations, laws passed in the aftermath of the rebellion threatened maroons guilty of "inveigling slaves" from plantations or "harbouring runaways" with banishment from the island.[8]

Not surprisingly, conflict and ambiguity complicated the history of this arrangement between the planter class and the maroons in the half century after 1740. On occasion, residents of the maroon towns faithfully outfitted parties to track down runaways in their areas, and the accounts brought back to the estates by recaptured runaways produced a marked animosity in the slave huts.[9] Such examples of loyalty led Governor Adam Williamson to assert hopefully in 1793 that "the Maroons are well affected, and would exert themselves either in the defence of the Island or quelling internal Insurrections."[10] The planters themselves, however, apprehended danger in the carefree mobility of ostensible black allies, and their concerns surfaced time and again. They observed that the laws restricting the movements of the maroons were indifferently enforced, and they watched

---

8   R. C. Dallas, *The History of the Maroons, from their Origin to the Establishment of their Chief Tribe at Sierra Leone*, 2 vols. (London, 1803), I, pp. 22–97; Frank Wesley Pitman, *The Development of the British West Indies, 1700–1763* (New Haven, 1917), pp. 113–18. For a general treatment of rebelliousness in the British Caribbean in this period, see David Barry Gaspar, "A Dangerous Spirit of Liberty: Slave Rebellion in the West Indies during the 1730s," *Cimarrons* 1 (1981), pp. 79–91.

9   See, for example, the harsh treatment suffered by one recaptured runaway described in Orlando Patterson, *The Sociology of Slavery: An Analysis of the Origins, Development, and Structure of Negro Slave Society in Jamaica* (Rutherford, Madison, and Teaneck, N.J., 1967), p. 263.

10   Adam Williamson to Henry Dundas, 9 March 1793, Colonial Office Records, Public Record Office, London, class 137/ volume 91 (hereinafter C.O. class/vol., PRO).

as the maroons wandered about with ease in the towns and through the countryside, where they had extensive contact with plantation slaves. The men of Trelawny Town, the largest of the maroon settlements, fathered "numerous Children by Female Slaves, residing on the Low Plantations" of the surrounding parishes, and, concluded a 1795 report, "the Nature of their Connections was alarming." When the Trelawny maroons took up arms against the government that same year, officials moved quickly to isolate the rebels by cutting off such communication, fully expecting their "Search for concealed Arms in all the Negroe Huts over the Island" to uncover and foil their networks.[11]

Finally, critics of the government's treaties pointed out, the agreement with the maroons hardly deterred groups of new runaways from seeking even greater independence and taking to the woods and mountains to establish towns of their own. Well known from estate to estate, the daring exploits of leaders of runaway groups sparked excited conversation among Jamaican slaves and constantly reminded them of both the hazards and the promise of such activity. Market days, dances, horse races, and other public occasions attracting large gatherings of slaves allowed news of these developments to circulate. When Mingo, a fisherman and former driver on a large Trelawny estate, "made a Ball ... after the Conclusion of Crop" in the fall of 1791, slaves from neighboring estates who attended were astonished to see Brutus present. An incorrigible runaway serving a life term in the parish workhouse at Martha Brae for his role in organizing unauthorized maroon towns in the 1780s, Brutus had recently escaped and had already set about his old ways. At the ball, Brutus scoffed at his owner's attempts to recapture him and affirmed rumors spread by recently returned runaways that he, together "with about eighteen other Negroes men slaves and three women of different Countries and owners" from Trelawny, Runaway Bay, and Clarendon, had established an impregnable new town in the backwoods of the parish. Many of those attending Mingo's ball must have already known of

---

11   Lord Balcarres to Duke of Portland, 11 August, 25 August 1795, C.O. 137/95, PRO.

Brutus Town; its residents had planted provisions and through "corre-spondence" with trusted plantation slaves kept the settlement stocked with "Rum, Sugar, Salt and other necessaries." Months after Brutus's dramatic appearance, slaves in St. Ann and Trelawny testified before local officials "that all the Negroes know of this Town" and "that if this Town is not destroyed [the planters] shall not be able to keep a single negroe from going there as they are all trying to get there." In fact, Brutus Town was only one of several similar runaway settlements inspiring the imaginations if not the active participation of slaves all over "cockpit country."[12]

The excitement of the fall and winter of 1791–92, magnified by the black revolution in neighboring Saint-Domingue, energized slave communication networks in Jamaica, and mobile runaway slaves like Brutus may have played a key if hidden role in spreading news from plantation to plantation. Two episodes from Jamaica's north coast during this period illustrate both that slaves paid close attention to developments around them and that they devised clandestine ways to transmit information quickly and effectively. In November 1791, John Whittaker, proprietor of an outlying plantation, discovered that his slaves learned of recent developments on the coast before he did. After one of his workers informed him of a recent development in Montego Bay the night before word of the incident arrived by a mes-senger on horseback, Whittaker reflected with amazement and alarm that there must be "some unknown mode of conveying intelligence amongst Negroes." In this instance, the grapevine of the slaves over-came several significant obstacles. Whittaker's estate lay in "a retired situation no publick Road leading through or near it," and Whittaker had his slaves under constant supervision and was certain that "no Negro of mine could have been absent from their employment during the day." Finally, the distance to Montego Bay, some thirty miles, "was too great to go and return in the night. Yet," Whittaker related, his slaves "were particularly informed of every circumstance there in less

---

12   See the examination of Luckey, "Examinations of sundry Slaves in the Parish of St. Ann Jamaica respecting an intention to revolt," 31 December 1791, 11 January 1792, and the examinations of Duke and Glamorgan, "Examinations of sundry Slaves in the Parish of Trelawny Jamaica," 5 January 1792, C.O. 137/90, PRO.

than 24 hours after these Circumstances had taken place." Around the same time, Montego Bay upholsterer Robert Parker caught an accidental glimpse of nocturnal communication when he left his bedroom one sleepless night. In front of his establishment he saw "four Negroes ... very earnest in discourse," evidently waiting for a scheduled meeting with "two more Negroes that were on the other side of the Bridge." As they waited, their conversation concerned the number of "Guns and Soldiers" of the whites. Parker received a further surprise when, after the arrival of their friends, the four original companions abandoned English and began to converse in what Parker identified as "Coramantee."[13]

The activities of runaway slave communities in Jamaica did not go unnoticed in nearby Cuba, underscoring the fact that the histories of maroon societies in the two islands in the eighteenth century were closely intertwined. First, maroons in the two islands virtually shared a common space. One of the centers of maroon activity in the Spanish colony, the steep and densely wooded Sierra Maestra ranging along the east–west coastline at Cuba's southeastern tip, was a short sail from the edge of Jamaica's "cockpit country," and from points high in the sierra the peaks of the British island's Blue Mountains were actually visible.[14] The short distance between the two islands concerned Spanish officials, who feared that communities of runaway slaves in the Sierra Maestra might make common cause with hostile British forces in Jamaica.[15]

One chapter of the common history of maroons in Jamaica and Cuba was written in the 1730s, when the timing of the First Maroon War in Jamaica coincided exactly with a similar uprising among slaves working near the east coast of Cuba. In 1731, at precisely the time when

13   John Whittaker to J. L. Winn, 11 January 1792 and report of Robert Parker, n.d., enclosed with "Minutes of the proceedings of the Committee of Secrecy and Safety in the Parish of St. James's, Jamaica," C.O. 137/90, PRO.

14   For descriptions, see Robert T. Hill, *Cuba and Porto Rico, with the other Islands of the West Indies* (New York, 1898), pp. 39–40, and Alexander von Humboldt, *The Island of Cuba*, trans. J. S. Thrasher (New York, 1856), 129n.

15   Juan Nepomuceno de Quintana to Eugenio Llaguno, Cuba, 31 December 1796, Archivo General de Indias, Sevilla, Spain, Sección de Gobierno, Audiencia de Santo Domingo, leg. 1264 (hereinafter AGI, Santo Domingo).

the rebels in Jamaica were beginning their armed struggle for independence, slaves in the state-run copper mines near Santiago de Cuba
revolted *en masse* and took to the mountains east of the city, near the
present-day site of El Cobre. Like their counterparts in Jamaica, these
so-called *cobreros* managed to resist repeated attempts to dislodge
them and caused considerable concern for the planters in the valley
below. By the 1780s, descendants of the original rebels, now numbering more than a thousand, had fanned out from El Cobre into smaller
settlements scattered throughout the surrounding sierra.[16] Again
during the 1790s, the cycle of unrest and official anxiety over maroon
activity affected Cuba as much as Jamaica. Governors of Santiago de
Cuba, now heavily involved in Cuba's full-fledged and growing investment in African slave labor, reported that their best efforts to bring the
cobreros under control had failed. In fact, by the middle of the decade,
El Cobre welcomed all kinds of fugitives from slavery, "*cobreros* as
well as other slaves," and was home for several infamous characters
who had been on the run for years.[17] Apprehensive that the Jamaican
Maroon War of 1795–96 would spread to the Cuban mountains, as it
apparently had in the 1730s, Cuban officials did not hesitate to show
solidarity with their British neighbors; when the Jamaica Assembly
requested that the Cubans send a number of their fierce tracking dogs
and *chasseurs* to bring the rebels under control, they complied with
uncharacteristic dispatch.[18]

During this uncertain and active period, mobile *cobreros* built a
network of news and rumor which stretched even across the Atlantic.
In the 1780s, Spanish authorities could not control rumors that the

---

16   See the section from Francisco Pérez de la Riva, *La habitación rural en Cuba*
(La Habana, 1952), translated and reprinted in Richard Price, ed., *Maroon Societies:
Rebel Slave Communities in the Americas* (Baltimore, 1979), esp. pp. 54–5.

17   Quintana to Llaguno, Cuba, 31 December 1796, AGI, Santo Domingo, leg.
1264.

18   Luis de las Casas to Príncipe de la Paz, La Habana, 14 November 1795,
AGI, Papeles procedentes de la isla de Cuba, leg. 1489 (hereinafter AGI, Cuba); Lord
Balcarres to Duke of Portland, 29 December 1795, C.O. 137/96, PRO. Pleased with
the results, the Jamaicans turned to this solution some weeks later in an attempt to
control runaways in areas of Saint-Domingue under British control. See Quintana
to Las Casas, Cuba, 25 February 1796, AGI, Cuba, leg. 1435.

king had finally granted freedom and land to the *cobreros* only to have his wishes thwarted by the resistance of local officials. Convinced that slaves should have independent sources of transatlantic information, a small group of *cobreros* delegated Gregorio Cosme Osorio to travel to Spain in order to represent the interests of the descendants of El Cobre's runaway slaves at court. Osorio's reports helped to keep the spirit of resistance alive into the mid-1790s. By 1795, Juan Baptista Vaillant, the governor of Santiago de Cuba, reported that a new wave of liberation rumors was sweeping the east coast of Cuba and that slaves were deserting plantations in disturbing numbers. Governor Vaillant blamed the wide circulation of several recent letters from Osorio for these developments.[19]

The geography of Saint-Domingue, with its rugged and majestic mountain ranges rimming the colony's long and jagged eastern border, also presented mobile slaves ample opportunity for escape. After 1700, maroon activity grew and expanded as rapidly as plantation slavery itself. Early in the century, bands of maroons inhabited the region surrounding the rich northern plain. By mid-century, the center of maroon activity had shifted southward along the rim of mountains overlooking the new boom areas of Mirebalais, Cul-de-Sac, and Anse-à-Pitre. Though marronage was a significant factor affecting the character of the slave system throughout Saint-Domingue, the east-central region between the Cul-de-Sac and the Spanish border would continue into the era of the Revolution to be the locus of the most stable maroon societies as well as the scene of continuous warfare between maroons and government-sponsored expeditions. As the rule of the slavocracy entered its final days in the 1780s, maroon groups of various sizes and descriptions stretched in a broken line from the northernmost reaches of Saint-Domingue all the way to its southern tip. The role of these Haitian maroons in advancing the coming revolution remains a topic of intense debate.[20]

---

19   José Luciano Franco, *Las minas de Santiago del Prado y la rebelión de los cobreros, 1530–1800* (La Habana, 1975), pp. 58–63; Juan Baptista Vaillant to Las Casas, Cuba, 14 September 1795, AGI, Cuba, leg. 1435.

20   Gabriel Debien, "Le marronage aux Antilles françaises au XVIIIe siècle," *Caribbean Studies* 6 (October 1966), pp. 3–41. The work of Haitian historian Jean

The activities of Saint-Domingue's maroon societies focused greater planter concern, but the tradition of short-term individual desertion was arguably of more consequence in the day-to-day functioning of plantations and among the slaves themselves. Whether visiting relatives, escaping an impending punishment, or engaging in trade and other proscribed activities, slaves who left for absences of short duration and distance bedeviled managers on every plantation. Proprietors and overseers became so accommodated to short-term absences from their plantations and so powerless to control them that they often did not even bother to delete the names of absent slaves, especially those of habitual leave-takers, from current plantation lists.[21] In addition, overseers frequently reported finding runaways from other area plantations hiding out in the quarters of their slaves. In 1790 the overseer of one plantation in the Cap Français district arrested twenty-seven fugitive slaves in his vicinity within a short time, "as many in the slave huts as in the hills."[22] Already, however, the relaxed attitude of the days before the arrival of the news of the French Revolution had begun to give way to new fears about what this news might mean to plantation slaves. By 1790, whites recognized the possibility that rebellion might spread easily to the countryside, and that they could ill afford to ignore even these short-term migrants any longer.[23]

While the mountains and backwoods with their maroon

Fouchard emphasizes the crucial role played by maroons in Saint-Domingue in the long struggle for Haitian independence and black freedom. See Jean Fouchard, *Les marrons du syllabaire* (Port-au-Prince, 1953), and *Les marrons de la liberté* (Paris, 1972), in addition to Edner Brutus, *Révolution dans Saint-Domingue*, 2 tomes ([Belgium], n.d.), and Leslie Manigat, "The Relationship between Marronage and Slave Revolts and Revolution in St-Domingue-Haiti," in Vera Rubin and Arthur Tuden, eds., *Comparative Perspectives on Slavery in New World Plantation Societies* (New York, 1977), pp. 420–38. For a view strongly critical of the "Haitian school," see David P. Geggus, *Slavery, War, and Revolution: The British Occupation of Saint-Domingue* (Oxford, 1982), pp. 27, 411, 457–8.

21   Debien, "Marronage aux Antilles françaises," pp. 3, 7–9.

22   Séguy de Villevaleix to Comte de Polastron, 31 September 1790, reprinted in Gabriel Debien, *Études antillaises (XVIIIe siècle)* (Paris, 1956), p. 170.

23   See, for example, Debien, *Études antillaises*, p. 164, and Pierre Léon, *Marchands et spéculateurs dans le monde antillais du XVIIIe siècle: les Dolle et les Raby* (Paris, 1963), p. 141.

communities provided hope in the popular imagination regarding individual escape and collective resistance throughout the eighteenth century, the growing coastal cities nurtured the most complex patterns of mobility and presented the most vexing problems of control for all the colonial powers. Caribbean cities were more than centers of commercial exchange, population, and government; they were in a real sense centers of education. Towns provided anonymity and shelter for a wide variety of masterless men and women, including but by no means restricted to runaway slaves, and they offered unique opportunities for these people to rub shoulders, share experiences, and add to their knowledge of the Caribbean world and beyond. By the 1790s, larger cities like Kingston, Cap Français, and Havana could properly be termed capitals of Afro-America, and dissidents in dozens of smaller coastal centers were engaging in the kinds of transactions which would play a crucial role in spreading the excitement of the Age of Revolution in the Caribbean.

At the start of the eighteenth century, however, these cities presented a very different picture. In 1700, Havana, with its impressive stone cathedrals and fortifications, had few rivals in the region. The future urban centers of the British and French Caribbean were fledgling settlements more closely resembling the "overgrown villages" of the eastern seaboard of British North America than the established capitals of the Spanish and Portuguese. Only about two thousand people inhabited Kingston, the city founded to replace Port Royal in 1692, at the turn of the eighteenth century. Similarly, Cap Français, destined to become Saint-Domingue's most important city and later the revolutionary capital of the Caribbean, had only recently inherited its role as a locus of settlement from buccaneering La Tortue across the channel. At the time of the founding of Kingston, "le Cap" was home for only 160 white men, sixty-three white women, and thirty-four black slaves, and twenty years later the town still contained barely a thousand residents.[24]

------

24   Colin G. Clarke, *Kingston, Jamaica: Urban Development and Social Change, 1692–1962* (Berkeley, Los Angeles, and London, 1975), pp. 6, 141. Clarke estimates Kingston's population in 1700 at 5,000. For the "overgrown villages" of Boston, New York, and Philadelphia, see Gary B. Nash, *The Urban Crucible: Social Change,*

The progress of cash crop agriculture in the region between 1700 and 1790 transformed these settlements in both size and function. Surviving periodic natural disasters and incessant warfare, these and other coastal centers had grown significantly by the era of the Haitian Revolution. A generation of intense economic activity and reform after 1763 found Havana by 1791 a teeming entrepôt whose population, including the web of surrounding suburbs, ranged somewhere between 44,000 and 50,000. The city continued to expand during the years of the revolution in Saint-Domingue, doubling in size between 1791 and 1810. Other Spanish-American cities, most notably Caracas, whose population almost doubled between 1772 and 1812, and Buenos Aires, experienced similar rapid development as population and trading centers.[25] By 1790, Kingston was the hub of overlapping networks of regional and transatlantic trade in the British orbit; of all the cities in English-speaking America, only New York and Philadelphia had more people.[26] Official figures issued in 1788 listed the population of Cap Français at 12,151 in the city proper, a statistic which did not include the tens of thousands of people living on plantations in the immediate highlands whose lives were intimately connected to the city.[27]

In addition to the maturation and growth of the region's largest cities, several smaller coastal centers also elbowed their way to a kind of urban status by the late eighteenth century. Whereas the largest cities dominated transatlantic trade, their aggressive competitors provided outlets for the produce of local plantations through a thriving coastal and short-distance regional trade of small locally built vessels. Unlike Havana and the surrounding cities of the western coast of Cuba,

---

Political Consciousness, and the Origins of the American Revolution (Cambridge and London, 1979), pp. 3–4. M. L. E. Moreau de Saint-Méry, Description topographique, physique, civile, politique et historique de la partie française de l'isle Saint-Domingue, nouvelle édition, 3 tomes (Paris, 1958), I, p. 479 has figures for Cap Français.

25   Alexander von Humboldt, Ensayo político sobre la isla de Cuba (La Habana, 1960), p. 108; Sánchez-Albornoz, Population of Latin America, p. 127.

26   Clarke, Kingston, p. 141, estimates the city's population at 23,500 in 1790. According to the first Census of the United States conducted that same year, New York had 49,401 residents, Philadelphia 28,522, and Boston 18,320.

27   Moreau de Saint-Méry, Description, I, p. 479.

which dominated the Straits of Florida and faced outward toward the Atlantic, the arc of towns encircling the island's eastern region, from Trinidad and Puerto Príncipe on the south coast to Holguin on the opposite side, focused inward toward the Caribbean. Older even than Havana and the site of the island's first colonial capital because of its proximity to the coast of Hispaniola, Santiago de Cuba was only slightly smaller than Kingston in 1791, with a total population of 19,703 residents.[28]

From its well-protected harbor, Santiago de Cuba looked out upon a system of smaller port cities in Jamaica and Saint-Domingue, linked by trade and geographical proximity. Barely twelve hours' sail to the southwest lay the excellent harbors of the north coast of Jamaica. As Jamaica's "North side" developed in the eighteenth century, they served as outlets to the sea for the northern tier of sugar-producing parishes—Hanover, St. James, Trelawny, St. Ann, St. Mary, and Portland. At the same time, these cities, situated close to foreign colonies and surrounded by "numerous creeks and bays, where small-decked vessels may run in at any time," provided staging areas for Jamaica-based smugglers and ports of call for their counterparts from Cuba, Saint-Domingue, and elsewhere.[29] By 1758, two of the busiest of these ports, Montego Bay and Port Antonio, had achieved sufficient stature to be named, along with Kingston and Savanna-la-Mar, official ports of entry and outfitted with proper courts and customs apparatus. The other northern towns—St. Ann's Bay, Falmouth, Martha Brae, and Lucea—became centers of commercial importance before

28 Juan Baptista Vaillant to Las Casas, 18 June 1791, "Resumen general de los moradores que comprehende la Ciudad de Cuba, y su respectivo territorio formado en el año de 1791," 18 June 1791, AGI, Cuba, leg. 1434; Antonio J. Valdés, *Historia de la isla de Cuba y en especial de la Habana*, rep. of 1813 edition (La Habana, 1964), pp. 63–4. See also the observations of Ramon de la Sagra, *Histoire physique et politique de l'isle de Cuba*, 2 tomes (Paris, 1844), I, pp. 34–5, regarding "the large number of anchorages for coasting vessels" along Cuba's east coast.

29 Jamaica Assembly, *Proceedings of the Honourable House of Assembly of Jamaica, on the Sugar and Slave-Trade* (London, 1793), p. 13. For Jamaica's pivotal role in regional contraband trade, see Allan Christelow, "Contraband Trade between Jamaica and the Spanish Main and the Free Port Act of 1766," *Hispanic American Historical Review* 22 (May 1942), pp. 309–43.

they attracted large numbers of permanent residents. One observer described the adjacent settlements of Falmouth and Martha Brae in 1794 as comprising between them "from 700 to 800 White Inhabitants, besides the People of Colour, who are pretty numerous," but so rapidly had the plantations of their hinterland expanded that officials predicted "in due course there will be more Sugar & Rum shipped there, than at any other Port." Martha Brae's application for free port status therefore received very serious consideration despite the town's diminutive size.[30] But when officials in Kingston and Port Royal spoke about the north coast of the island, they stressed the region's vulnerability as much as its commercial progress. Defenseless against "the frequent Depredations made by the Spanish Boats from Cuba," residents of the northern ports also lived under the long shadow of "cockpit country" and the maroon towns. For all these reasons, reported Governor Williamson in 1792, "the Spirit of discontent has usually first shewn itself" among the slaves of the north coast.[31]

Just fourteen leagues, or about forty-two miles, southeast of Spanish Cuba lay Môle Saint-Nicolas on the coast of Saint-Domingue, the strategic key to the vital Windward Passage, and only one among a dozen equally vibrant coastal towns of varying sizes dotting the jagged coast of the rich French colony.[32] Sandwiched in a strip of land between the mountains and the coast, the colony of Saint-Domingue showed an even stronger orientation toward its cities and the sea than either Cuba or Jamaica. Like Santiago de Cuba, Montego Bay, and their smaller satellites, the cities of Saint-Domingue's western and southern provinces owed their development and outlook as much to intra-Caribbean factors as to metropolitan intervention. Isolation from Cap Français because of the rugged mountains of the interior often left the cities of western and southern Saint-Domingue to their

30   Sir Alan Burns, *History of the British West Indies* (London, 1954), p. 495; Stephen Fuller to Duke of Portland, 18 February 1794, C.O. 137/93, PRO; Fuller to Henry Dundas, 18 February 1794, Letterpress Books, Stephen Fuller Papers, Duke University Library (hereinafter FLB).

31   Philip Affleck to Philip Stephens, 7 June 1790, Admiralty Records, PRO, class 1/ volume 244 (hereinafter ADM class/vol., PRO); Adam Williamson to Henry Dundas, 5 August 1792, C.O. 137/90, PRO.

32   Sagra, *Historia*, I, p. 19.

own devices; residents of Gonaïves, Saint-Marc, and Port-au-Prince in the west, and Jérémie, Cayes, and Jacmel in the south might easily have felt closer, both geographically and otherwise, to Cuba, Jamaica, and the northern coast of the South American mainland than to the Cap or to France. Largely ignored by vessels from France and accustomed to looking to foreign colonies for supplies in lean times, merchants and planters in these cities would raise the loudest cries for commercial and political independence in the early years of the French Revolution.

Even before revolutions in North America, France, Saint-Domingue, and Spanish America drew these cities into struggles for independent home rule, Caribbean port cities were natural magnets for all types of people seeking personal independence. Colonial authorities were ever mindful of the many invitations to masterlessness which the cities held out but also of the difficulties attached to regulating life in the towns. By comparison, life in the country, even with the many problems associated with controlling slave labor, was idyllic, ordered, and properly regimented. Whereas country life revolved around the predictable and steady regimen of the plantation, cities turned these work values on their heads in ways most inimical to the slave system. An 1801 visit to busy Kingston moved one British traveler to remark that "the desire of acquiring wealth without adequate exertion is a most vituperative and pernicious passion. Hence in all depots of trade we find a greater proportion than elsewhere of gamblers, swindlers, thieves, beggars, mountabanks and 33 pedlars."[33] White observers already familiar with this diverse panorama worried that the masterless tenor of life in the towns posed ever-present dangers of sedition. The governor's description of the same city a year earlier accurately reflected the agonies and fears of planters all over Afro-America. "Every kind of Vice that can be found in Commercial Towns," wrote Lord Balcarres in 1800,

---

33   Robert H. Fisher, "Narrative of a voyage to the West Indies, for the purpose of attempting the establishment of an Ice Market in the Island of Jamaica," (West Indian Travel Journal, 1800–1801), University of Virginia Library, pp. 26–7.

is pre-eminent in Kingston: here the imagination of Pandora's Box is fully exemplified. Turbulent people of all Nations engaged in illicit Trade; a most abandoned class of Negroes, up to every scene of mischief, and a general levelling spirit throughout, is the character of the lower orders in Kingston ... Should there be at any time an Insurrection among the Slaves

he projected, "here is not only a place of refuge in the first instance, but in a moment the Town might be laid in ashes."[34]

As Balcarres knew very well, cities had furnished places of refuge for plantation dissidents for generations. By mid-century, the larger towns attracted many runaway slaves from the surrounding countryside. In 1744, police authorities in Kingston attacked this problem by restricting the huts in outlying areas of the city, inhabited by free Negroes and the runaways they protected, to only one door, and compounds of more than four huts to one common entrance.[35] The earliest runaway notices for Saint-Domingue, printed in the newly founded *Gazette de Saint Domingue* in 1764, show that runaway slaves in the northern parishes of the French colony sensed a greater prospect of making a successful escape in Cap Français and its environs than either in the mountains or near the beckoning border of the neighboring Spanish colony.[36]

As the Caribbean's port towns grew in size, their attraction for runaway slaves increased apace. In the 1790s reports from the Spanish colonies confirm the active presence of bands of runaways in and around the coastal cities. In Caracas, such groups inhabited the vast plains, or *llanos*, which fanned out from the capital city. A conservative estimate placed the number of runaway slaves living and operating in the Caracas vicinity at around three hundred in 1791, and the number climbed rapidly over the next decade. The make-up of these groups probably included both fugitives from plantations and

---

34   Lord Balcarres to Commander-in-Chief, 31 July 1800, C.O. 137/104, PRO.

35   Pitman, *British West Indies*, 40n.

36   Gabriel Debien, "Les marrons de Saint-Domingue en 1764," *Jamaican Historical Review* 6 (1966), p. 15.

cattle farms and others who worked in the city itself.[37] Similar contingents centered around the Havana district in Cuba, where runaways were as active as they were in the mountains of the Santiago de Cuba region at the other end of the island. In June of 1791, problems in the "rounding up of fugitive blacks, so necessary to their owners, in the capturing of deserters, who fill up the countryside, and finally, in containing the disorders carried out all over by the malefactors sheltered in the mountains" severely stretched the capacities of municipal officials in Havana to deal with them.[38] Less than a year later, the *alcalde* of Jaruco, a sparsely populated satellite of Havana on Cuba's east coast, requested government aid in suppressing the recurrent "robberies and other scandals" perpetrated by fugitive slaves in the area.[39] By 1798, new regulations drawn up for controlling runaways from Cuba's rapidly expanding slave economy recognized both the problem of slaves running to cities as well as that of keeping the urban slaves themselves from absconding, as "most of the runaway slaves belong to residents of the city of Havana."[40]

Runaway slaves were also active in and around the cities of the French and British colonies in the 1790s. Between October 1790 and August 1791, French authorities apprehended 500 runaways in the vicinity of Cap Français alone. Figures recording the numbers of recaptured slaves and the place of their arrest seem to indicate that fugitives who found their way to the city proper eluded the authorities more successfully than those who roamed outlying districts.[41] In

37 See the *resumen* of "Expediente relativo al recurso de los Ganaderos y Hacendados de la Provincia de Caracas … Años de 1790 a 92," AGI, Sección de Gobierno, Audiencia de Caracas, leg. 15 (hereinafter AGI, Caracas).

38 Manuel Ventura Montero y Uriza to Las Casas, La Habana, 3 June 1791, AGI, Cuba, leg. 1465.

39 Las Casas to Marques de Cárdenas, La Habana, 10 February 1792, Marques de Cárdenas to Las Casas, La Habana, 14 February 1792, AGI, Cuba, leg. 1460.

40 "Supplemento al reglamento sobre esclavos cimarrones, mandado publicar por el Exmo. Sr. Gobernador y Capitán General," La Habana, 1 June 1798, Conde de Santa Clara to "Alcaldes de Hermandad de esta Ciudad y Pueblos de su Jurisdicn.," La Habana, 20 July 1798, AGI, Cuba, leg. 1508-A.

41 Jean Fouchard et Gabriel Debien, "Aspects de l'esclavage aux Antilles françaises: le petit marronage à Saint-Domingue autour du Cap (1790–1791),"

Jamaica, runaways crowded into busy Port Royal in the 1790s. Citing "the number of runaway negroes with which [the town] is infested," white inhabitants petitioned the Assembly in 1801 for funds to erect "a place of confinement" to control this population and to discourage others from coming.[42]

In addition to providing some unique opportunities for runaway slaves, Caribbean cities also held special attraction for free blacks and browns, the most marginal of the various groups comprising the masterless Caribbean. Whether plying trades, seeking work, or living by their wits, free nonwhites tended to settle in the towns, and the number of urban free people of color increased steadily during the period of the French Revolution. Always feared for their abilities to move about and disrupt the smooth functioning of the plantation economy, urban communities of free coloreds and free blacks imbibed the egalitarian spirit of the times and rapidly assumed a political voice which emerged and matured during the 1790s.

Free people of color were most numerous in the Spanish Caribbean, where they occupied a prominent demographic niche in urban areas. Free coloreds comprised twenty-two percent of the population of Havana and its suburbs in 1791. The populations of the towns along the Caribbean-oriented east coast contained even higher percentages of free black and brown residents. In Santiago de Cuba, figures from 1791 listed 6,698, or thirty-four percent, of the city's 19,703 residents as either free "Negroes" or free "mulattoes." A census taken the following year showed a similar pattern for Bayamo, where half the black population was free, and free nonwhites accounted for more than thirty-seven percent of the city's population of 22,417.[43] During the revolutionary period after 1791, the urban concentration of this

---

Cahiers des Amériques Latines: série "Sciences de l'homme" 3 (janvier–juin 1969), pp. 31–67.

42   Jamaica Assembly, *Journals of the Assembly of Jamaica*, 14 vols. (Jamaica, 1811–29), X, p. 491.

43   Vaillant to Las Casas, Cuba, 18 June 1791, "Resumen general de los moradores que comprehende la Ciudad de Cuba," 18 June 1791, Vaillant to Las Casas with enclosed *estados*, Cuba, 22 June 1792, AGI, Cuba, leg. 1434; Kenneth F. Kiple, *Blacks in Colonial Cuba, 1774–1899* (Gainesville, 1976), p. 85; Humboldt, *Island of Cuba*, pp. 112–14.

population expanded significantly. Alexander von Humboldt, visiting Cuba in the early years of Haitian independence, commented at great length upon the recent increase in the size of the free Negro population in urban Cuba. Because "Spanish legislation … favors in an extraordinary degree" their aspirations for freedom, he remarked, "many blacks (*negros*) acquire their freedom in the towns." Humboldt also cited an 1811 population study conducted by the *ayuntamiento* and *consulado* of Havana which found the black population, both free and enslaved, more thoroughly urbanized than ever. In the Havana district, where the number of free Negroes equaled the number of slaves, blacks and browns in the countryside outnumbered those in the towns by a slim ratio of three to two. On the east coast, fully half of all blacks and browns lived in the towns, and free people of color dominated some of the more sizable settlements. "The partido (district) of Bayamo," recorded Humboldt, "is notable for the large number of free colored (forty-four percent), which increases yearly, as also in Holguin and Baracoa." Indeed, he concluded, with a note of warning to Caribbean slavocracies, "since Haiti became emancipated, there are already in the Antilles more free negroes and mulattoes than slaves."[44]

Even before the watchwords of the French Revolution reached their ears, urban free coloreds in Spanish territories tested the limits of their masterless status and pressed for certain types of equality. This spirit surfaced most visibly within the ranks of the military. Since incorporation of free men of color into separate but ostensibly equal militia battalions began in the 1760s, the assertive behavior of these armed troops had drawn steady complaint from civil authorities. When officers of *pardo* and *moreno* militia units in Caracas demanded the same funeral observances and ceremonial garb as white officers early in 1789, Spanish officials worried that such attacks against the structure of inequality in the military would lead inevitably toward more general attacks on the structure of colonial society. This latest episode, feared the captain-general, represented the dangerous thin edge of an egalitarian wedge—or perhaps the sharp blade of a two-edged sword. "As much as I am aware of the grave difficulties which

---

44   Humboldt, *Island of Cuba*, pp. 187, 190–1, 212–13, 242.

every day of this so-called equality will bring," he wrote in April, "I also fear other evil consequences if their pretensions are denied. In the first case there is the risk of more haughtiness and audacity on the part of the officers; in the second ... disloyalty, the spirit of vengeance, and sedition."[45] Crown policy took a hard line against all evidence of such restiveness. In Cuba, just days before the first plantations were burned in neighboring Saint-Domingue, Luis de las Casas, governor and captain-general, received instructions from the Crown to silence the "old complaints" against white officers levelled by officers of the *pardo* and *moreno* units at Havana.[46]

In the British and French colonies, free people of color were considerably fewer in number than in Cuba and the other Spanish possessions, a fact which ironically underscored even more strongly their visibility as a masterless urban presence. Though rarely counted as carefully in population censuses, free blacks and browns seemed to cause much greater day-to-day concern among government officials and white residents in both Jamaica and Saint-Domingue than in the Spanish colonies. Jamaica's free people of color migrated to the area around Kingston. Almost sixty percent of the 3,408 "black and coloured" persons taking out certificates of freedom under a 1761 legislative act calling for the registration of all free persons in the island resided in Kingston and Spanish Town, the nearby capital city. In 1788, more than one-third of all the island's free colored people lived in Kingston alone, compared to twenty-two percent of all whites and seven percent of all slaves.[47]

---

45   Juan Guillelmi to Antonio Valdés, Caracas, 14 February, 30 April 1789, AGI, Caracas, leg. 113; Allan J. Kuethe, "The Status of the Free *Pardo* in the Disciplined Militia of New Granada," *Journal of Negro History* 56 (April 1971), p. 109. Though such racial terminology is never without its ambiguities, in general the Spanish used the term "*moreno*" to describe free blacks, and "*pardo*" to refer to the people whom the English called "mulattoes." See Magnus Mörner, *Race Mixture in the History of Latin America* (Boston, 1967), p. 44.

46   Las Casas to Conde del Campo de Alange, La Habana, 16 August 1791, AGI, Santo Domingo, leg. 1255.

47   "Return of the number of White Inhabitants, Free People of Colour and Slaves in the Island of Jamaica—Spanish Town, Nov. 1788," C.O. 137/87, PRO; George W. Roberts, *The Population of Jamaica* (Cambridge, 1957), pp. 38–9; W. J.

By 1788, white Jamaicans were sufficiently troubled about both the growth of this population and its mobility to bring such persons under more careful scrutiny. Concerned that the line between slavery and freedom should remain clearly demarcated to foil the efforts of slaves sliding imperceptibly into the free colored caste, the Assembly called upon "justices and vestry" from all parishes to

> cause diligent inquiry to be made within their respective parishes, as to the number of negroes, mulattoes, or Indians of free condition, and cause them to attend at their next meeting, and give an account in what manner they obtained their freedom, that their names and manner of obtaining their freedom may be registered in the vestry books of such parishes.[48]

But even this effort to weed out the slaves from the ranks of the masterless did little to check the tremendous growth of the free nonwhite population during the ensuing decade. As in Cuba, these numbers swelled during the period of the Haitian Revolution, as large numbers of free coloreds, many of them immigrants from Saint-Domingue, crowded into Kingston. When parish officials in Kingston petitioned for incorporation in 1801, they referred pointedly to the fact that "the population has of late greatly increased, and particularly as to foreigners and free persons of color," and called for more stringent law enforcement and "an efficient and strict police" to minimize the dangers posed by these masterless immigrants.[49]

In Saint-Domingue, free blacks and browns of the cities actively identified with the ideas of the French Revolution in an effort to improve their status, and in doing so unwittingly opened the door for the slave revolt of 1791. The presence of mulattoes and free blacks in

Gardner, *A History of Jamaica, from its Discovery by Christopher Columbus to the Year 1872*, reprint, new ed. (London, 1971), p. 173; Bryan Edwards, *The History, Civil and Commercial, of the British Colonies in the West Indies*, 4th ed., 3 vols. (London, 1807), I, pp. 260–1; Clarke, *Kingston*, p. 141.

48 *The New Act of Assembly of the Island of Jamaica ... Commonly Called. The New Consolidated Act ... Being the Present Code Noir of that Island* (London, 1789), article LXIX.

49 *Journals of the Assembly of Jamaica*, X, p. 507.

the cities was causing increased concern and comment as early as the 1770s. In addition to the brown artisans who were familiar fixtures, wrote one observer in 1775, "there are now in the Cities Mulattoes and Negroes, calling themselves free, who have no known means of subsistence." Questions concerning the loyalty of this class complicated the earliest efforts to regiment free colored men into police units to keep them off the streets. Opponents of such a measure reasoned that since "public tranquillity is assured, why give arms to the only men who might disrupt it?"[50] Such confidence in uninterrupted "public tranquillity" eroded quickly in the years leading up to the arrival of the French Revolution. By the 1780s, white observers saw free nonwhites in cities as sources of sedition to be carefully watched and controlled, and government functionaries took extra care to count the numbers of urban *affranchis* in their occasional censuses. For example, official figures noted only 195 free colored residents in 1775 in Cap Français, but in 1780, in what was apparently a more careful count, almost 1,400 people appeared in this category, ample testimony both to an expanding presence and to a mounting concern.[51] By the time the drama of the early French Revolution gripped Saint-Domingue's coastal cities, planters all over the island were expressing fears that agitation in the towns might spread to plantation areas through the agency of the blacks and mulattoes in nearby cities. "The idle negroes of the cities are the most dangerous," wrote a typical sugar planter from the western parish of Arcahaye in 1790. Moves were already under way "to expel from the towns all the vagrants, people who had nothing to lose," and who were at the center of all the agitation.[52]

Such concerns were not misplaced. Throughout the eighteenth century, planters found the links between city and country both vexing and essential. Acutely aware that cities with their free populations loomed as ever-present enticements to desertion for dissident slaves, they also recognized that the survival of their plantations

---

50   Michel René Hilliard d'Auberteuil, *Considérations sur l'état présent de la colonie française de Saint-Domingue*, 2 tomes (Paris, 1776), II, pp. 85–6.

51   Figures taken from Moreau de Saint-Méry, *Description*, I, pp. 479–80.

52   Joseph Laurent to Antoine Dolle l'Américain, Bordeaux, 4 August 1790, quoted in Léon, *Marchands et spéculateurs*, pp. 140–1.

depended upon the access to markets and the sea which port cities provided. Therefore, they actively worked to assure the free flow of goods between the interior and the coast, even though its potential costs to their social regime were obvious.

The growth of internal marketing systems in Caribbean societies, an eighteenth-century phenomenon closely tied to the growth of cities, presented further opportunities for individual mobility even as it brought the worlds of town and country closer together. In both Jamaica and Saint-Domingue, masterless people of all descriptions controlled in large measure the movement of foodstuffs and cheap consumer goods between cities and outlying areas. In the British colony, the practice of slaves raising their own fruits and vegetables on garden plots set aside for that purpose was well established through-out the island by mid-century. As the free population of the cities expanded, slaves found ready markets for their produce, which they exchanged for money or other items.[53]

From its inception, the Jamaican marketing system involved slave women and their free black and brown counterparts as the key agents. The Jamaican "higgler," a social type prominent in the society to the present day, became the broker in the lively commerce between country and city. Attracted by the profits to be gleaned as a go-between and by the measure of freedom and mobility which the life of the higgler promised, many women fled plantations to pursue higgling on a full-time basis. Phebe, a seamstress who left her Kingston plantation in 1787, was still at large and "passing" for free five years later. She was "said to be living either at Old-Harbour, Old-Harbour market, or in their vicinity, and to be a higgler."[54] Planters and town merchants tried hard to control these "wandering higglers," who "fore stal so many of the necessaries of life that are sold in our markets," and who brought news from the city to slaves on the plantations.[55]

---

53   See the seminal article by Sidney W. Mintz and Douglas Hall, "The Origins of the Jamaican Internal Marketing System," *Yale University Publications in Anthropology* (no. 57, 1960), esp. pp. 12–13, 15, 20.

54   Kingston *Royal Gazette*, 20 October 1792, file in National Library of Jamaica, Kingston (hereinafter NLJ).

55   Matthew Gregory Lewis, *Journal of a Residence among the Negroes in the*

For both economic and security reasons, therefore, higglers and other itinerant traders and peddlers found their chosen professions severely circumscribed by law, especially in times of tension like the early revolutionary era in the Caribbean. "No character is so dangerous in this Country as that of a Pedlar," reported a group of north coast planters in 1792, "and perhaps there was never a rebellion among the Slaves in the West India Islands which was not either entirely, or in part carried on through this Class of People."⁵⁶

In Saint-Domingue, internal marketing played the same role in linking the plantations with the cities. The opportunities within the domestic economy of the French colony attracted all types of people: poor urban whites out of work, free blacks and mulattoes, and privileged slaves, all dealing in produce and small European manufactures. In the cities themselves, free black and brown women took the central roles; many of them owned commercial "houses" and slaves of their own. And like the higglers of Jamaica, country women rose early to travel from plantation to plantation and buy produce from slaves to sell in city markets. Planter concern with the mobility of all these wandering buyers and sellers involved not only their pesky ability to control a large share of internal markets, but extended to their larger social role as well. The legendary maroon leader called Mackandal, who led a campaign to poison all the whites of the northern province in the 1760s, made brilliant use of a network of itinerant traders to predict and control events at long distances, thereby enhancing his status as a powerful religious mystic among his slave followers.⁵⁷ These intermediaries would play a pivotal role in bringing from the cities to the plantations news of the excitement brewing after 1789.⁵⁸

West Indies (London, 1845), p. 41; *Royal Gazette*, 2 March 1793. For a description of the working life of a modern higgler which emphasizes her role in communication between her community and "former neighbours now living in town," see Margaret Fisher Katzin, "The Jamaican Country Higgler," *Social and Economic Studies* 8 (December 1959), pp. 421–35.

56   "Minutes of the proceedings of the Committee of Secrecy and Safety in the Parish of St. James's, Jamaica," [1792], C.O. 137/90, PRO.

57   "Minutes of the proceedings of the Committee of Secrecy and Safety," C.O. 137/90, PRO.

58   See Hénock Trouillot, "Les sans-travail, les pacotilleurs et les marchands à

A wide variety of masterless types joined the slaves, runaways, and free blacks in Caribbean towns. Colonial governments experienced as much difficulty controlling many of the European immigrants as they did managing slaves. From early in the eighteenth century, for example, white immigrants in search of fortune or imported for the purpose of moderating the widening black/white population imbalance proved troublesome to the authorities in the British and French Caribbean. A 1717 experiment of the British Parliament that shipped convict laborers to the colonies as indentured servants soon backfired. Just months after the arrival of the first wave of bonded immigrants, Jamaica's governor reported that

> so farr from altering their Evil Courses and way of living and becoming an Advantage to Us, ... the greatest part of them are gone and have Induced others to go with them a Pyrating and have Inveigled and Encouraged Severall Negroes to desert from their Masters ... The few that remains proves a wicked Lazy and Indolent people, so that I could heartily wish this Country might be troubled with no more of them.

Just as displeasing to government officials were the results of the so-called Deficiency Laws, annual acts dating from 1718 which stipulated that plantation owners maintain fixed ratios of whites to blacks and livestock or pay fines. Governor Robert Hunter complained in 1731 that the whites introduced under this plan, many of them Irish Catholics, were liabilities to the community, "a lazy useless sort of people" whose loyalties were always suspect.[59] By the 1780s, however, the planter class had swallowed at least some of its distaste for whites of lower station, though the price for this precarious white solidarity seemed a bit high for some. Planter-historian Bryan Edwards described the white commoner who "approaches his employer with an extended hand, and a freedom, which, in the countries of Europe, is seldom displayed by men in the lower orders of life towards their

---

Saint-Domingue," *Revue de la société haïtienne d'histoire* 29 (1956), pp. 47–66.

59   Nicolas Lawes to Board of Trade, 1 September 1718, C.O. 137/13, PRO, Robert Hunter to Board of Trade, 13 November 1731, C.O. 137/19, PRO, both quoted in Pitman, *British West Indies*, pp. 54, 55–6.

superiors;" Edwards found these pretensions to equality almost as disturbing as he later would find those of the free coloreds.[60]

French officials in Saint-Domingue echoed the same sentiments in the 1770s and 1780s, when the fabled "prosperity" of the colony attracted large numbers of European immigrants seeking to carve out a share of the profits for themselves. According to one observer, the new arrivals consisted largely of sturdy artisans, including "carpenters, joiners, masons, coopers, locksmiths, wheelwrights, saddlers, coach-builders, watchmakers, goldsmiths, jewelers, and barbers," seeking to escape tough economic conditions at home.[61] But a Cap Français police report of 1780 speaks anxiously of the "people arriving daily from Europe, who, for the most part, have crossed the ocean to flee their families and their country, and have come to America in order to escape the reprisals of relatives and of the law."[62] Distinctly multinational in character, the wave of immigration of these ambitious and often desperate people, mostly young men, brought to Saint-Domingue's cities a new and restless population of *"petits blancs"* of boundless mobility and suspect loyalties. When British forces invaded Saint-Domingue in 1793, remembered a colonel involved in that effort, they encountered considerable resistance from urban whites whom he could only describe as "adventurers from every part of Europe" who had come to the Caribbean "in quest of fortune."[63]

Like the free Negroes, mulattoes, and runaway slaves with whom they came into contact upon their arrival, unruly European immigrants soon found themselves unwelcome guests in a society where the power of masters depended to such a degree on the maintenance of social order. Hilliard d'Auberteuil reflected the prevailing sentiment of Saint-Domingue's establishment when he referred contemptuously

---

60   Edwards, *History, Civil and Commercial*, II, pp. 7–8.

61   S. J. Ducoeurjoly, *Manuel des habitans de Saint-Domingue*, 2 tomes (Paris, 1802), II, p. 63.

62   "Mémoire sur la police du Cap" (1780), reprinted in Pierre de Vassière, *Saint-Domingue: la société et la vie créoles sous l'ancien régime (1629–1789)* (Paris, 1909), pp. 337–8.

63   Colonel Chalmers, *Remarks on the Late War in St. Domingo, with Observations on the Relative Situation of Jamaica, and Other Interesting Subjects* (London, 1803), pp. 8–9.

to this vicious "mob of vagabonds and adventurers hurling themselves upon these shores ... without trade or property ... No citizen or inhabitant dares to trust them."[64] They shared equally with the free people of color in the blame for a rise in urban crime, and authorities at the Cap accused them of bringing with them all the vices of the European urban proletariat, among them "robberies, brawls, gambling, libertinism, mutinies, even sedition."[65] The governor of Martinique, another French Caribbean colony, even breathed a sigh of relief when large numbers of restless urban whites departed his island for Saint-Domingue, "where they may give themselves up to hunting and disorder, and where licentious liberty is complete."[66] A lieutenant in the French navy who saw service in the Caribbean in 1790 and 1791, presciently predicted that the urban *petits blancs*, this "refuse of all nations," would become "one of the best elements of propaganda for revolutionary agitation."[67]

The lower orders of whites in the cities consisted of more than just poor adventurers. A substantial number of them were deserters from the military, masterless men by choice whom colonial authorities mentioned in the same breath with runaway slaves. All over the Caribbean, commanders of colonial regiments complained both about the quality of the men sent out from home and of the willingness of their charges to shirk their prescribed duties in favor of the chance for independence. The British governor of St. Vincent expressed this frustration in 1777, calling the latest crop of recruits "the very scum of the Earth. The Streets of London must have been swept of their refuse, the Gaols emptied ... I should say the very Gibbets had been robbed to furnish such Recruits, literally most of them fit only ... to fill a pit with."[68] The unenviable reputation of European servicemen

---

64 Hilliard d'Auberteuil, *Considérations*, II, pp. 55–6.

65 "Mémoire sur la police du Cap."

66 Quoted in T. Lothrop Stoddard, *The French Revolution in San Domingo* (Boston and New York, 1914), p. 4.

67 Chevalier Camille de Valous, *Avec les "rouges" aux Iles du Vent: souvenirs du Chevalier de Valous (1790–1793)* (Paris, 1930), p. 5.

68 Quoted in Lowell Joseph Ragatz, *The Fall of the Planter Class in the British Caribbean, 1763–1833* (New York and London, 1928), pp. 31–2.

posted to the West Indies as "undisciplined men" of "irregular habits" stalks them in the recent literature as relentlessly as it did in the eighteenth century.[69]

Rates of desertion climbed when war and rumors of war drove soldiers away from the barracks and sailors off the ships, but, like all the other forms of popular resistance present in the Caribbean, desertion was a time-honored tradition in both war and peace by the close of the eighteenth century. Invitations to desert were not lacking. Discipline in colonial regiments was rigid and uncompromising; frequent epidemics ravaged the ranks of newly arrived troops, confined as they often were in close and unsanitary quarters; and many opportunities to participate in local cultures beckoned. Deserters from Spanish regiments enjoyed the unique option of taking refuge in churches, where law and custom protected them from apprehension. But others of all nationalities eagerly shipped themselves aboard small merchant or contrabanding vessels, lost themselves in cities, or wandered from place to place as vagrants.

In the early 1790s, the political currents then swirling about the Atlantic basin also led soldiers and sailors to desertion and other more direct forms of resistance to military authority. Advertisements for deserters in Jamaica regiments suggest such political avenues of explanation. For example, many reports describe deserters of Irish background. James Regan, whose heavy brogue branded him as distinctive, deserted the Kingston barrack in 1792, taking with him the clothes, money, and even the commission of his English captain. He then hired a horse and a young black guide, traveled across the island to "one of the Northside ports," and tried unsuccessfully to pass himself off as his captain in an effort to gain passage off the island.[70] A group of five deserters from the 62nd Regiment which absconded around the same time included only one Englishman and three Irishmen.[71] Henry Hamilton, another native of Ireland and a weaver by trade, left the barrack at Stony Hill with an older Scottish comrade,

---

69 See Roger Norman Buckley, *Slaves in Red Coats: The British West India Regiments, 1795–1815* (New Haven and London, 1979), pp. 3, 166n.

70 *Royal Gazette*, 4 August, 1 September 1792.

71 *Royal Gazette*, 20 October 1792.

also a weaver, in August, 1793.[72] The apparent unrest among Irish soldiers and seamen in royal service in the early 1790s coincides closely with the emergence of nationalist republicanism in Ireland, a new and vital stage in the developing opposition to British rule. If deserters from British regiments in the West Indies included Irish dissidents, such activity provides some background to the role which the United Irishmen would play in the naval mutinies of 1797 at Spithead and the Nore. In the Caribbean itself, such a radical stream might sometimes find an immediate outlet in local struggles against the British. Just after the black rebels of Saint-Domingue captured Cap Français in the late spring of 1793, the commander of a British armed cutter serving off the coast of the rebellious colony identified a notorious "Irishman of prodigious size" and thick brogue as "a deserter from his cutter, on board of which he had acted as boatswain." The deserter had recently been spotted as one of the motley crew of a large "rowboat, armed with fifty or sixty men of all colors" which preyed on British and American shipping and had apparently made common cause with the black rebels on land.[73]

The wide-ranging efforts of colonial governments to discourage such behavior echo parallel efforts to control runaway slaves. In Jamaica, advertisements for military deserters appeared in newspapers on the same pages as notices for slave deserters, and apprehended deserters could expect the kind of swift and severe punishment routinely meted out to rebellious slaves. Early in 1791, military authorities sentenced "a marine and a seaman" guilty of deserting one of the king's warships in Port Royal to receive 500 lashes each, though later "the Admiral humanely remitted half the punishment."[74] Governors,

72 *Royal Gazette*, 17 August 1793.

73 Samuel G. Perkins, *Reminiscences of the Insurrection in St. Domingo* (Cambridge, 1886), pp. 72–3. See Marianne Elliott, *Partners in Revolution: The United Irishmen and France* (New Haven and London, 1982), pp. 17–34, for a general discussion of the early development of Irish republicanism and its relationship to the French Revolution.

74 *Kingston Daily Advertiser*, 6 January 1791, file in American Antiquarian Society, Worcester, Massachusetts (hereinafter AAS). See also the case of the deserted sailor apprehended and brought to trial in Port Royal in June 1792. The court sentenced him "to be flogged from ship to ship" as an example to the other

officers, the Assembly, and private citizens also offered bounties for aid in the recovery of deserters, in much the same fashion as they did for absent slaves. Often the lines between different forms of desertion became blurry indeed. For example, when authorities apprehended mulatto Josef Isidro Puncel at two in the morning near the gates of the central plaza in Havana, they jailed him as a runaway slave, only to find upon closer investigation that he was actually a free deserter from the armada.[75] On the other hand, since the security of planters, merchants, colonial officials, and their families depended in large measure upon the strength, loyalty, and readiness of military forces, they enjoyed some leeway which runaway slaves did not possess. Early in 1789 and again four years later, as the prospect of war loomed on the horizon, the Spanish Crown attempted to bring deserters back into the fold by issuing an amnesty covering all those found guilty of desertion and contrabanding, both at large and in prison.[76]

One particular incident of desertion involving a group of British regimental musicians provides a rare glimpse into Governor Balcarres's "Pandora's Box"—the complex urban underground protecting fugitives from the discipline of Caribbean slave society. Too often ignored by military historians, musicians were integral to British army regiments in the West Indies and elsewhere, and their role as well as their numbers appear to have expanded between the middle of the eighteenth century and the era of the Napoleonic wars.[77] As military bands in Europe broadened both in size and instrumentation during this period, black musicians became increasingly prominent and by the 1780s could be found playing beside whites in all parts

---

sailors in the fleet entertaining similar ideas. The punishment added up to a painful total of eighty-four lashes. *Royal Gazette*, 23 June 1792.

75   Juan Manuel García Chicano to Las Casas, La Habana, 12 July 1794, AGI, Cuba, leg. 1465.

76   Juan Guillelmi to Valdés, Caracas, 30 April 1789, AGI, Caracas, leg. 113; Pedro Carbonell to Campo de Alange, Caracas, 31 July 1793, AGI, Caracas, leg. 94; Las Casas to Campo de Alange, La Habana, 11 June 1793, AGI, Santo Domingo, leg. 1261.

77   H. C. B. Rogers, *The British Army of the Eighteenth Century* (New York, 1977), pp. 43–4.

of the continent. Crashing cymbals and beating kettledrums, tambourines, bass drums, triangles, and so-called "Jingling Johnies," blacks in British bands brought with them new sounds which the bands eagerly incorporated as part of the ongoing process of cultural borrowing which had always characterized British military music.[78] More extensive borrowing occurred in the West Indies. In the islands, blacks appeared in European military bands very early in the century; black drummers performed in French regiments at least as early as the 1720s. By the end of the century, British regimental bands also drew readily upon black talent. The presence of local black musicians in these bands not only affected their music, but also provided disaffected British musicians routes of access to the vibrant musical culture of the islands and ultimately to the underground which nourished it.

In the 1790s in Jamaica, musicians from British regiments appear especially prone to desertion. This was certainly the case in the 10th Regiment of Foot stationed near Kingston. In April of 1793, the commanding officer of the 10th Regiment circulated in local newspapers notices for musicians who had absconded at different times that month. One of these deserters was Samuel Reed, an Irish "labourer" of about twenty-five who had played the clarinet and other instruments. Just days after Reed's disappearance, Joseph Lees, a drummer, left the barracks to join him.[79]

Perhaps Reed and Lees were attempting to join two fellow musicians who had been absent for more than a year. In dramatic fashion late in February 1792, ten musicians—no doubt most of the band— had deserted from the 10th Regiment and headed for Kingston. Apparently the escape was well planned. The deserters first found shelter at the home of an old friend, a brown man called Jacob Hyam, who had himself recently served as a fifer to an artillery company in the same regiment. Closely following their trail, military authorities apprehended three of the musicians at Hyam's home; the rest escaped. Several days later, three more of the deserters were caught, this time hiding out at the home of "an old white woman named Mary Ellis"

---

78 Henry George Farmer, *Military Music* (London, 1950), pp. 35–7.
79 *Royal Gazette*, 4 May 1793.

who lived in a dark and seamy section of Kingston popularly known as "Damnation-alley." Here those tracking the four who remained at large discovered that only a day or two before, "finding themselves warmly pursued," the alert musicians "parted company, and took different routes." Two of the remaining four were soon taken up shortly before they boarded a vessel at Savanna-la-Mar.[80]

By late March, then, only two of the original ten had managed to elude the authorities, George Theodorus Eskirkin (a native of Ireland known to friends simply as "Dorus") and Quebec native John Sims. Both Eskirkin and Sims were accomplished musicians whose talents and interests included but ranged beyond mastery of the staple instruments issued to military musicians—the flute, hautboy, fife, and clarinet. Eskirkin, in the words of his commander, could "beat the drum," and Sims enjoyed the "violin, violin-cello, harpsichord … basoon, and guitar." Although the musical backgrounds of these two men differed in fundamental ways from those of the local musicians, their interests in the types of percussive and stringed instruments popular among black musicians in Jamaica may have enabled them to find kindred spirits in the underground who continued to help them evade the clutches of their pursuers. After leaving Jacob Hyam (now confined in the parish jail for having harbored the fugitives) and Mary Ellis, Sims and Eskirkin remained a step ahead of the law and moved to nearby Spanish Town, where they were often seen in the company of another notorious musician, "a black man named Jack Nailor," like Sims "a Fiddler" who made his home somewhere "in the Jew market." Either under Nailor's tutelage or on their own, the two deserters began taking up disguises in order to lose themselves amid the comings and goings of the capital. Sometimes they appeared as British seamen, dressed in long black stockings and tarred baggy trousers; at other times they became Spanish, effecting accents and walking about with "coloured handkerchiefs tied about their heads, and striped linen jackets and trousers." By mid-summer, exasperated authorities had all but given up on trying to apprehend Eskirkin and Sims, whom they

---

80   The saga of these deserters may be followed in the *Royal Gazette*, 24, 31 March, 5 May, 22 June 1792.

now described as literally indistinguishable from their darker-skinned companions in Kingston and Spanish Town. Said to be "fishing and shooting" along the southern coast, the two musicians had come to "look as brown as some people of colour." There is no record of either having been taken up and returned to military duty.

For Dorus and John, music proved to be the thread of common experience linking their adventure to the struggles of masterless men and women in Kingston's urban underground attempting to fashion a life outside the scrutiny of Caribbean officialdom. Their success reflects the difficulties these officials faced in disentangling the networks which permitted people of all types and descriptions to resist authority and assert a mobile existence. Such popular resistance and mobility would become key factors allowing for the transmission of the excitement of social revolution in the Caribbean. It is essential to recognize, however, that these networks were not confined discretely to single islands or areas but stretched to encompass entire regions. It is to this vital inter-island mobility—the world of ships and sailors— that we now turn our attention.

2.

"Negroes in Foreign Bottoms"

Sailors, Slaves, and Communication

After planters and merchants forced them off the land in the late 1600s, Caribbean buccaneers took to the sea as pirates. As slavery expanded in the next century, sailing vessels remained a refuge for the disaffected. By the 1790s, residents of the region recognized a close symbolic connection between experience at sea and freedom. In typical fashion, when Tom King, a Kingston slave "well-known in this Town, Spanish-Town, and Port Royal," slipped away in November 1790, his owner warned that King, "having been at sea may attempt to pass for a Free Man."[1]

In the same spirit as King's owner, many slaveholding whites in the eighteenth-century Caribbean commonly observed that "it was a very dangerous thing to let a negro know navigation." Olaudah Equiano, a slave who became a sailor in the 1760s and 1770s and eventually worked his way to freedom, felt that his mobile occupation placed him on a more equal footing with his owner, and he did not hesitate to "tell him my mind."[2] Whites often accused non-plantation and skilled black workers of insolence, but slaves who looked to the sea for either employment or escape posed special problems of control, as did those masterless blacks and browns who arrived in vessels from foreign colonies. Whether runaways like Tom King or sailors like Equiano, many slaves found it in their interest to orient themselves toward the sea and

---

1 *Kingston Daily Advertiser*, 4 February 1791.

2 [Olaudah Equiano], *The Life of Olaudah Equiano, or Gustavus Vassa the African. Written by Himself* (London, 1837; reprint ed., New York, 1969), pp. 137, 141.

the world beyond the horizon. The movement of ships and seamen not only offered opportunities for developing skills or escaping, but provided the medium of long-distance communication and allowed interested Afro-Americans to follow developments in other parts of the world.

Deep sea sailors from European vessels made up a highly visible segment of the Caribbean underground, where they formed local connections, kept people abreast of developments overseas, and often ran afoul of local authorities. In the late eighteenth century, these seamen arrived in the colonies in substantial numbers, especially considering local population levels. By the late 1780s, roughly 21,000 British mariners traveled to the West Indian colonies each year. In 1788, Jamaica's trade alone employed close to 500 ships and well over 9,000 seamen. More than twice as many French sailors arrived in Saint-Domingue in 1789, when 710 vessels brought 18,460 mariners to the booming French colony. In a small but growing city like Cap Français, this dockside constituency represented a sizable percentage of the population. By multiplying numbers of ships in the harbor "in normal times" by average crew sizes, Moreau de Saint-Méry estimated that about 2,550 seamen occupied Cap Français at any given time. In a city whose official population was barely above 12,000 in 1788, sailors outnumbered both white and free colored residents.[3]

While the population of arriving seamen saw considerable turnover, individual sailors might remain in the islands for considerable periods of time. Depending upon the time of year, the state of the market, prices, and other factors, ships' masters and supercargoes often required several weeks to put together a full cargo for the return voyage; preparing the vessels for sea compounded these inevitable delays. Disease, one of the many occupational hazards of life before

---

3 Minutes of the West India Planters and Merchants, London, 19 May 1789, West India Committee Archives (microfilm, 17 reels), M–915, Institute of Commonwealth Studies, London, reel 3 (hereinafter Minutes of WIPM); Dallas, *History of the Maroons*, I, pp. 6–7; William Walton, Jr., *Present State of the Spanish Colonies: including a Particular Report of Hispañola, or the Spanish Part of Santo Domingo*, 2 vols. (London, 1810), I, pp. 298–9; Moreau de Saint-Méry, *Description*, I, pp. 479–80.

the mast, also lengthened the stay of many seamen. In Jamaica for example, sailors made up eighty-four percent of the persons—301 of 359—checking in to the Island Hospital in Kingston in 1791; the following year, they comprised seventy-eight percent of the hospital's patients.[4] Finally, some of the sailors undoubtedly decided to linger in the colonies rather than subject themselves again to the rigid discipline and absolute authority of ship captains.

The behavior of seamen left to their own devices ashore caused steady complaint among Caribbean officials and presented a social control problem for police authorities throughout the region. Jamaican newspapers decried the "riotous and disorderly" conduct of sailors in Port Royal, Kingston, and the port cities of the north coast, and carried frequent accounts of clashes between transient Jack Tars and local militia units. Kingston's Town Guard, whose primary task consisted of controlling the movements of slaves after dark, routinely turned out to round up groups of rowdy sailors accused of disturbing the peace, whom the guardsmen shepherded to the parish jail or confined aboard royal vessels at anchor in Port Royal.[5] Collective resistance to such displays of authority, however, became a vital part of the ethos of the Anglo-American merchant seaman, as Jamaican authorities knew only too well. When a town magistrate in St. Ann's Bay sentenced one of their number to jail for "harassing" a local resident, "a mob of sailors" collected in front of the guilty official's home, "determined to rescue the prisoner from the constable." The frightened magistrate sounded the alarm, summoning the Light Infantry, which finally dispersed the gathering crowd and enabled "a file of men" to escort the prisoner to jail.[6]

Like the many laws designed to regulate the conduct of slaves, legislation directed against British seamen in the West Indies aimed to maintain their loyalty through a combination of half-hearted "reforms" and rigid restrictions. Legal pressure increased in times of international tension such as the late 1780s and 1790s, when navies

4   "Account of the Sick admitted into the Island Hospital, in Kingston," printed in *Royal Gazette*, 26 January 1793.

5   *Royal Gazette*, 7 July 1792.

6   *Royal Gazette*, 5 May 1792.

expected merchant marines to provide a reserve of able-bodied and experienced seamen to man the warships. A royal proclamation of 1788, for example, prohibited British seamen in the West Indies "from serving foreign Princes and States." In the early 1790s, Jamaica's House of Assembly brought forward measures "for the better order and government of the sea-port towns in this island," one of which promised to prevent "cheats, frauds, and abuses, in paying seamen's wages." With the declaration of war against France in 1793, however, the resistance of merchant sailors to service in the Royal Navy forced the Assembly to adopt another approach. "The Seamen having fled into the Country the moment they discovered by the public Papers ... that War had taken place," the Assembly drafted a tougher bill "to prevent their deserting from the ships or vessels to which they belong, and also to prevent their being harbored or concealed by persons keeping tippling or punch houses, and retailing rum and other spiritous liquors." Three years later, however, exasperated military officers continued to complain that "Crimping Houses and [other] Suspected places" where sailors congregated still protected deserters.[7]

Legislators seldom expressed openly the full range of their motives in putting such legislation into effect, but laws regulating the behavior of seamen undoubtedly aimed at driving a wedge between the mariners from Europe and local blacks and browns and at preventing any mutual sharing of interest or information. Subject to arbitrary punishments (including the lash) and often pressed or tricked into merchant vessels against their will, sailors might have easily found some common cause with local slaves. The language of these statutes usually cited the necessity of maintaining public order after hours. Grenada's "Police Act" of 1789 singled out for stiff penalties male slaves, free coloreds, and sailors who "to the ruin of their own health and morals, and to the evil example and seduction of others" gambled and caroused in the island's gaming houses by night.[8]

---

7 John Orde to Lord Sydney, 11 May 1788, C.O. 71/14, PRO; *Journals of the Assembly of Jamaica*, IX, pp. 93, 115, 336, 345–7; John Ford to Philip Stephens, 14 April 1793, ADM 1/245, PRO; Council to Hyde Parker, 1 July 1797, C.O. 137/98, PRO.

8 Cited in Edward L. Cox, *Free Coloreds in the Slave Societies of St. Kitts and Grenada. 1763–1833* (Knoxville, 1984), pp. 94–5.

Controlling other activities which brought together slaves and sailors from abroad, however, presented greater difficulty. Sailors provided a natural market for the produce grown by slaves in their garden plots—"yams, cocoas, plantains, bananas, fruits, &c."—which they swapped for the salted beef, linens, shoes, or other goods which made up the "private adventures" of the seamen—portions of their ships' cargo which they were allowed to trade on their own account. Irish merchant James Kelly, who inherited a wharf on the north coast of Jamaica early in the nineteenth century, observed with fascination the operation of this system of internal marketing and the interaction which grew up around it. "Sailors and Negroes are ever on the most amicable terms," he remarked, describing a "mutual confidence and familiarity" and "a feeling of independence in their intercourse" which contrasted sharply with the "degradation" blacks suffered in their everyday relationships with local whites.[9] Contact between sailors and West Indian blacks also had enduring cultural consequences. Many popular sea shanties, maritime work songs which traveled with sailors on British ships to all parts of the globe in the nineteenth century, bear striking resemblances to Caribbean slave songs; in fact, considerable evidence exists to show that the very practice of shantying may have its roots in the interaction of sailors and black dockworkers on the shorelines of the West Indian islands. One theory of the origins and development of pidgin and creole languages in the Caribbean region likewise emphasizes contact and borrowing between European sailors and African slaves.[10]

The commerce of Saint-Domingue brought to that colony an extraordinarily diverse group of European sailors. Like their British counterparts in Jamaica, many of these seamen participated actively

---

9   James Kelly, *Voyage to Jamaica, and Seventeen Years' Residence in that Island: Chiefly Written with a View to Exibit Negro Life and Habits*, 2nd ed. (Belfast, 1838), pp. 17, 29–30.

10   Roger D. Abrahams, *Deep the Water. Shallow the Shore: Three Essays on Shantying in the West Indies* (Austin and London, 1974), pp. 3–21; John E. Reinecke, "Trade Jargons and Creole Dialects as Marginal Languages," *Social Forces* 17 (October 1938), pp. 107–18; Loreto Todd, *Pidgins and Creoles* (London and Boston, 1974), pp. 32–3.

in the local underground and economy. In 1790, French Minister of the Marine La Luzerne reported that Saint-Domingue teemed with French mariners but also "Majorcans, Minorcans, Italians, Maltese, and other seafarers" laying over "in the course of a longer voyage" or "attracted to Saint-Domingue by the hope of a better lot." By this time, the island's port cities had long experience with accommodating these sailors. One observer in the 1770s counted no less than fifteen hundred "cabarets" and "Billiards," small drinking and gambling joints which catered to an unending stream of "twelve thousand Navigators and seafarers" who frequented these establishments and "make them profitable."[11]

Though municipal governments passed ordinances in response to the complaints of colonists about the sailors leading masterless lives in "cabarets, in dark gambling houses, or among the slaves," these laws registered little effect. In the Cap, for example, bar owners, slaves, and the authorities alike simply ignored regulations passed in 1780 limiting the number of such establishments and setting down rules for their operation. Bars remained open long after the appointed hour of closing, and owners violated other provisions by exceeding the restrictions on the amount of rum which they could dispense and by refusing to clear slaves from their places of business. A special division of the police force of Cap Français charged with keeping the sailors in line and with finding "all deserted mariners" was similarly ineffective.[12]

As in the British islands, extensive contact between seamen and local slaves and free coloreds occurred in the daylight hours as well as after dark. According to contemporary observers in Cap Français, sailors traditionally set up stands along the wharves on Sundays and holidays to barter and trade with all comers, including slaves. This so-called "white market," almost as old as the city itself, survived despite official opposition because sailors violently resisted several attempts

---

11 *Mémoire envoyé le 18 juin 1790, au Comité des Rapports de l'Assemblée Nationale, par M. de la Luzerne* (Paris, 1790), p. 27, RSD; Hilliard d'Auberteuil, *Considérations*, II, 42n.

12 Hilliard d'Auberteuil, *Considerations*, II, pp. 55–56; Moreau de Saint-Méry, *Description*, I, pp. 469, 475.

to close it down. Perhaps as a result of interaction with sailors, certain aspects of the language and culture of the slaves of Saint-Domingue suggest an orientation toward the world of the sea. Mingled with French, Spanish, and African components, several "sea terms also found their place" in the island's distinctive creole language. In addition, African women in Saint-Domingue sometimes referred to each other as "sailors," a custom which Moreau de Saint-Méry traced back to the old buccaneers who used the term as a way of confirming their solidarity.[13]

The constant yet shifting stream of itinerant seafaring folk provided the masterless underground in the colonies with a crucial transatlantic connection. As developments in Europe began to affect the future of slavery in the colonies, these sailors brought with them reports of great interest to both slaves and their owners. By 1790, British sailors arrived with news that an antislavery movement was gathering momentum in England, while French seamen wearing tricolored cockades had even more exciting stories to tell of political developments in France.

As outposts of European empires, each of the American colonies operated, at least in theory, within autarkic commercial schemes designed to keep colonial trade inside the imperial system and to protect this trade from the meddling of outsiders, thereby enhancing the state treasury. But from the beginning, fraud, bribery, smuggling, and other forms of illegal commerce linked together the colonies of the European powers in the Caribbean region despite the numerous official barriers. By the end of the eighteenth century, the British Navigation Acts, the French *exclusif*, and the Spanish *flota* system had gradually given way to modified approaches which precariously balanced the competing interests of free trade and imperial revenue. These concessions to local practice reflect the Caribbean reality of a regional community where geographic proximity was often more important than national boundaries. The easing of commercial restrictions had the effect of increasing intercolonial communication.

---

13   Moreau de Saint-Méry, *Description*, I, pp. 57, 81–2, 315–16.

Denmark created the first Caribbean "free port" in 1724, opening St. Thomas to the ships of every nation as a place where seafaring folk from all over the region could come together to exchange goods and information without the intrusion of mercantilist regulations. Before 1800 all the colonial powers followed suit and experimented with similar measures to attract the shipping of their rivals and undercut smugglers by taking away part of the incentive for illegal intercolonial trade. The slow movement toward less restricted, if not "free," trade picked up steam after 1763. In 1766, the first of the British Free Port Acts provided French and Spanish ships controlled access to ports in Jamaica and Dominica. The next year the French followed suit, opening Môle Saint-Nicolas to foreign shipping, and they extended these provisions to include Cap Français, Port-au-Prince, and Cayes in 1784. Meanwhile the Spanish Crown, following the devastating defeats of the Seven Years' War, began to institute similar reforms along the lines suggested by the Bourbon reformers in France. After first breaking the Sevilla-Cádiz monopoly on trade with the Indies, the new policies allowed Spanish ports in the colonies (with the exception of those belonging to the Captaincy-General of Caracas) to trade directly with one another in 1778.[14]

Even though they exclude the large number of ships which continued to engage in contraband trade after 1780 and record only how many vessels took advantage of these new regulations, official trade figures testify to the extent to which seagoing commerce bound the Caribbean community together. Jamaica's entry into the free port system, devised primarily to attract the trade of the French and Spanish, brought ships from Cuba, from the Spanish and French colonies on Hispaniola, and from as far south as the island of Curaçao and the port of Coro on the coast of Venezuela. These foreign vessels, while never constituting a majority of entering ships, nevertheless represented a significant

---

14 Armytage, *Free Port System*, pp. 54–5; Léon Deschamps, *Les colonies pendant la Révolution, la Constituante et la réforme coloniale* (Paris, 1898), pp. 21–2; *resumen* of the report of the Regente de la Real Audiencia de Santo Domingo on the commerce of Saint-Domingue up to 1788, Santo Domingo, 25 September 1793, AGI, Santo Domingo, leg. 1031; John Lynch, *Spanish Colonial Administration, 1782–1810: The Intendant System in the Viceroyalty of Río de la Plata* (London, 1958), pp. 1–24.

percentage. In the last quarter of 1787, Jamaican customs agents registered eighty-nine British ships and sixty-four foreign vessels. During
the next six months, eighty-six more Spanish vessels and seventy-two
French vessels, over fifty of them from Saint-Domingue, called at
Kingston alone. In the early 1790s, Jamaican newspapers recorded
the daily arrivals of foreign vessels, but were careful to hide specif-
ics in order to protect them from reprisals in their home territories,
where such activity might still be considered illegal. Even during the
war year of 1793, almost 350 foreign vessels successfully eluded the
privateers to land at Jamaica.[15]

The kinds of goods which flowed into the British colonies from
this regional trade touched the everyday lives of people throughout
the social structure and therefore probably attracted general interest.
Jamaica's commercial connection with the Spanish in Cuba brought to
the island vitally needed livestock, fresh beef, and specie. Ships arriving from Saint-Domingue, on the other hand, provided foodstuffs for
the consumption of slaves and the king's soldiers and sailors. In 1790
and 1791, "frequent supplies" of plantains arrived from Hispaniola to
ease the effects of high prices induced by shortages of "that most valuable article of food for Negroes" in the British island. At the same time,
military authorities noted that "regular arrivals" of cocoa from Saint-
Domingue, which continued even after the slave rebellion in 1791,
enriched the breakfasts of the troops and were thought to reduce their
rates of mortality and morbidity.[16]

In Saint-Domingue, geographic factors, combined with the chronic
inability of the French merchant fleet to satisfy the colony's rising
demand for all types of commodities, lent both motive and opportunity to merchants and planters to develop extensive contacts with

---

15   Armytage, *Free Port System*, pp. 10, 64; Alured Clarke to Lord Sydney, 30
May 1788, C.O. 137/87, PRO; *Royal Gazette*, 31 March 1792; "Number of Ships
which have Entered and Cleared, in the Island of Jamaica, during the year 1793,"
n.d., C.O. 137/91, PRO.

16   Jamaica Assembly, *Report from the Committee of the Honourable House of
Assembly. Appointed to Inquire into the State of the Colony, as to Trade, Navigation,
and Culture* (St. Jago de la Vega, 1800), pp. 5–6; *Kingston Daily Advertiser*, 3 January
1791; Philip Affleck to Stephens, 14 January 1792, ADM 1/244, PRO.

the English, Spanish, Dutch, and Danish. In lean times, colonists in smaller ports often depended on contacts with foreign territories for their very survival. In the 1770s, French colonists were taking matters into their own hands in order to battle shortages of grain and live-stock; they outfitted vessels to travel to North America for flour and to Cuba and the Spanish Main for horses and mules. When British cruis-ers cut off the western and southern ports from French ships during the American Revolution, Jérémie and Cayes relied on ships coming from Dutch Curaçao to ward off impending famine.[17] But these activities involved more than simply emergency measures or wartime expedients. Illicit commerce had always flourished in peacetime and continued after the peace of 1783. For decades, Saint-Domingue vessels took indigo and cotton worth thousands of pounds sterling to Jamaica in clear violation of the letter and spirit of the *exclusif*. Two-thirds of this amount came from the ports lying between Jérémie and Cap Tiburon, just thirty-three leagues, or half a day's sail, from Jamaica's east coast.[18]

Saint-Domingue's many good harbors attracted foreign shipping as well. In spite of the measures of 1767 and 1784 opening the Môle, the Cap, Port-au-Prince, and Cayes, merchants still pressed local officials to loosen restrictions against foreign shipping even more. Bowing to this mounting pressure by extending free trade regula-tions to Jacmel and Jérémie in 1789, the French governor-general was quickly dismissed.[19] Foreigners valued the opportunity to trade to Saint-Domingue as much as the French colonists valued the presence of their ships. As the revolutionary era approached, foreign colors flew proudly in Saint-Domingue's ports. In 1788, more than one thou-sand foreign vessels, the vast majority of them small ships averaging between sixty and seventy-five tons in weight, called at these ports. Of

---

17   Hilliard d'Auberteuil, *Considérations*, I, p. 279; Maurice Begouën-Démeaux, *Memorial d'une famille du Havre: Stanislas Foäche* (1737–1806) (Paris, 1951), p. 99.

18   Hilliard d'Auberteuil, *Considérations*, I, pp. 281–2; Balcarres to Commander-in-Chief, 31 July 1800, C.O. 137/104, PRO.

19   Clarke to Sydney, 12 July 1789, "Ordonnance concernant la liberté du Commerce pour la Partie du Sud de Saint-Domingue," 9 May 1789, C.O. 137/88, PRO; Affleck to Stephens, 14 September 1789, ADM 1/244, PRO.

this number, 259 were Spanish traders from all parts of the Americas which exchanged bullion for European manufactures and slaves. The following year 283 Spanish ships came to trade in the French colony. Moreau de Saint-Méry's extraordinarily detailed description of the French colony in 1789 placed 140 vessels at anchor in the harbor of Cap Français when commerce was normal, sixty of which would bear foreign registry.[20] To the west and south, Port-au-Prince and Cayes more closely resembled free ports than colonial cities in the fall of 1790, with vessels registered in the United States, Jamaica, Curaçao, St. Croix, and St. Thomas far outnumbering French vessels. From January to September, customs figures counted 272 foreign arrivals at Port-au-Prince, an average of more than one per day, and eighty even at smaller and more remote Cayes.[21]

Though foreign trade produced clear advantages, the movement of ships in this short-distance trade increased inter-island mobility, and many observers expressed concern about the many strangers who arrived aboard these vessels. Soon after Jamaica opened its first free ports in 1766, for instance, French, Spanish, Dutch, and Portuguese seamen, merchants, and commercial agents began to appear in large numbers in the island's port cities. Residents worried about the loyalty of these strangers. Far from solving the island's problems of provisioning, argued Rose Fuller in 1773, the Free Port Act had only succeeded in lending an air of legality to the annoying presence of "many Foreigners" who had no intention of becoming naturalized British citizens, did nothing to support the government of the island, and therefore represented possible dangers to the island's security.[22]

White Jamaicans registered stronger reactions to the presence of foreigners of color. In 1782, Jamaica's Grand Jury of the Quarter

20   Edwards, *History, Civil and Commercial*, III, p. 219; Walton, *Present State of the Spanish Colonies*, I, p. 300; Moreau de Saint-Méry, *Description*, I, pp. 479–80. His figures do not include the numbers of slave ships.

21   *Affiches américaines* (Port-au-Prince), 11 septembre 1790.

22   [Rose Fuller], *Additional Reflections: Serving as a Supplement to a Paper relative to the Consequences of the Free Port Act on the Island of Jamaica transmitted to the Earl of Dartmouth in 1773* (Jamaica, 1774), n.p., MS 368, National Library of Jamaica, Kingston (hereinafter NLJ).

Sessions called attention to the many people of color from Dutch Curaçao, like Jamaica a hub of trade, and other foreign territories living on the island. A "multitude of this description" had settled in Kingston, while "others [roamed] at large." The Grand Jury proposed that the legislature oblige these foreign Negroes to carry tickets to be produced on demand or, better, that "they should have a label round their necks describing who and what they are." In addition, they recommended that captains of foreign ships post a bond promising "to take away such people as they may bring into port."[23] By the 1790s, foreign blacks and browns continued to be fixtures in Jamaican port cities where they attracted the suspicion of municipal authorities. In July 1791, officials in Montego Bay took "Hosa, a Spanish Negro" off a Spanish sloop and placed him in the workhouse as a runaway slave over his protestations that he was free. The following year, "two Spanish mulattoes" received one month's hard labor in the Kingston workhouse after a row with a local "free negro."[24] The revolution of slaves in Saint-Domingue would soon provide a major pretext for authorities in both the British and Spanish colonies to take much stronger measures to discourage the immigration of foreign blacks.

The regional trade in re-shipped African slaves, a specialized branch of intercolonial Caribbean free trade, allowed ships and people to travel to places where they were otherwise prohibited. Because trading slaves provided a convenient cover for ships engaging in illegal commerce, this trade brought foreign shipping to the otherwise restricted Spanish territories. The British showed the way. From early in the eighteenth century, Jamaica was the center of a thriving network of contraband trade which included a substantial illegal trade in African labor to French and Spanish ports. Moreover, under British control the *asiento* to provide Spanish America with slaves enabled smugglers posing as slave traders to unload a wide variety of illegal goods. Occasionally, free seamen even resorted to passing themselves

---

23   *Kingston Daily Advertiser*, 3 February 1791.

24   *Cornwall Chronicle and Jamaica General Advertiser* (Montego Bay), 2 July 1791, file in AAS; *Royal Gazette*, 17 March 1792.

off as slaves in order to land and barter with the locals.[25] The rising demand for slaves throughout the Caribbean justified the free port system and the general loosening of commercial restrictions which occurred after 1763.

When the end of the American Revolution brought peace to the Caribbean, all the colonial powers once again turned their attention to questions of economic development. Awed with the opulent success of Saint-Domingue, policymakers in other parts of the Caribbean set about making their ports as attractive to ships loaded with cargoes of Africans. In 1789, news concerning these latest commercial loopholes buzzed everywhere. The French in Saint-Domingue were not the only ones devising new schemes for increasing their black labor force.[26] The newly appointed governor of the Dutch entrepôt of St. Eustatius left word in Dominica in May that he brought "orders to fortify, and to open the Port for the importation of negroes in foreign bottoms." News that a Spanish royal decree of 28 February 1789 allowed foreign vessels of less than 300 tons to land and sell cargoes of slaves at ports in Cuba, Santo Domingo, Puerto Rico, and Caracas sparked even greater interest. In addition to granting foreign vessels opportunities to trade directly with the Spanish, the decree of *comercio libre* allowed Spanish ships to travel to foreign colonies for the purpose of purchasing slaves.[27]

Under these new dispensations, the movement of small vessels carrying either slaves or produce for their purchase was the most active form of intercolonial commerce linking the Greater Antilles in the years immediately prior to and after the outbreak of the revolution in Saint-Domingue, and commercial activity picked up in other Caribbean subregions as well. In the Greater Antilles, Jamaica

---

25   George H. Nelson, "Contraband Trade under the Asiento," *American Historical Review* 51 (October 1945), p. 59.

26   See the copy of Saint-Domingue's "Ordonnance concernant la liberté du Commerce," 9 May 1789, C.O. 137/88, PRO.

27   John Orde to Lord Sydney, 31 May 1789, C.O. 71/15, PRO; James Ferguson King, "Evolution of the Free Slave Trade Principle in Spanish Colonial Administration," *Hispanic American Historical Review* 22 (February 1942), pp. 44, 51; Juan Guillelmi to Antonio Valdés, Caracas, 14 June 1789, AGI, Caracas, leg. 114.

continued to be the major transshipping point for this trade, and the French and later the Spanish depended greatly on the ability of the British to provide slaves for their colonies. In the 1770s, merchants from Saint-Domingue outfitted vessels with rum and molasses and headed for Jamaica, where they traded for slaves over the objections of the island's sugar planters. French agents engaged in putting together black cargoes for the return voyage were already familiar sights in Kingston and other ports.[28] Small Spanish ships operating out of Cuban ports also made hundreds of such voyages. Whereas Havana could receive foreign slavers under the *cédula* of 1789, merchants and planters in cities like Santiago de Cuba relied on locally registered vessels to travel to foreign ports to make slave purchases. Between September 1789 and June 1791, ships from Santiago de Cuba made 157 authorized trips abroad in search of slaves. They visited Saint-Domingue and even called as far away as Curaçao, but nine of ten made their purchases in Jamaica.[29] Along the coast of Caracas, nearby Curaçao served the same function as did Jamaica for its French and Spanish neighbors, though on a considerably smaller scale. Many of the 3,300 African laborers whom traders brought to Caracas in the first two-and-a-half years of *comercio libre* came through the Dutch entrepôt.[30]

Merchants, planters, and government authorities welcomed this free trade in slaves, but with reservations. Despite rules restricting foreign slavers to twenty-four hours in Spanish ports, officials soon reported that this supposed commerce in slaves smacked of the age-old abuses of the *asiento* system. Suspicious vessels arrived with only a few slaves to sell, and even some of these proved to be sailors posing as slaves in order to land contraband goods. Similarly, when small

---

28   Hilliard d'Auberteuil, *Considérations*, I, p. 279; [Fuller], *Additional Reflections*, n.p.

29   Juan Baptista Vaillant to Diego de Gardoqui, Cuba, 22 June 1791, "Estado que manifiesta el Total de Negros bozales introducidos de las Colonias Extrangeras en este Puerto consequente à la R1. Gracia de 28 de febrero de 1789," Santiago de Cuba, 22 June 1791, AGI, Santo Domingo, leg. 1256.

30   Esteban Fernández de León to Gardoqui, Caracas, 6 July 1792, AGI, Caracas, leg. 503.

Spanish boats came to Jamaica's north coast to trade livestock for slaves, the British suspected them of engaging in mischief, particularly because their crews frequently included free black or brown sailors.[31] Lingering uneasiness about the kinds of slaves which their competitors offered for sale also tempered French and Spanish enthusiasm for the new methods of obtaining Africans. French planters experimenting with buying slaves from British smugglers in the early 1770s worried that Jamaicans had already bought "all the good Negroes" and that those remaining, while cheaper in price, might very well be unhealthy "rejects" or, worse, "mischievous or corrupt characters" transported for crimes. The voracious appetites of the French planters for more slaves in the 1780s caused some observers to fear that indiscriminate slave buying might make Saint-Domingue a repository for refractory creolized slaves from all over the Caribbean. A French memorialist expressed this sentiment in 1789. Not only was Saint-Domingue's dependence on the neighboring British colony for much of its labor supply unhealthy for the nation's commerce, he argued; furthermore, "the Slaves which our rivals furnish are almost always the refuse of their 32 colonies."[32]

Certainly, many of the English-speaking slaves whose names appear in newspaper notices announcing auctions for captured runaways were plantation dissidents from Jamaica and other places. In March 1789, officials at Petit-Goave announced the sale of a forty-year-old "English" slave claiming to have escaped from a watchmaker in Port-au-Prince. In September, Moïse, another English-speaker recently sold to an owner in Cap Dame-Marie, was apprehended by police in Port-au-Prince. Attracted by the relative anonymity of the capital city, Moïse may also have been attempting to secure a passage to Jamaica. In early December officials auctioned three more English-speaking runaways, Williams and Joseph Phillips in Port-au-Prince, and an intriguing character calling himself "Sans-Peur" ("Without Fear")

31   Guillelmi to Pedro de Lerena, Caracas, 25 October 1790, AGI, Caracas, leg. 115; Manuel Gilavert to Luis de las Casas, Batabano, AGI, Cuba, leg. 1468.

32   "Mme. Lory à M. de la Tranchandière, 20 mars 1773," reprinted in Gabriel Debien, *Plantations et esclaves à Saint-Domingue* (Dakar, 1962), p. 46; *Mémoire sur la commerce de la France et de ses colonies* (Paris, 1789), pp. 60–1, RSD.

at Cap Français.[33] Slaves from English-speaking territories were not the only foreign slaves represented in these notices. In addition, they recorded slaves from Curaçao and others who spoke Portuguese and probably came from Brazil.[34]

Experience justified the French planters' concern with the influx of foreign creole slaves. Slaves from other colonies, especially from the British territories, engaged in rebellious activity in Saint-Domingue before 1790, and they played a pivotal role again during the revolutionary years. Plymouth, who led a ban of maroons in the 1730s, came to Saint-Domingue from one of the British colonies. Mackandal, leader of another outlying group of rebels in the 1760s, escaped from Jamaica, as did Boukmann, the religious figure credited with organizing the initial revolt which signaled the oncoming revolution in August 1791. And Henry Christophe, a rebel commander who later became independent Haiti's second president, was born on the British island of St. Kitts.

On the Venezuelan coast, Spanish officials registered similar misgivings about some of the slaves introduced through the island of Curaçao. The arrival in September 1790 of a shipment of thirty-one slaves, nine of whom were said to have been "educated" in the Dutch colony, prompted *intendente* Juan Guillelmi to act to prohibit the creoles from landing. He explained that "it has been observed that creole slaves brought up in foreign colonies are harmful to these provinces."[35] Five years later, a runaway slave from Curaçao led the largest revolt of slaves and free coloreds in Venezuelan history. But even as Guillelmi spoke, portents of revolution in the French colonies had already forced colonial officials to examine anew the issues of black mobility, communication, and sea travel in the Caribbean.

---

33   *Affiches américaines*, 11 mars, 9 septembre, 4 décembre 1790; *Affiches américaines* (Supplément) (Cap Français), 4 décembre 1790.

34   See *Affiches américaines* (Supplément), 13 février, 16 octobre 1790, and Fouchard et Debien, "Petit marronage autour du Cap," p. 57.

35   Quoted in Miguel Acosta Saignes, *La trata de esclavos en Venezuela* (Caracas, 1961), p. 39.

f commercial and political networks connected the islands with each other and significantly affected their development, the same web of contact linked the West Indies to British North America. Beginning long before 1776 and continuing into the decades following the independence of the thirteen colonies, ships transported goods and people between the Caribbean and the Atlantic coast of the northern continent. Just as residents of the Caribbean felt the effects of the American Revolution, the black rebellions in the Caribbean at the end of the eighteenth century frightened slaveholders and inspired slaves in the United States as much as in the islands.

In the seventeenth and eighteenth centuries, commerce between the mainland and the Caribbean islands shaped the history of both regions. Beginning in the 1600s, the temperate zone of North America and the tropical areas to the south took separate but complementary paths of development. By the next century, the North Americans supplied flour, dried fish, salted beef, lumber, horses and other livestock, and the dry provisions which allowed the sugar, cotton, and tobacco planters of the islands to specialize in the cultivation of these and other tropical staples. This trade represented such a vital element in the economic structures of both regions that its continuation and control became one of the most contentious issues leading to the rupture of the thirteen colonies with Great Britain. On the eve of the American Revolution, John Adams referred to the precious West India trade as "an essential link in a vast chain, which has made New England what it is, the southern provinces what they are, [and] the West India islands what they are," and predicted that "tearing and rendering" would result inevitably from the British effort to control that trade.[36]

From the perspective of North Americans like Adams, this "essential link" encompassed the non-British Caribbean islands as well as the British possessions. Beginning around 1700, especially close relations built up between the thirteen colonies and Saint-Domingue and

36   Quoted in Charles W. Toth, ed., *The American Revolution in the West Indies* (Port Washington, N.Y. and London, 1975), ix. For the development and differentiation of north and south, see Richard Pares, *Yankees and Creoles: The Trade between North America and the West Indies before the American Revolution* (Cambridge, 1956), pp. 1–24.

the other French West Indies. As North American supply outstripped demand in the British islands, French ports presented valuable outlets for surplus goods while offering Yankee traders cheaper rum and molasses in return. As the British moved after 1763 to close off this flourishing but illicit trade, the French countered by liberalizing trade regulations in order to continue to attract North American vessels. During the American Revolution, these commercial connections proved especially valuable to the rebels, who bought powder and ammunition in French ports which allowed them to sustain the rebellion. After 1783, commerce with the Caribbean and in particular with Saint-Domingue expanded greatly. Trade figures demonstrate vividly the extent of mutual dependence as the post-revolutionary era in North America began to give way to the age of the French Revolution. By 1790, the value of United States trade with Saint-Domingue, a colony of barely more than half a million inhabitants, exceeded that of trade to all the rest of the Americas combined, and was second only to Great Britain's share in the overall foreign trade of the new nation. More than 500 North American ships engaged in the trade with Saint-Domingue, and the French West Indies produced two-thirds of all the coffee and sugar consumed in the United States. For their part, the French islands consumed one-fourth of all flour, three-fourths of all salted beef, sixty percent of the dried fish, eighty percent of the pickled fish, and seventy-three percent of the livestock exported from the American states. North American commercial interests in the Caribbean region continued into the Napoleonic era; between 1790 and 1814, one-third of all United States exports went to the Caribbean and South America.[37]

Social, political, and cultural contacts between north and south naturally resulted from this expanding commercial network. Before the Revolution, blacks were among the thousands of sailors who worked the North America–West Indies trade. Black New Englanders

---

37 Rayford W. Logan, *The Diplomatic Relations of the United States with Haiti, 1776–1891* (Chapel Hill, 1941), pp. 7–31; Ludwell Lee Montague, *Haiti and the United States, 1714–1938* (Durham, 1940), pp. 29–32; John H. Coatsworth, "American Trade with European Colonies in the Caribbean and South America, 1790–1812," *William and Mary Quarterly*, 3rd ser., 24 (April 1967), pp. 243, 245–6.

like Massachusetts native Paul Cuffe, who would later acquire his own vessel and become active in the colonization of Sierra Leone, made voyages to the Gulf of Mexico and the West Indies in the 1770s.[38] Caribbean blacks moved in the other direction as well. "I, who always much wished to lose sight of the West Indies," wrote Olaudah Equiano of his experiences and travels as a seaman in the 1760s, "was not a little rejoiced at the thoughts of seeing any other country." During that memorable decade, Equiano made friends in Savannah, witnessed demonstrations over the repeal of the Stamp Act in Charleston, and heard George Whitefield preach in Philadelphia.[39] Occasionally black visitors from the south chose to remain and begin new lives on the continent. In 1762, for instance, a carpenter from Saint-Domingue sued successfully for his and his family's freedom in the New York vice-admiralty court.[40]

In the 1770s, several hundred blacks and mulattoes from Saint-Domingue participated directly in the war for North American independence, and they took back with them experiences in fighting for liberty which they may have applied to their later struggles. As a result of a 1778 commercial treaty between the United States and the French West Indies, French forces joined the Americans in military engagements against the British in the West Indies. In 1779, however, French admiral D'Estaing sailed from Saint-Domingue to Savannah with several battalions of black and mulatto troops in an effort to break up the British siege. Though the poorly coordinated attack failed to dislodge the British, observers credited one of these detachments from Saint-Domingue with covering the retreat of the American forces, thereby averting a major defeat. The lasting impact of this engagement on the minds of the black and brown soldiers proved of greater importance than their heroism in 1779. Considering that these troops,

---

38   Lorenzo Johnston Greene, *The Negro in Colonial New England* (New York, 1942), pp. 114–17, discusses blacks in seagoing trades. For Cuffe see Sheldon H. Harris, *Paul Cuffe: Black America and the African Return* (New York, 1972), pp. 18–19.

39   [Equiano], *Life of Equiano*, pp. 142–155.

40   John Franklin Jameson, ed., *Privateering and Piracy in the Colonial Period: Illustrative Documents* (New York, 1923), p. 586.

NEGROES IN FOREIGN BOTTOMS" 57

numbering at least 600 and perhaps twice that many, included among their ranks Henry Christophe, André Rigaud, Martial Besse, and other leaders of Saint-Domingue's fight for freedom, a nineteenth-century student of their role at Savannah has argued persuasively that "this legion ... formed the connecting link between the siege of Savannah and the wide development of republican liberty" in the New World.[41]

The aftermath of the American Revolution brought thousands of black and white loyalists from the mainland to the Caribbean in the early 1780s. This emigration from southern ports in 1782 foreshadowed the exodus from Saint-Domingue after the slave rebellion a decade later. When the British fled Savannah in July 1782, they allocated ample room aboard their vessels for Tory inhabitants and "their effects"—mostly slaves—and large numbers of both slaves and free people ended up in Jamaica. On August 15, an unspecified number of white loyalists landed in Jamaica along with some 1,400 blacks. It is estimated that 400 white families and perhaps as many as 3,500 additional slaves, making a total near 5,000, reached Jamaica as a result of the evacuation of Savannah alone. Jamaica also received more than half of the 5,327 blacks, both free and enslaved, who left aboard British vessels during the hurried evacuation of Charleston in December 1782. Smaller contingents of black loyalists ended up in the Bahamas and other British islands.[42]

The fates of these highly visible refugees varied as widely as their backgrounds. A 1786 petition to the Jamaica House of Assembly boasted of those Americans in Kingston who were "opulent and industrious [and] practice commerce," but the authors complained in the same breath that many of the new arrivals were "extremely indigent and wholly supported at the expense of the parish." The petitioners

41   T. G. Steward, *How the Black St. Domingo Legion Saved the Patriot Army in the Siege of Savannah, 1779* (Washington, 1899), p. 13; Logan, *Diplomatic Relations of the United States with Haiti*, p. 25.

42   Wilbur H. Siebert, *The Legacy of the American Revolution to the British West Indies and Bahamas: A Chapter out of the History of the American Loyalists* (Columbus, 1913), pp. 14–16; James W. St. G. Walker, *The Black Loyalists: The Search for a Promised Land in Nova Scotia and Sierra Leone 1783–1870* (London, 1976), pp. 8–10; Benjamin Quarles, *The Negro in the American Revolution* (Chapel Hill, 1961), pp. 163–7; Ragatz, *Fall of the Planter Class*, p. 194.

urged repeal of a 1783 act exempting the North Americans from paying taxes as a means of driving out these undesirables.[43]

Black North American immigrants to the Caribbean region show a similar, if not quite so stark, diversity. Currents of Afro-North American thought followed the ex-slaves to the islands. For example, even a "successful" free black immigrant like George Liele could prove a troublesome presence in Jamaica. Liele, a Baptist minister, was responsible for introducing the Baptist faith to Jamaica and enlisted hundreds of black converts. Because of his race and his religion, he suffered to an extreme degree the persecution which the planter class directed at all Protestant evangelical believers in the late eighteenth century.[44] By the 1790s, other black immigrants in Jamaica appear in runaway slave notices and in workhouse records. Two North Americans followed different routes to arrive at the Kingston workhouse late in 1791. Solomon Dick, who claimed to be free, was arrested under vagrancy laws, while Daniel had escaped some three years earlier from his owner, a French planter living near Fort Dauphin in Saint-Domingue, and was apparently one of the many English-speaking slaves who escaped from the French colony to Jamaica in the late 1780s and early 1790s.[45]

At the same time, whites in the eastern Caribbean registered various complaints about the presence of North American blacks in that subregion. When a Nevis merchant reported that slave sailors had appropriated his small sloop late in 1790, he described two members of the crew as "Virginians," including Long Jem, an "arch dog."[46] Another telling illustration comes from September 1791, when a Dominican slaveowner expressed his thanks to a resident of Charleston who had recently returned a runaway slave who was "secreted" in the Carolina capital. If only the British government would reciprocate, he sighed, as there were presently "not less than

---

43   Brathwaite, *Establishment of Creole Society*, pp. 89–91.

44   See Carter G. Woodson, *The History of the Negro Church* (Washington, 1921), pp. 42–7.

45   *Royal Gazette*, 29 October 1791.

46   *Gallagher's Weekly Journal Extraordinary* (Dominica), 21 December 1790, copy in C.O. 71/18, PRO.

four hundred slaves, the property of the people of Carolina, brought off at the evacuation," making their home on the British island.[47] Inevitably, some of the black North Americans who had been shipped to the islands against their will desired to return to the less tropical and more familiar environment they had left behind. Young Daniel, "a native of Virginia" was "so much attached to his country," warned his owner after Daniel disappeared, that "he will endeavour to get on board some vessel for America."[48]

If ships and boats sailing among the island colonies of the Caribbean brought the region together commercially, their movement also aided those seeking to escape the rigorous social control of these slave societies. The prospect of attaining a masterless existence at sea or abroad lured every description of mobile fugitive in the region, from runaway slaves to military deserters to deep-sea sailors in the merchant marines of the European empires. While huge oceangoing vessels and warships continued to symbolize the power of planters and merchants, smaller vessels designed for local use became vehicles for hardy souls willing to brave the elements and the possibility of stiff punishment to seize their opportunity. For all the colonial powers, the mobility of these unauthorized seaborne travelers presented social dilemmas at home as well as diplomatic problems abroad.

Though advocates of free trade tried to undercut the contrabandists and interlopers, they still found ways to elude Spanish *guarda-costas*, British patrol boats, and customs officers to land and sell their goods. Illegal trade continued to thrive among Cuba, Jamaica, and Saint-Domingue in the 1780s in spite of the measures which each power took to stifle this trade. Most of the hard currency which circulated in Saint-Domingue in the years leading up to the revolution, for example, consisted of *pesos fuertes* earned in the illicit trade with Cuba. While Spanish boats from Cuba slipped into Saint-Domingue with fresh meats and bullion, British boats from Jamaica engaged in illegal trade with the Cubans. All kinds of people participated in

---

47   "Extract of a letter from Dominica," *Royal Gazette*, 17 December 1791.
48   *Royal Gazette*, 25 May 1793.

unlawful commerce. In July 1790, Jamaican officials asked that the Spanish release several British sailors in a Cuban jail for illicit trading.[49] Mariners from outlawed vessels filled the jails in other colonies as well. In 1789, the British demanded the release of a crew of contrabandists taken off the coast of Puerto Rico and held in Caracas. The long exposed coast of the mainland invited scores of illegal traders. After disease and desertion decimated the Spanish fleet anchored at Puerto Cabello in 1793, officials in the capital considered a plan to raise 2,000 sailors by rounding up vagrant seamen and emptying prisons of many of the mariners found guilty of trading illegally. Especially in the western provinces, where free people of color were most numerous, many of these imprisoned sailors were listed as "*de color.*"[50]

Deserters from military service often ran to foreign colonies to escape their pursuers. To stem frequent unauthorized travel from Cuba, officials issued licenses in order to control militiamen from taking advantage of their position to leave the island. During the war later in the decade, the Crown extended amnesty to deserted soldiers and sailors both in other Spanish possessions and in foreign territories. In like fashion, shipwrecked British sailors fled to Cuba, where they could "call themselves Americans with a view of avoiding the British Service," rather than return to Jamaica.[51]

Finally, runaway slaves were prominent among this varied group which took advantage of commercial interaction to find both work and shelter on the seas or in foreign colonies. The commonplace ease of inter-island travel, slave access to transportation, and intercolonial rivalries combined to make both short- and long-distance, colony-to-colony slave flight possible. Most often, these seaborne runaways sought territories where plantations did not yet dominate the economy

---

49   *Resumen* of the report of the *regente* of the Audiencia de Santo Domingo, 25 September 1793, AGI, Santo Domingo, leg. 1031; Vaillant to Las Casas and enclosures, Cuba, 22 July 1790, AGI, Cuba, leg. 1434.

50   Guillelmi to Valdés, Caracas, 17 July, 24 August 1789, AGI, Caracas, leg. 114; Gabriel Aristizábal to León, Puerto Cabello, 11 October 1793, León to Gardoqui, Caracas, 11 December 1793, AGI, Caracas, leg. 505.

51   Vaillant to Las Casas, Cuba, 21 June 1791, AGI, Cuba, leg. 1434; Conde de Santa Clara to Ministro de Guerra, La Habana, 7 July 1797, AGI, Cuba, leg. 1526; J. Brice to Las Casas, La Habana, 24 February 1794, AGI, Cuba, leg. 1469.

or where political considerations lessened the possibility that they would be returned to their original owners. But even a fully developed slave society like Jamaica received its share of runaway slaves from other colonies. When Parliament inquired in 1788 about whether any Jamaican slaves practiced Catholicism, officials cited several black immigrants "who were brought from Guadeloupe" during the Seven Years' War, and "some Runaways from the neighbouring Spanish and French Islands." Jamaican newspapers frequently listed black vagrants in parish workhouses claiming to be residents of other Caribbean islands. In the spring of 1792, for example, William, a Barbadian, languished in the Kingston workhouse while Sam, from Curaçao, was imprisoned in St. Elizabeth parish.[52]

For Jamaican and other British officials, however, slaves leaving the island presented a greater challenge than incoming deserters. From the late seventeenth century through the era of the French Revolution, the Spanish colonies attracted the largest number of maritime refugees from slavery. Even before 1700, runaways fleeing slavery in the British dominions began to arrive in canoes and ask for asylum in Spanish territories. The Crown's early decision to protect black fugitives in both Florida and Cuba as refugees from Protestant heresy in search of instruction in Catholicism initiated a policy of welcoming slaves fleeing foreign colonies which lasted, though sometimes shakily, for a century. In the 1730s, the Spanish reconfirmed this policy of extending religious asylum to runaways, and word of the possibility of freedom quickly spread to distant slave communities through slaves working on trading vessels.[53]

52 Great Britain, Board of Trade, *Report of the Lords of the Committee of Council appointed for the consideration of all matters relating to trade and foreign plantations*, 6 pts. ([London], 1789), pt. III, Jamaica, n.p. (hereinafter *Privy Council Report* [1789]); *Royal Gazette*, 14 April 1792.

53 Jane Landers, "Spanish Sanctuary: Fugitives in Florida, 1687–1790," *Florida Historical Quarterly* 62 (January 1984), p. 297; John J. TePaske, "The Fugitive Slave: International Rivalry and Spanish Slave Policy, 1687–1764," in Samuel Proctor, ed., *Eighteenth-Century Florida and Its Borderlands* (Gainesville, 1975), pp. 3–4; Patterson, *Sociology of Slavery*, p. 263; Peter H. Wood, *Black Majority; Negroes in Colonial South Carolina from 1670 through the Stono Rebellion* (New York, 1974), pp. 306–7.

In the 1750s, runaways to Spanish colonies created diplomatic stresses in Spain, as other nations began to raise legitimate questions about the religious justification for Spanish policy toward slave fugitives. In 1752, the Dutch demanded the return of runaways who had deserted to Puerto Rico from their colonies on St. Maarten and St. Eustatius, but the French ambassador called attention at the same time to slaves from Guadeloupe, a colony under a Catholic king, who had also found their way to that Spanish island.[54] Five years later, the governor of French Martinique reported that slaves had departed his island for Puerto Rico, and in 1760 the captain-general at Havana discovered a group of "French Negroes," most likely runaways from Saint-Domingue, at large "in the vicinity of the Moro Castle."[55] At the same time, the movement of slaves from the French islands in the eastern Caribbean to Trinidad, part of the captaincy-general of Caracas, gave that island a reputation as a sanctuary similar to Puerto Rico.[56]

The peace following the end of the Seven Years' War threatened to reduce this mobility, because the Bourbon reformers in Spain reassessed Spanish policy regarding slaves and other fugitives from foreign colonies and directed colonial officials to begin returning them. On Hispaniola, tensions between French and Spanish officials eased considerably in 1764 after the Spanish governor allowed a detachment of the *maréchaussée* (mounted militia) from Saint-Domingue to cross the border in pursuit of a band of runaways which had inhabited the mountainous stretches separating the colonies since 1728.[57] In July 1767, Spain and Denmark moved to cut off movement between Puerto Rico and the Danish islands of St. Croix, St. Thomas, and St. John in a treaty calling for the reciprocal return of runaway slaves and other

54   H. H. Wassender to Joseph de Carvajal y Lancaster, Madrid, 13 October 1752, "Expediente sobre unos Negros, que de la Ysla de Guadalupe se pasaron a la de Puerto Rico, y reclama el embasador de Francia" (1752), AGI, Sección de Indiferente General, leg. 2787 (hereinafter AGI, Indiferente General).

55   See the *expediente* regarding fugitives to and from the Danish islands dated 9 May 1768, Madrid, AGI, Indiferente General, leg. 2787.

56   Angel Sanz Tapia, *Los militares emigrados y los prisioneros franceses en Venezuela durante la guerra contra la Revolución: Un aspecto fundamental de la época de la preëmancipación* (Caracas, 1977), pp. 42–3.

57   Debien, "Marronage aux Antilles françaises," pp. 5–6.

fugitives traveling between Spanish and Danish territories.[58] But such delimitations were piecemeal and always subject to the vagaries of international politics. As Spain and Denmark finalized their agreement, the British argued in vain that a similar arrangement be applied to the many runaways from Jamaica in Cuba and those from the British Virgin Islands in Puerto Rico, where a British frigate arrived in 1770 in a futile effort to reclaim the most recent cohort of black fugitives from St. Kitts.[59] Black desertion from the British islands continued through the era of the American Revolution. By 1790, absentee lobbyists in London termed the losses of British slaves to Trinidad "very considerable," and reported that runaways to Puerto Rico "are supposed now to amount to some Thousands, including their descendents."[60]

While seaborne black runaways from the Windward and Leeward Islands headed for Trinidad and Puerto Rico, Cuba's shores beckoned slaves from the islands farther west. On the north coast of Jamaica, black desertion to Spanish Cuba was a well-established custom by the 1790s. The earliest "boat people" leaving Jamaica for Cuba appear in the records in 1699, when twenty slaves arrived by canoe and were granted religious asylum in the Spanish colony. In 1718, the Jamaica Assembly first began to tackle the problem of "Negroes going off the Island to the French or Spanish Colonies" by ordering that such unauthorized emigrants be "tried by Two Justices and Three Freeholders, and suffer such Pains and Punishments (according to the Nature of their Crime) as they shall think fit."[61] Judicial measures of this nature, however, assumed that Jamaican slaveowners would first be able to recover their slaves from the Cubans, an extremely difficult task during this century of unceasing tension between Spain and England. Hundreds of English-speaking slaves traveled to Cuba in the rebellious 1730s, and in 1751, barely a year after the publication of a royal *cédula*

---

58   *Expediente*, 10 April 1768, AGI, Indiferente General, leg. 2787.

59   *Expediente*, 9 May 1768, Miguel de Muesas to Julien de Arriaga, Puerto Rico, 15 May 1770, AGI, Indiferente General, leg. 2787.

60   Minutes of WIPM, 6 April 1790, reel 3.

61   Patterson, *Sociology of Slavery*, p. 263; Appendix, Act 66 (1718), reprinted in *Privy Council Report* (1789), pt. III, Jamaica, n.p.

reaffirming that Jamaican runaways embracing Catholicism would be protected by the Spanish in Cuba, reports stated that black Jamaicans were escaping to the protection of Catholic priests.

Through the 1760s and the 1770s, the Assembly stepped up efforts to stem the tide of out-migration, leveling stiffer punishments upon slave runaways and their free abettors. By 1789, slaves attempting to leave the island could by law receive the death penalty. In addition, free coloreds aiding such escapes risked banishment from the island, and guilty whites suffered prohibitive fines.[62]

After reaching the shores of Cuba, some of these runaway slaves found and became a part of whole communities of deserters of many descriptions and nations. An outlaw society near Bayamo, for example, amounted to a multinational guild of traders in illegal goods and all kinds of fugitives. The governor of Santiago de Cuba, capital of the Bayamo district, reported in 1771 that "deserters from the army, escaped convicts, and other fugitives," including runaway slaves, arrived in eastern Cuba in small vessels to take off hides, livestock, and dyewoods for sale in the British and French colonies. Investigating officials found the area's small unguarded harbors "full of ships engaged in illicit trade—French, English, and ours." Six years later, Bayamo's governor voiced concern about these same interlopers. Heavily armed, they resisted the government troops sent out against them, and their numbers were growing. "The refuge of all the trouble-makers of the district," these outlying communities of illegal traders "welcomed" deserters from the army and militia and "thieves, vaga-bonds, foreigners, American-born runaway slaves, and all of those pursued by Justice." Jamaican planters often blamed illicit traders for seducing their slaves to run away to foreign colonies, and the observa-tions of Cuban officials suggest that at least some of the black fugitives to the Spanish island arrived aboard the vessels of renegades engaged in illegal commerce.[63]

---

62   Governor Trelawny to Board of Trade, 4 July 1751, C.O. 137/25, PRO; Acts of 1768, 1771, and 1777, reprinted in *Privy Council Report* (1789), pt. III, Jamaica, n.p.; *New Act of Assembly of the Island of Jamaica* (1789), articles LXIV, LXV, LXVI.

63   Juan Antonio Ayanz de Vreta to Pasqual de Cisneros, Cuba, 6 September

The long struggle between north coast planters and runaway slaves continued on the eve of the Haitian Revolution, as Jamaican slaves were still braving the elements in search of freedom in Cuba. In the spring of 1788, Richard Martin of St. Mary's parish reported to the Assembly that eleven of his slaves had absconded in a canoe and had arrived in Cuba aboard a Spanish brigantine which had picked them up *en route*. On a trip to the Spanish island shortly thereafter, Martin to his surprise encountered several other recent runaways from Jamaica boasting their new freedom under the Catholic Church in the coastal towns of Trinidad and Puerto del Príncipe. Havana officials confirmed that Martin's slaves were "at present in this City instructing themselves in the Catholic religion, which was their object in coming here," adding that "the laws of Spain ... put it beyond the power of this Government to deliver them up."[64] The following April, yet another small group of slaves left St. Ann's Bay for Cuba. A week later, they appeared off the eastern coast of the Spanish island in the company of a local fisherman. In June their owner, John Wilcox McGregor, hired a vessel and traveled to Cuba in pursuit, where he soon found them working in the employ of the governor and "town-major" in Santiago de Cuba. After the runaways claimed freedom under Spanish law, McGregor was "Struck with amazement" when Juan Baptista Vaillant, governor of Santiago de Cuba, blocked his attempts to recover his workers. Surely, he pleaded, Vaillant was not so credulous as to take seriously the "Sham pretences" which his and other Jamaican slaves were using to escape slavery. "Every set of people in Bondage," McGregor implored, "will use every Artifice and try every Subterfuge, to obtain Emancipation." Equally infuriated with Spanish conduct, Governor Effingham excoriated this "most Jesuitical excuse which their Governors have made these many years." Just months after a remarkably similar incident in which he had a difficult time negotiating the release of British sailors accused of trading in contraband, the governor petitioned the King's ministers to bring diplomatic pressure

1771, Juan Germin Lleonar to Cisneros, Bayamo, 7 September 1777, AGI, Indiferente General, leg. 2787.

64 *Journals of the Assembly of Jamaica*, VIII, pp. 457, 460; Joseph de Ezpeleta to Alured Clarke, 25 March 1789 (translation), C.O. 137/88, PRO.

to bear, as "on the North Side of this Island, some have been I am told Actually Ruin'd by such Losses repeated."[65]

Interestingly, some north coast planters every bit as concerned as McGregor about the desertion of their slaves to the Spanish seemed considerably less anxious to have them back. Blacks who had tasted freedom or had traveled the seas and seen other colonies were likely to attempt another escape. More importantly, hearing returned slaves recount their experiences abroad might tempt fellow workers to elope to Cuba or some other Spanish colony. On one occasion, these considerations led to an incident in which some rather complicated dynamics came into play. After several planters from Trelawny and St. Ann's succeeded in finding and bringing back to Jamaica a group of runaway slaves living in Bayamo, their prisoners agreed to (or were forced to) make public statements about the cruel treatment they had received at the hands of the Spanish. They then threw themselves upon the mercy of their captors and "earnestly supplicated that any other punishment, short of death, might be inflicted upon them rather than go back to Cuba." Apparently satisfied that they had made their point, the planters proceeded to "punish" the deserters by sending them back to Cuba with a warning never to return to Jamaica.[66]

Despite the remonstrances of British planters and officials, royal orders to Spanish governors in the Indies continued to encourage the immigration of runaway slaves from foreign colonies as late as the summer of 1789. In November of that year Jamaica's House of Assembly petitioned London asking that diplomatic pressure be applied in order to keep Spanish officials from "protecting the slaves eloping from this island, and refusing to deliver them up." At the same time, the frenzied search for local solutions intensified. Having discovered "a conspiracy ... in a much larger number of negroes to desert this island, and take refuge in ... Cuba," the Assembly attacked the

65   *Journals of the Assembly of Jamaica*, VIII, pp. 514–15; John Wilcox McGregor to Vaillant, 7 June 1789, Lord Effingham to Grenville, 13 June, 9 October 1790, C.O. 137/88, PRO.

66   Jamaica Assembly, *Further Proceedings of the Honourable House of Assembly of Jamaica, Relative to a Bill Introduced into the House of Commons, for Effectually Preventing the Unlawful Importation of Slaves* (London, 1816), p. 98.

problem in a different fashion, by restricting canoes "to a size not exceeding fourteen feet in length"—still large enough for fishing, but also sufficiently small to make "adventuring" at sea hazardous.[67]

During that eventful spring, however, Spanish policy shifted decisively. In May 1790 the Crown abruptly reversed its position of the previous year and issued new orders to governors in the colonies that they no longer protect foreign fugitives seeking shelter in Spanish territory. By mid-summer, word of this change in policy reached the colonies. Soon governors in Cuba refused to accept foreign runaways, and Spanish officials in Trinidad announced that incoming fugitives would be arrested and sold abroad.[68] The British at Jamaica received the news with guarded skepticism, but gave it high public profile nevertheless, knowing that the slaves' network of communication provided the most effective way of informing them of the change in Spanish policy. In the absence of a public statement from the Spanish governors themselves, the Assembly settled for publishing private official correspondence, a move which, reported the governor in March 1791, "has given an alarm at least to our Negroes which has been of some use." Later in the year British officials were confident that, "as the measure appears now to be generally known among the Slaves, it will … have the good effect of checking their desertion in future.[69]

Other governments seized this opportunity to bring to an end the absconsion of slaves to the Spanish. In the spring of 1791, the governments of Spain and Holland, "moved by the reiterated complaints of

67   *Journals of the Assembly of Jamaica*, VIII, pp. 519, 565–6, 596; Stephen Fuller to Committee of Correspondence (Jamaica), 30 January 1791, "Mr. Stephen Fuller's Account as Agent from the 31st December 1785 to the 31st December 1790," FLB.

68   Antonio Porlier to Pedro de Lerena, Aranjuez, 14 June 1790, AGI, Indiferente General, leg. 2787; Joaquín García to Porlier, Santo Domingo, 25 July 1790, AGI, Santo Domingo, leg. 953; Las Casas to Porlier, La Habana, 7 August 1790, AGI, Cuba, leg. 1490.

69   Effingham to Grenville, 19 March 1791, Henry Dundas to Effingham, 8 August 1791, C.O. 137/89, PRO. If this news did have such an effect, it was short-lived. Jamaican slaves continued to desert to Cuba during the 1790s, and as late as 1798 Spanish officials recognized their claims to freedom. See Isidro Joseph de Limonta to Santa Clara, Cuba, 26 August 1798, AGI, Cuba, leg. 1499-A; Santa Clara to Ministro de Gracia y Justicia, La Habana, 5 October 1798, AGI, Cuba, leg. 1528.

desertion in their colonies in America and desiring to remove the causes for desertion, and to make further complaints of desertion impossible," agreed to a "plan for the mutual return of deserters and fugitives." The Convention of 1791 was designed to cut off the communication between Puerto Rico and St. Eustatius, western Venezuela and Curaçao, and the Orinoco and the Dutch colonies along the Guiana coast.[70]

The intense diplomatic pressure which other European governments were bringing to bear against the Spanish in 1789 and 1790, and the threat of war with the British, clearly influenced the reversal of Spain's century-old practice regarding black fugitives from foreign colonies. But the British accepted too much of the credit. By the middle of 1790, the French Revolution had already begun to shape Spanish policy. Closing the door to slaves from other territories represented a first step in the attempt to guard the colonies against the spread of French revolutionary ideas. The action of Spanish officials in 1790 prefigured the concern which strangers—especially strangers of color—would cause as the Haitian Revolution developed.[71]

Seagoing vessels of different sizes and functions sailed back and forth along the coasts of colonies throughout the Americas. The canoes which brought runaway slaves from Jamaica to Cuba had a variety of uses, from fishing to piloting to transport. Other open vessels which the English called "wherries" and "long boats" carried passengers from port to port or ferried freight and fresh water between the merchantmen at anchor and the wharves. Single-masted "shallops" and "droggers," larger decked boats ranging in size from twenty to one hundred tons burden, transported sugar casks, puncheons of rum, and other heavy articles, while smaller "plantain boats" carried cargoes of fresh fruit for local consumption. In the coastal waters of Saint-Domingue, as off Jamaica, small boats of every size and description

---

70   "Convención entre el Rey Nuestro Señor y los Estados Generales de las Provincias Unidas, para la recíproca restitución de desertores y fugitivos," 23 June 1791, AGI, Indiferente General, leg. 2787.

71   Chapter Four will examine more closely the resolution of 1790 within the context of the early French Revolution in the Caribbean.

"swarmed like bees" in the years prior to the revolution, according to one contemporary observer. Because incoming deep-water vessels tended to focus on only the major ports, the bustling "interior traffic and navigation" controlled by the smaller boats linked the many coastal cities of the French colony to each other. In Jamaica, where the center of agricultural activity was located at a considerable distance from the seat of government and the island's major deep-water port, this coastwise commerce in small vessels not only aided north coast planters in getting their produce to market, but also brought provisions and food to support the population of the towns.[72]

Already saddled with collecting duties and trying to detect the smuggled goods and contraband, customs officials often left the small locally registered boats to accomplish their errands with a minimum of supervision. When officials did move to exercise more control over the coasters, they met with considerable resistance. In 1787, Jamaican customs officers attempted without success to implement a Parliamentary statute which called for registration of every ship of fifteen tons burden or above. Soon owners of plantain boats and piloting vessels complained of interminable delays in moving fruits, wood, and lime into Kingston and Port Royal and petitioned the Assembly to return to the old system of allowing these boats to move freely without having to clear customs. The Assembly's inquiry showed, however, that many owners took advantage of the system. For instance, while the exemption from customs clearance officially applied only to plantain boats of ten tons or smaller, owners of much larger vessels simply registered as plantain boats in order to avoid the customs. Moreover, examinants from the customs cited other reasons besides inconvenience for the resistance of boat owners, having "the strongest reasons to believe that illicit practices are carried on, to a very great degree, in all kinds of small vessels." These practices included trips to foreign colonies for prohibited goods. While the Assembly agreed that irregularities did exist and applauded the efforts of customs officers to detect them, the members could not come up with a feasible set of

---

72 *Resumen* of the report of the *regente*, Santo Domingo, 25 September 1793, AGI, Santo Domingo, leg. 1031.

regulations which would not at the same time damage the efficiency of the system.[73]

All over the Caribbean region, the vital work of coastal commerce involved slaves and free people of color at every level, from loading and unloading to navigation. A French traveler to Havana in 1788 observed that "almost all the commission merchants there were free Negroes," whose responsibilities often included "superintending the loading of cargo for a whole ship."[74] In Jamaica, owners of plantain boats, some of whom were free blacks and browns, customarily hired black crews and captains to operate and navigate them. Other types of coastal vessel also made extensive use of black mariners. Newspaper advertisements made frequent reference to blacks employed as fishermen, as "sailor negroes," or as being "used to the Drogging business"; sometimes these skilled seaborne slaves were offered for sale as part of a package which included the wharves and boats which they worked. Barbados's Governor Parry reported in 1786 that "the Numbers of Negro slaves employed in navigating the Trading Vessels in these Seas … seem to me to increase so much as to require the attention of the British Legislature, as it throws so many English Seamen out of employment."[75]

On both sides of the Atlantic, service at sea had always sheltered the masterless, from runaway slaves and indentured servants to fugitives from the law. In the insular slave societies of the Caribbean, the mystique of the sea existed to an even stronger degree than elsewhere. Life aboard one of the modest vessels which plied the coasts or engaged in small-scale intercolonial commerce presented an attractive alternative to the life of regimental hierarchy to be found aboard a

---

73   *Journals of the Assembly of Jamaica*, VIII, pp. 287–8, 294–301.

74   J. P. Brissot de Warville, *New Travels in the United States of America, 1788*, trans. Mara Soceanu Vamos and Durand Echeverria, ed. Durand Echeverria (Cambridge, 1964), p. 64.

75   *Journals of the Assembly of Jamaica*, VIII, pp. 295, 298. For examples of advertisements, see *Royal Gazette*, 26 May 1787, 28 January 1792, 24 August 1793, and *The Charibbean Register, or Ancient and Original Dominica Gazette* (Roseau, Dominica), 26 March 1791, copy in C.O. 71/20, PRO. Parry is quoted in Ruth Anna Fisher, "Manuscript Materials Bearing on the Negro in British Archives," *Journal of Negro History* 27 (January 1942), p. 88.

larger ship or ashore on a standard sugar plantation. While a Jamaican editorialist could lament the "vicissitudes of Fortune" which plummeted one Francis Duchesne "from a life of ease and affluence" to "a wretched existence in the humble character of a foremast-man on board a drogger," considerable evidence suggests that both free blacks and slaves valued the opportunity to go to sea or to work in the coastal trade.[76] Olaudah Equiano, who began a long career at sea aboard a drogger in Montserrat in the 1760s, relished his occupation for several reasons. Working as a sailor enabled him to see other islands, meet new people, and deepen his understanding of regional politics; to "get a little money" by doing some trading on his own account; and, most importantly, to look his owner in the eye and demand respect. Both because of the ever-present opportunities for escape and because he could bid his services to other merchants, Equiano jealously defended his "liberty," resolving that he would desert his master before being "imposed upon as other negroes were."[77]

Like Equiano, other black workers on the shoreline hammered out a semi-independent status which their employers were forced to recognize. When the midday winds blew too strongly for the coastal boats to put to sea, Jamaica wharfinger James Kelly allowed his "wharf Negroes" to "go where they were inclined" with the implicit understanding that he "could, with confidence, count on their attendance" once the winds shifted. Often, however, black maritime workers used their privileged positions to make both individual and collective escape attempts. Caribbean newspapers are replete with accounts of such instances. In August 1790 a "well known" slave sailor in Grenada named William disappeared from the drogger which employed him, as did three slave pilots "all well acquainted" on the southern coast of Jamaica who absconded in a canoe in November 1792.[78] Late in 1790, a crew of slaves aboard the *Nancy*, a small sloop which moved goods

---

76 Jesse Lemisch, "Jack Tar in the Streets: Merchant Seamen in the Politics of Revolutionary America," *William and Mary Quarterly*, 3rd ser., 25 (July 1968), pp. 374–7; *Savanna-la-Mar Gazette* (Jamaica), 15 July 1788, file in AAS.

77 [Equiano], *Life of Equiano*, pp. 110, 131, 137, 141–2.

78 Kelly, *Voyage to Jamaica*, pp. 30–31; *St. George's Chronicle and New Grenada Gazette*, 13 August 1790; *Royal Gazette*, 24 November 1792.

among the closely situated islands near St. Kitts, mutinied against their captain and took over the vessel. This crew of four reflected in micro-cosm a broad segment of the Atlantic world: the leader of the rebellion was a native of the British island of Nevis, and his co-conspirators consisted of a sailor "of the congo nation" and two "Virginians." In a desperate attempt to recover his property, owner Jeremiah Neale rec-ognized the wide range of options available to the black "pirates," and published detailed descriptions of the vessel and its rebellious crew in newspapers from Jamaica to Grenada.[79]

Aware that the proximity of the sea constantly beckoned slave dis-sidents from the plantations, owners of runaway slaves sternly warned ship captains and sailors that they would be prosecuted for admitting deserted slaves aboard their vessels, warnings which many captains apparently chose to ignore. Slaves with experience at sea were often successful in making escapes from estates and finding new jobs (and shelter) aboard ships. References to runaways as having seen service "on board some type of vessel" were commonplace in newspaper notices for runaways. Early in 1792, Bob, a Jamaican slave who had "been occasionally employed as a fisherman and as a sailor negro," left his owner, who expected that "he will endeavour to get on board some vessel." More than a year later, Bob landed in the workhouse at Black River after being apprehended aboard a shallop whose captain, inci-dentally, was also black.[80] Even slaves without experience at sea could pick up some key nautical terms or perhaps a verse or two of a popular sea shanty, and pass themselves off as free sailors. Captains looking to put together crews were often not disposed to inquire carefully after their background. Daniel, a young brown man learning the carpenter trade in Kingston, was seen attempting to flee Jamaica "on board his Majesty's Ship the Diana at Port Royal" in November 1791.[81]

---

79   *Gallagher's Weekly Journal Extraordinary* (Roseau, Dominica), 21 December 1790, copy in C.O. 71/18, PRO; *St. George's Chronicle and New Grenada Gazette*, 17 December 1790; *Kingston Daily Advertiser*, 14 February 1791.

80   *Royal Gazette*, 14 January 1792, 29 September 1792, 20 April 1793.

81   *Royal Gazette*, 12 November 1791. For other examples of slaves who may have boarded vessels under similar circumstances, see *Royal Gazette*, 21 April 1792, 14 September 1793.

As if the desire for freedom were not sufficiently compelling of itself, some slaves had more complex individual motives for seeking passages aboard seagoing vessels. Emy left her employer in St. Andrew parish and traveled to Kingston "in a drogger or a plantain boat" in order to visit her husband in neighboring St. Thomas. Even the religious awakenings of the late eighteenth century encouraged slaves to think about experiencing the wider world represented by ships and boats. Spiritual considerations led Jemmy, a precocious youngster who had "associated at times ... with some of those description of people called *Methodists*" to try to "get on board some vessel, and thereby effect his escape from the island." Another slave named Adam, like the apostle Peter "a fisherman by trade," was described by his owner as "a great smatterer in religious topics." After embracing the Baptist faith, Adam was "always preaching or praying." Late in 1790, perhaps Adam decided to broaden his ministry and become "a fisher of men": he boarded a merchantman gathering an outward cargo with the intent to "sail out with her when she is completely loaded."[82]

Like the daring runaway slaves whose exploits quickly became topics of conversation in slave communities, many "sailor Negroes" achieved considerable notoriety. This was partially a function of their mobile jobs; descriptions of sailors and other blacks in maritime professions which appear in runaway notices refer repeatedly to the fact that they were "well known" in the areas in which they worked. In Jamaica, some black sailors earned legendary status, while many others were colorful and familiar local fixtures. Bermuda-born Joe Anderson, "a stout ... sailor negro," successfully eluded his owner by jumping aboard a ship at Port Antonio on the north coast in 1779, despite being shackled with "an iron collar, rivetted, and about 5 or 6 links of chain." For the next fourteen years, Anderson continually managed to evade the grasp of his persistent master, finding work and shelter "all that time on board of vessels." By 1793, though still pursued, Anderson was "well known in Kingston" and continued to ply his trade. The people who frequented the working-class haunts in

---

82 *Royal Gazette*, 23 February, 13 April 1793; *Kingston Daily Advertiser*, 7 January 1791.

the west end of Kingston near the harbor, as they recounted the legend of Joe Anderson, must also have known the elder statesman called "Old Blue." This "tall … long-visaged sailor negro" enjoyed a reputation as long and distinctive as his graying beard. When he was not "skulking about the west of town," Blue worked aboard droggers and plantain boats to make ends meet, or found jobs ashore "at some of the leeward parishes." By night, one could find him spinning stories and hoisting glasses with fellow seamen in local grog shops. Apparently, drinking was among Old Blue's favorite pastimes; his owner revealed that the runaway sailor was "not unfrequently intoxicated."[83]

Besides being the refuge for masterless characters and runaways, the coastal trade was a vital source of information about happenings elsewhere in the region. In British Honduras, officials accused the Spanish in neighboring settlements of "enticing away the slaves of British Settlers under a pretence of granting them freedom," and cited one example of an official's aid disguising himself as a Spanish sailor and wandering "among the negro houses very late at night" trying to convince them to desert.[84] But largely through black and brown sailors, Jamaican slaves learned of the possibility of making a successful escape to Cuba. Sometimes they received more direct encouragement. The five runaway slaves whom John McGregor followed to Cuba in June 1789 consisted of a "Compleat Washer Woman," a "Ship and House Carpenter," and "three Sailor Negroes." When McGregor's slaves arrived on the coast of Cuba, they were accompanied by a sixth fugitive, a "French Negro" who had also been working in local vessels off St. Ann's Bay. McGregor was convinced that this foreign-born sailor, with the added appeals of the "low trading Spaniards" from Cuba who frequented Jamaica's north coast, had induced his slaves to desert. McGregor may very well have been correct. Testifying before Spanish officials, the alleged culprit told of having been taken off a French ship during the American Revolution and sold as a slave in Jamaica;

---

83   *Royal Gazette*, 24 March 1792, 11 May 1793.

84   Colonel Hunter to Governor of Yucatan, [November 1790], C.O. 123/13, cited in Sir John Alder Burdon, ed., *Archives of British Honduras*, 3 vols. (London, 1931–35), I, 190n.

he had fled in order to regain his freedom.[85] In 1790, a black dock-worker in Kingston revealed that crewmembers of the "Two Brothers" shallop had "asked him to go with them to the Spanish Country where he should have his freedom." Officials identified the three sailors as a "Curracoa brown man," a "Spanish negro" who spoke no English, and "an old negro man named Edinburgh." The following day, the vessel disappeared, and officials surmised that this motley crew of "Foreigners" had "raised upon the captain and carried the vessel to some Foreign Port."[86]

During the 1790s, both before and after the outbreak of the revolution in Saint-Domingue, people involved in all of the various forms of seaborne activity—sailors from the large deep-water vessels and those from the small boats engaged in intercolonial trade; runaway slaves and other deserters; and "sailor Negroes"—assumed center stage. Whether at sea or on land, masterless people played a vital role in spreading rumors, reporting news, and transmitting political currents as antislavery movements and finally a republican revolution gathered momentum in Europe.

The strongest evidence of their influence would come later, when officials all over Afro-America moved to suppress this uncontrollable communication of ideas by circumscribing the boundaries of human mobility in the region.

---

85   Vaillant to McGregor, 1 September 1790, "Narration of Facts ... by John Wilcox McGregor of the Island of Jamaica," London, 1 September 1790, C.O. 137/88, PRO; "Testimonio de las Diligencias originales obradas sobre la aprehensión de seis negros ... que profugaron de uno de los Pueblos de la Colonia Británica," 1789, AGI, Indiferente General, leg. 2787.

86   *Kingston Daily Advertiser*, 1 January 1791.

3.

"The Suspence Is Dangerous in a Thousand Shapes"

News, Rumor, and Politics on the Eve of the Haitian Revolution

The mobility which characterized the masterless Caribbean at the end of the eighteenth century provided a steady undercurrent of opposition to the "absolute" power of masters, merchants, and military officers in the region. In passing from plantation to plantation, from country to city, from town to town, or from island to island, people on the move challenged the social control which symbolized imperial authority. But the movements of runaway slaves, free people of color, deserters from military service, and sailors did not take place in a vacuum; their traditions of mobile resistance assumed an even wider significance when political currents swirling about the Atlantic world brought excitement and uncertainty to the shores of the American colonies, as they did during the revolutionary 1790s. In such times, officials worried openly about possible connections between mobility and subversion.

In the oral cultures of the Caribbean, local rulers were no more able to control the rapid spread of information than they were able to control the movements of the ships or the masterless people with which this information traveled. The books, newspapers, and letters which arrived with the ships were not the only avenues for the flow of information and news in Afro-America. While written documents always had a vital place, black cultural traditions that favored speech and white laws that restricted literacy gave a continuing primacy to other channels of communication. For the harbors where the master-less congregated also buzzed with an assortment of orally transmitted accounts—scraps of news, conflicting interpretations, elusive facts, and shifting rumors. A spicy story or telling anecdote could furnish attentive listeners with news of slave unrest, an impending imperial conflict, unstable sugar prices, or new departures in colonial policy. Whatever their form, reports of developments abroad which might have a tangible effect on American slave societies brought to the surface underlying tensions about authority, legitimacy, and belief. In cultures where people depended upon direct human contact for information, news spread quickly and became part of a shared public discourse.

As emancipation drew near in the British West Indies, the effective "grapevine" of slaves would baffle British colonists and officials. In the early 1830s, colonial governors commented—sometimes in amazement, most often in exasperation—on the slaves' facility in gath-ering and transmitting information. Slaves learned quickly of each new initiative in Parliament and each move in their behalf, and the ripples which such news caused in black communities complicated efforts to control the slave population. "The slaves have an unaccount-able facility in obtaining partial, and generally distorted, information whenever a public document is about to be received which can in any way affect their condition or station," wrote Governor Smith of Trinidad in 1831. The governor of British Guiana discovered a similar dynamic among the slaves in that colony, and concluded that "nothing can be more keenly observant than the slaves are of all that affects their interests."[1]

What was true in the abolition era in the British colonies was equally applicable generations before. Of all the types of intelligence which arrived either on the printed page or by word of mouth in

---

1   Governor Smith to Lord Goderich, 13 July 1831, C.O. 295/87, PRO, Benjamin D'Urban to John Murray, 20 April 1830, C.O. 111/69, PRO, reprinted in Eric Williams, ed., *Documents on British West Indian History, 1807–1833* (Port-of-Spain, 1952), pp. 189, 190.

Afro-American societies, none was more eagerly anticipated or potentially explosive than news which fueled hopes of black emancipation. Just as planters and traders sought news on prices and market conditions and soldiers and sailors watched and listened for word of war or peace from all the publications and people crossing the local dock, so slaves too developed a keen sense of their own interest and kept their ears open for news relevant to their concerns. As the example of Spanish policy regarding runaway slaves makes clear, circulation of such reports among slave societies could spread uncontrollably and galvanize dissident slaves into action.

In addition, local black activists themselves created, transmitted, and utilized combinations of news and rumor to advance their interests independently. Several examples suggest some of the ways in which forceful rumors could raise expectations when carefully placed within slave communities. In 1749, slaves in Caracas, taking advantage of the confusion in the aftermath of a popular uprising of coastal traders against the monopoly of the Caracas Company, seized upon a rumor of impending freedom to organize a revolt of their own. The agitation centered around Juan de Cádiz, a free black recently arrived from Spain, who circulated news that the king had decreed that all Spanish slaves in the Indies be liberated. Promptly, Caracas slaves were whispering among themselves that His Majesty had dispatched the historic *cédula* in the care of a replacement for the local bishop who had recently died. While some slaves looked out for the new bishop's arrival, others were certain that the spirit of the deceased bishop would deliver them by bringing the decree back as his last act in this world.[2] In Martinique in 1768, several slaves who gave voice to an equally powerful liberation rumor discovered how effective—and perilous—such manipulation of public opinion could be. French authorities identified them as the original sources of the rapidly spreading news that a powerful African king had arrived, had purchased from the colonial government all the slaves on the island, and that they could soon expect to board vessels to return to Africa.

---

2   Héctor García Chuecos, "Una insurrección de negros en los dias de la colonia," *Revista de historia de América* 29 (junio de 1950), pp. 67–76.

The bearers of these tidings were placed in irons and publicly suffered thirty-nine lashes for three successive days.[3]

In the 1770s, news of developments across the sea focused even more sharply the attention of Afro-Americans and energized their culture of expectation. This excitement centered in the British Empire. From England, accounts of Lord Mansfield's historic decision in the case of former Virginia slave James Somerset arrived quickly in the American slave colonies. By 1773, barely a year after Somerset won his freedom in England, planters reported anxiously that word had reached Somerset's fellow black Virginians, and some were attempting to board vessels for England "where they imagine they will be free (a Notion now too prevalent among the Negroes, greatly to the Vexation and Prejudice of their Masters)." The following year, another slave deserted an Augusta County plantation "to board a vessel for Great Britain … from the knowledge he had of the late determination of Somerset's Case."[4]

The coming of the American Revolution presented a wide range of opportunity for blacks to express their aspirations for freedom and to demonstrate their ability to absorb and transmit the revolutionary excitement in the air. Free blacks and slaves working in coastal occupations near Charleston, for example, clearly recognized the implications of the impending revolution in 1775, and passed word among themselves of the "great war coming soon" which would "come to help the poor Negroes."[5] Likewise anticipating the drama about to unfold, white patriots in the coastal South viewed with dismay their vulnerability in the event of a British invasion. Two Georgia delegates to the Continental Congress in 1775 shared with John Adams their

---

3 Lucien Peytraud, *L'esclavage aux Antilles françaises avant 1789. d'après des documents inédits des archives coloniales* (Paris, 1897), pp. 372–3.

4 *Virginia Gazette* (Purdie and Dixon), 30 September 1773, 30 June 1774, cited in Gerald W. Mullin, *Flight and Rebellion: Slave Resistance in Eighteenth-Century Virginia* (New York, 1972), p. 131.

5 These are the words of Thomas Jeremiah, a free black Charleston pilot, quoted through court records in Peter H. Wood, "'Taking Care of Business' in Revolutionary South Carolina: Republicanism and the Slave Society," in Jeffrey J. Crow and Larry E. Tise, eds., *The Southern Experience in the American Revolution* (Chapel Hill, 1978), pp. 284–85.

fear that, if promised freedom, twenty thousand slaves from Georgia and South Carolina would fly to the British camp. They also related how recent news had stimulated the networks of black communication in the southern colonies. "The negroes have a wonderful art of communicating intelligence among themselves," noted an obviously impressed Adams in his diary after their discussion. "It will run several hundreds of miles in a week or fortnight."[6]

Subsequent events fulfilled some black hopes and proved white fears prophetic. After the outbreak of hostilities, thousands of North American slaves in quest of freedom fled their masters to join the British; others hoped to gain freedom by fighting with the patriots. Not only did the revolt against British rule affect Afro-Americans in the rebellious colonies, the winds of the revolution swept into other neighboring areas of Afro-America. In Bermuda, black sailors took to the sea in privateers running powder and ammunition to the rebels. The dislocations and ideological currents of the revolt also affected Jamaica. Just as the Declaration of Independence appeared in the mainland colonies in July 1776, planters in Hanover parish barely averted an attempt of blacks along the coast to strike a blow for freedom. In the aftermath of the scare of 1776, white Jamaicans spoke anxiously of the danger posed by the currents of revolutionary ideology in slave societies. "Dear Liberty has rang in the heart of every *House-bred Slave*, in one form or other, for these Ten years past," wrote one observer after the plot had been thwarted. "While we only talk'd about it, they went no farther than their private reflections upon us and it: but as soon as we came to blows, we find them fast at our heels. Such has been the seeds sown in the minds of our Domestics by our Wise-Acre Patriots."[7]

The peace of 1783 virtually extinguished the hopes kindled by the era of the American Revolution. In the years following the British defeat, the colonial powers in the Caribbean moved to recast their

---

6   Diary entry, 24 September 1775, in Charles Francis Adams, ed., *The Works of John Adams*, 10 vols. (Boston, 1850–1856), II, p. 428.

7   Richard B. Sheridan, "The Jamaica Slave Insurrection Scare of 1776 and the American Revolution," *Journal of Negro History* 61 (July 1976), p. 301. For the activities of black seamen from Bermuda, see Cyril Outerbridge Packwood, *Chained on the Rock: Slavery in Bermuda* (New York and Bermuda, 1975), pp. 42–6.

empires by closing loopholes (the new Spanish policy regarding runaway slaves provides the best example) and revitalizing the trade in African slaves. To the north, the victorious rebels did not extend their revolutionary principles to include the unfree, and by 1787 it was clear that the new nation would be built in large measure on the backs of the enslaved black workers who constituted fully a fifth of the population of the United States.

Beginning in the late 1780s, however, another wave of expectation and rumor gripped Afro-America. This time, the excitement encompassed a substantial cross-section of American slave societies, extending beyond the British colonies to include directly those of the Spanish and French. Not only did the revolutionary rumblings in Europe reverberate in the Americas, but slavery was everywhere under close and often critical metropolitan scrutiny. In Britain, whose slave trade was expanding again after declining during the war, popular pressure forced Parliament in 1787 to begin the long and slow process which would finally result in the trade's abolition twenty years later. Similarly, the Bourbon reformers in Spain turned to the issue of slavery in the Spanish territories in the 1780s, and in 1789 attempted to place legal restraints on the absolute power of slaveholders and overseers on plantations. By 1789, of course, momentous news began to filter in from France. The storming of the Bastille, the Declaration of the Rights of Man, and the tentative colonial policy of the revolutionary government all held serious implications for the future of slavery in the French colonies.

By 1790, the debates in Parliament over the slave trade, the Spanish reforms concerning slavery, and the French Revolution were not only topics of heated debate behind the closed doors of local government bodies; they were also the subjects of irrepressible speculation and rumor aboard ships, in city streets, and on plantations. From colony to colony, slaves and other disfranchised groups spread the news and shared their excitement, bending and stretching the conflicting accounts to build hopes that Atlantic "society was on the verge of a major transformation that would hasten their liberation."[8] This

---

8 Carol V. R. George, *Segregated Sabbaths: Richard Allen and the Emergence of Independent Black Churches, 1760–1840* (New York, 1973), p. 15. George's study

culture of expectation anticipated and helped to fuel the outbreak of revolution in the heart of Afro-America.

Sixteen long and eventful years passed between the Somerset ruling of 1772 and Parliament's decision to examine the legality and conduct of the British slave trade. Even as Mansfield handed down his judgement, the number of ships clearing British ports on slaving missions to the coast of Africa had reached its all-time peak. Between 1771 and 1773, more than one hundred vessels per year left Liverpool, Europe's busiest slave trading port, on the first leg of the Atlantic triangle, and many more departed from London and Bristol. The revolt in North America sharply reduced the volume of Britain's lucrative trade in African labor, but only temporarily. At war's end, vessels which had outfitted as warships once again became Guineamen, and merchants in the slave trade quickly regained their secure commercial position of the prewar years. After 1783, the trade revived as speedily as it had languished a decade earlier.[9]

But the recovery of the slave trade in British ports did not abate the popular opposition to the trade which had surfaced during the lean years. In Liverpool, where confrontations between merchant seamen and the hungry press gangs of the British Navy became commonplace during the war, sailors took the lead by mounting violent protests against the exploitative working conditions of the slave trade. In the fall of 1775, unemployed seamen took to the streets to call attention to low wages and cruel treatment of mariners on slaving vessels. Marching under a red flag and sporting red ribbons in their caps, the protesters pulled down the rigging of slavers at anchor, sacked and burned the

---

identifies a similar culture of expectation surrounding the response of North American slaves to itinerant Baptist and Methodist exhorters in the same period, but this statement applies equally to the effect of the political currents of the late eighteenth century.

9   See the figures for Liverpool in Richard Brooke, *Liverpool as it was during the last quarter of the Eighteenth Century. 1775 to 1800* (Liverpool and London, 1853), p. 234; Gomer Williams, *History of the Liverpool Privateers and Letters of Marque, with an Account of the Liverpool Slave Trade* (London and Liverpool, 1897), p. 678; and J. A. Picton, *Memorials of Liverpool Historical and Topographical, Including a History of the Dock Estate*, 2 vols. (London and Liverpool, 1875), I, p. 224.

homes of prominent merchants and shipowners engaged in the trade, and attacked the Exchange.[10] After the war, local groups—Quakers and non-Quakers alike—kept alive the opposition to the slave trade. As the revolution ended, John Pinney, heir to several family-owned West Indian plantations, found public opinion in Bristol to be a major obstacle blocking efforts to resurrect the slave trade. "The people here seem devoted to our destruction," Pinney intimated to a Caribbean correspondent in 1783. "They entertain the most horrid ideas of our cruelties—it now pervades all ranks of people—they think slavery ought not to be permitted in any part of the British dominions."[11] A decade after the seamen's revolt of 1775, the slave trade remained at the center of public controversy in Liverpool as well. Prominent abolitionist James Currie reported in 1786 that "the general discussion of the slavery of the negroes has produced much unhappiness in Liverpool ... and the struggle between interest and humanity has made great havoc in the happiness of many families."[12]

Four years after the treaty ending the American Revolution, the struggle within Britain against the slave trade started to surface on many fronts. Black Londoners, whose efforts to avoid re-enslavement had brought the issue of slavery to public notice and set the context for the *Somerset* decision, channeled information to abolitionists and provided eyewitness accounts of the horrors of slavery and the trade it fostered. By 1787, such accounts were appearing in print for the first time.[13] Other developments occurring that same year pointed more

10   R. Barrie Rose, "A Liverpool Sailors' Strike in the Eighteenth Century," *Transactions of the Lancashire and Cheshire Antiquarian Society* 68 (1959), pp. 85–6. Rose ranks this uprising, together with the better known Gordon Riots of 1780 and the "Church and King" riots of 1791, as the "three most serious town riots which shocked England at the close of the eighteenth century." See also Brooke, *Liverpool during the last Quarter of the Eighteenth Century*, pp. 325–47, an invaluable account which includes extensive reprinting from newspapers.

11   John Pinney to James Tobin (1783), quoted in Charles Malcolm MacInnes, *A Gateway of Empire* (London, 1939), p. 334.

12   Quoted in Picton, *Memorials of Liverpool*, I, p. 225.

13   See Ottobah Cugoano's influential *Thoughts and Sentiments on the Evil and Wicked Traffic of the Slavery and Commerce of the Human Species. Humbly Submitted to the Inhabitants of Great Britain* (London, 1787), thought to be the first published attack on the slave trade written by a black author.

directly toward a parliamentary solution to the problem of the slave trade. On the organizational front, an informal committee of London Quakers was recast as the Society for Effecting the Abolition of the Slave Trade, with Granville Sharp (one of two non-Quakers among the twelve committee members) as chairman. By identifying and circulating "such information as may tend to the abolition of the Slave Trade," the so-called "London Committee" hoped to spearhead the effort to pressure Parliament into action. Later in 1787, thousands more voices joined the movement after abolition committees in Manchester and London, working independently, initiated campaigns to saturate Parliament with signed petitions urging consideration of the slave trade. The petition drive quickly spread to other cities, and more than one hundred petitions bearing thousands of signatures would reach Parliament by the early summer of 1788. In February, however, with the stack of petitions piling high, Prime Minister William Pitt had already issued an order-in-council to submit the slave trade to a parliamentary inquiry. As a first step, Pitt directed the Committee for Trade and Plantations of the Privy Council to conduct a preliminary investigation and to gather evidence on a wide range of subjects touching every aspect of Britain's involvement in the slave trade. He charged the Privy Council to bring in evidence on African societies, the procurement of slaves, conditions aboard slave ships, treatment of slaves on West Indian plantations, black demography in the West Indies, and the slave trade practices of Britain's colonial rivals.[14]

By the time of Pitt's official pronouncement, however, supporters of the slave trade on both sides of the Atlantic were already busy building opposition to abolition. Liverpool and Bristol merchant-shipowners petitioned Parliament, arguing that the slave trade was the very linchpin of the nation's mercantile system and warning that its disruption would cripple economic activity in the ports, throw thousands of people out of work, and ultimately redound to the advantage

---

14   For summaries, see Reginald Coupland, *The British Anti-Slavery Movement* (London, 1964), pp. 86–101; Roger Anstey, *The Atlantic Slave Trade and British Abolition 1760–1810* (London, 1975), pp. 255–78; and James Walvin, "The Public Campaign in England Against Slavery," in David Eltis and James Walvin, eds., *The Abolition of the Atlantic Slave Trade* (Madison and London, 1981), pp. 63–79.

of the French and Spanish.[15] Just as active was the so-called "West India interest"—absentee planters and merchants with considerable holdings in the islands. Meeting at the London Tavern, the West India Planters and Merchants organized a subcommittee to pressure members of Parliament and government officials and to manipulate the flow of information through publication of pro-slavery tracts and sympathetic articles to be placed artfully in the public prints.

News of Parliament's action reached the colonies swiftly, and by April 1788 further accounts arrived daily. Pitt's announcement came as no surprise in the islands, where colonists, well informed of developments, had already opened discussions about ways to head off the coming parliamentary assault. Both public and private channels carried accounts of the building sentiment for abolition. In Barbados, newspapers appearing in early April reported the growing interest in Britain and throughout Europe in the "iniquitous and inhuman traffic." John Orde, governor at Dominica, an eastern island which served both as a slave market and as a way station for British slavers headed farther west, reported in mid-April that "the intention of bringing the subject of the Slave Trade before Parliament is generally known here, and has been for some time." Despite his efforts to quiet public discussion, he disclosed, "many letters received from Liverpool in particular have had a different tendency." In Jamaica, news of the petition drive and its apparent effect on public opinion in England had "already occasioned great alarm in all ranks of the people here" when the first official dispatches arrived, and concerned white observers proposed calling the legislature into special session to calm the situation.[16]

Because of the seasonal nature of the shipping cycle, the coming of late winter and early spring always brought long-awaited news of events in England to the Caribbean. With the hurricane season

---

15   See, for example, the petitions reprinted in Elizabeth Donnan, *Documents Illustrative of the History of the Slave Trade to America*, 4 vols. (Washington, 1930–35), III, pp. 574–5, 602–12.

16   *Barbados Gazette* (Bridgetown), 2 April 1788, (microfilm copy of file in Barbados Museum), AAS; John Orde to Lord Sydney, 13 April 1788, C.O. 71/14, PRO; Alured Clarke to Sydney, 22, 25 April 1788, C.O. 137/87, PRO.

safely behind them, merchant ships began to arrive in profusion late in December, and for the next three to four months incoming vessels greatly outnumbered departures; harbors swarmed with ships at anchor; taverns overflowed with seamen; and wharves hummed with activity. As events in England developed in the first three months of 1788, seventy-four British ships arrived at Dominica, by far the island's busiest quarter of the year in terms of trade with Britain.[17] More dramatic was the end-of-the-year infestation of British ships at Jamaica. From late December 1787 to the end of the following March, 204 vessels arrived from Britain while only ninety cleared for the return voyage.[18] Colonist William Beckford remembered that Jamaicans awaited "with no small impatience and anxiety" the wave of ships which began to arrive every December. Between Christmas and Easter, all residents of the port cities had their reasons for frequenting the quay. During this time, the docks became "a scene of bustle and confusion," with "boats passing to and from the different shipping, … strings of negroes … passing and repassing upon a variety of avocations; and … the groups of white people whom curiosity, friendship, or trade assemble together."[19]

Furthermore, in all seasons the reception of incoming news had developed into something of a publicly shared ritual by the late eighteenth century. The flurry of activity attending the arrival of a boat bearing letters and newspapers from England strongly impressed a British traveler to Barbados in the 1790s. The mail packet's approach touched off a wave of popular excitement:

> On the packet making the harbour it caused a crowd not unlike what you may have seen at a sailing or rowing match upon the Thames. Each wishing to be first, and all eager to learn the reports, the vessel was beset on every quarter before she could come to anchor, and the whole bay became an animated scene of crowded ships and moving boats. Many

---

17   Orde to Sydney, 10 May 1788, 1 September 1788, C.O. 71/14, PRO; Orde to Sydney, 13 December 1788, 22 January 1789, C.O. 71/15, PRO.

18   Alured Clarke to Sydney, 30 May 1788, C.O. 137/87, PRO.

19   William Beckford, *A Descriptive Account of the Island of Jamaica*, 2 vols. (London, 1790), I, pp. 319–20.

who could not go to the packet as she entered the harbour, repaired on shore to be ready, there, to meet the news. The people of the town, also, thronged the beach in anxious multitudes. All was busy expectation. Impatience scarcely allowed the bags to reach the office: every avenue to which was so closely blockaded that the house was quite in a state of siege, and the post-master and his mansion in danger of being taken by storm.[20]

Aware of the public way that news arrived in the colonies, proslavery lobbyists brought forward one of the most compelling arguments against parliamentary interference. Very early in the contest over the slave trade, its supporters began to stress the dangerous impact which such deliberations would have on slaves in the British Caribbean. The fears of the planter class on this subject, transmitted to colonial policymakers through their representatives in London, are strikingly reminiscent of the concerns of the Carolina plantocracy on the eve of the American Revolution, "Your Lordship may depend upon it," wrote Stephen Fuller, agent for Jamaica and a longtime resident of the West Indies, to Lord Sydney in January 1788, "that during the time this business is agitated in Parliament, the slaves will be minutely acquainted with all the proceedings." Falsely encouraged by public discussions of abolition, he warned, slaves might well choose to "strike while the iron is hot, and by a sudden blow finish the business themselves in the most expeditious and effectual manner, without giving their zealous friends [in England] any further trouble." While clearly designed to make officials in England think carefully about tampering with labor arrangements in the West Indies, Fuller's caveat nevertheless expressed the deepest private concerns of his planter clients. By the summer, even Caribbean newspapers wondered aloud whether slaves would "be so elevated and enraptured with the news" about Parliament's deliberations that "the excess of their joy and frantic zeal for their general emancipation" would cause unrest.[21] In deference to such concern, officials in both England and the colonies moved with

---

20   George Pinckard, *Notes on the West Indies*, 2 vols. (London, 1816), I, p. 229.
21   Stephen Fuller to Lord Sydney, 29 January 1788, FLB; *Barbados Gazette*, 23 August 1788.

caution as the showdown in Parliament approached. Lord Sydney's private dispatches to colonial governors urged them to be alert to the possibility of slave unrest, and the governors themselves reported that they were, in the words of the governor of Jamaica, paying "particular attention to prevent any disturbance in Consequence of the rumours which must necessarily be spread among the Negroes upon this occasion, avoiding as much as possible, to create unnecessary Suspicion or alarm."[22]

Despite such efforts, or perhaps because of them, alarm ran high. As the packets arrived in Jamaica in late April bringing the so-called "Heads of Inquiry"—queries from the Privy Council regarding slave laws and treatment in the colonies—anxious planters prematurely surmised that slavery was at an end. Upon the emancipation of the slaves, asked one of Stephen Fuller's Jamaica correspondents late in April, "how, or where are they to be settled? ... Are our Lands too to be taken away for their support and residence?" Even Pitt's postponement of open debate in Parliament until 1789 had done little to relieve the tension; in fact, the long wait seemed interminable: "The very suspence is dangerous in a thousand Shapes," disclosed Fuller's friend, "but we must encounter them with our utmost efforts."[23]

Evidence of just how suspenseful and dangerous the situation could become for white Jamaicans soon materialized. An abortive uprising of slaves at St. John's parish in Jamaica in April confirmed planters' expectations "that the Negroe business will cause some trouble in this Island."[24] Similar warnings echoed from other British territories. By late June, the absentee West India Planters and Merchants in London reported "several Letters received from the Sugar Colonies" testifying to local slave unrest and anticipating that "when the Ships in the Merchant's service leave the Islands on the approach of the Hurricane season, a Spirit of Mutiny will break forth amongst the Negroes, especially in the island of Jamaica." Only a speedy deployment of "an

22   Clarke to Sydney, 22 April 1788, C.O. 137/87, PRO.
23   "Extract of a Letter from Spanish Town Jamaica dated 25th April 1788 to Stephen Fuller Esq. Agent for Jamaica," C.O. 137/87, PRO.
24   T. J. Parker to George Hibbert, 21 April 1788, extract reprinted in Stephen Fuller's petition of 2 July 1788, C.O. 137/87, PRO.

additional adequate Force" of ships and troops, they implored, would deter the slaves from acting upon their "erroneous conclusions" that slavery might be coming to an end.[25]

A year later, in May of 1789, William Wilberforce, the young member from Yorkshire who had agreed two years earlier to bring the concerns of the London Committee to the halls of Parliament, rose in the House of Commons to deliver his historic first speech calling for an end to Britain's share in the African slave trade. Though his motion was narrowly defeated, the vote was only the beginning of a new round of evidence gathering and debate. By 1790, the continuing agitation was entering its third year and had become a more public issue than ever in the islands. In Kingston, a local newspaper poked fun at a "gentleman of this parish" recently returned from London who had since his return proclaimed himself "a perfect disciple of the humane Mr. Wilberforce" and determined to make his slaves free laborers. Upon his arrival, however, he discovered to his dismay and to the delight of the columnist, that his slaves had "taken care to save him the trouble of emancipation, by *taking their own freedom*."[26] London's absentee planters, hearing of the recent edict published in Spanish Trinidad which welcomed runaway slaves from the English and French, complained that the Spanish maneuver could not have come at a more inopportune time. "The late discussions of the Slave Trade, confounded with an Idea of general Emancipation" found British slaves at present "unusually agitated," they argued, "and the danger of Insurrections cannot but be augmented, by this insidious Invitation to Freedom from a Foreign Power."[27] Later that year, such apprehensions gained credibility after a slave revolt on the island of Tortola. Official inquiries found that the uprising "proceeded from a Report that has prevailed among the Slaves that there is already in the Island as Act sent out from England by Government for the Purpose of abolishing Slavery but that it is suppressed at the Instance of the Inhabitants."[28]

25   Minutes of WIPM, 30 June 1788, reel 3.

26   *Kingston Daily Advertiser*, 16 January 1790, reprinted in Edward Brathwaite, *The Development of Creole Society in Jamaica 1770–1820* (London, 1971), p. 35.

27   Minutes of WIPM, 6 April 1790, reel 3.

28   Turnbull to Shirley, 1 June 1790, C.O. 152/69, quoted in Elsa Goveia, *Slave*

That slaves would express such an interest in the progress of the abolition movement in England is not surprising. But how did they gain
access to such news? Explaining to the world the slaves' ability to learn
about and stay abreast of developments in England—and how they
could be so misled as to expect that their liberation was involved—
Jamaican planters pointed to an active conspiracy of misguided British
humanitarians and mobile black agents. "Means of information were
not wanting," according to planter-historian Bryan Edwards. These
sources included oral accounts from "the black servants continually returning from England" in the company of traveling absentee
owners; the many antislavery pamphlets which found their way to
the islands; and finally more symbolic materials such as the variety
of medallions and woodcuts suggesting black oppression and resistance.[29] The Assembly echoed Edwards, blaming the "Industriously
Circulated … Essays and harangues of the Abolishers" on the printed
page, but also the London Committee's equally ill-advised publication of antislavery testimony before Parliament in booklets "sent out
by Persons in England, and explained to our slaves by Free People of
their own Complexion."[30]

But the steady expansion of the very trade which abolitionists
attacked and planters and merchants sought to protect also brought
to the islands another source of information whose presence has been
ignored by modern historians as it was passed over by contemporary
observers—seamen working the slave ships themselves. Several

Society in the British Leeward Islands at the End of the Eighteenth Century (New
Haven, 1965), p. 95.

29   See Edwards's comments in Jamaica Assembly, *The Proceedings of the Governor
and Assembly of Jamaica, in Regard to the Maroon Negroes* (London, 1796), 1.

30   Address of the Council to Williamson, [29 November 1791], C.O. 137/90,
PRO; *Petition of Stephen Fuller. Esq., Agent for Jamaica, to the House of Commons*,
30 March 1792, MS 1731, National Library of Jamaica, Kingston (hereinafter NLJ).
Only in 1771 had Parliament begun to loosen the absolute restriction on the public
reporting of debates and speeches on the floor, and it was not until 1783 that visitors
were allowed to take notes on the proceedings. See Arthur Aspinall, "The Reporting
and Publishing of the House of Commons' Debates 1771–1834," in Richard Pares
and A. J. P. Taylor, eds., *Essays Presented to Sir Lewis Namier* (London, 1956),
pp. 227–57.

factors point to slave trade seamen as likely sources of information for black West Indians. First, the majority of British sailors arriving in the Caribbean in the late 1780s came on slave ships. Though considerably smaller in tonnage, slavers carried much larger crews than the vessels engaged in the direct trade between Britain and the Caribbean, both to facilitate trading on the African coast and to suppress shipboard rebellions during the Middle Passage. Roughly sixty percent of the more than 10,000 Liverpool seamen who journeyed to the West Indies between 1785 and 1787 worked on board slave ships. During 1787, while the movement to abolish the slave trade gathered momentum, 2,524 of 4,264 sailors departing Britain's most active port for the West Indies sailed by way of Africa.[31]

Not only did seamen from the slave trade outnumber those in other branches of Britain's West India trade, but they were most likely to remain in the islands, either voluntarily or against their will, after their vessel's return to England. Desertion and forcible discharge by captains seeking to defraud sailors of their wages combined to effect what abolitionist Thomas Clarkson, the first serious student of this aspect of the British slave trade, termed in 1788 the "continual disgorgement of seamen from [slaving] vessels into the islands."[32] Researching in customs records in London and Liverpool in the summer of 1787, Clarkson found, in addition to high rates of mortality for seamen in the slave trade, disproportionately high rates of desertion and discharge from slave trade service. Of Clarkson's sample of 5,000 seamen embarking on slaving voyages in 1786, fewer than half, 2,320, returned to Britain in the vessels in which their voyage had originated. Taking into account the sailors who perished during the first and second legs of the deadly triangular voyage still left some 1,500 deserters and dischargees—thirty percent of the original number—unaccounted for. The next year, Clarkson found that only 1,428 of the 3,170 sailors

---

31 Herbert S. Klein, *The Middle Passage; Comparative Studies in the Atlantic Slave Trade* (Princeton, 1978), pp. 164–70; "Mr. Tarleton's Calculation of the Trade of Liverpool to Africa and the West Indies" (1787), *in Privy Council Report* (1789), pt. IV.

32 Thomas Clarkson, *An Essay on the Impolicy of the Slave Trade, In Two Parts* (London, 1788), 55n.

shipping out of Liverpool on slavers returned, and modern scholars have pieced together a similar picture for Bristol seamen.[33]

Whether deserters or dischargees, many former seamen from the slave trade tried to construct new lives in the Caribbean, where they had ample opportunity to interact with both slaves and masterless people. Some found casual employment ashore, while others used their seafaring skills and either signed aboard vessels "employed in other Trades" or worked alongside slaves and free black seamen "navigating the small Vessels which go from one Island to another." Others less fortunate festered as beggars, sick and destitute. Local residents called these people "wharfingers," suggesting cynically that they had become so numerous as to "own" the wharves which they frequented. Common sights in Jamaica and other islands where slaving vessels unloaded their cargoes, "wharfingers" were sometimes "taken in by the Negro-women out of Compassion," and blacks often buried seamen who died in the islands in their own cemeteries.[34]

The commonality of experience which brought together slaves from Africa and seamen from Europe contributed to a broader mutual identification between the two groups. While some slaves longed to escape the plantation and find a freer life at sea, European seafarers had long recognized the striking parallels between life before the mast and life on the plantation. Seamen subject to rigid and arbitrary discipline, to the absolute power of ships' masters, to press gangs and the lash, found an appropriate analogy for their lives in the slave experience. One contemporary description of the dreaded Liverpool press gangs finds the poor victim "seized as if he were a common felon, deprived of his liberty, torn from his home, his friends, his parents, wife or children, hurried to the rendezvous house, examined, passed,

---

33   Thomas Clarkson, *The History of the Rise, Progress, and Accomplishment of the Abolition of the African Slave-Trade by the British Parliament*, 2 vols. (London, 1808), II, p. 60; Clarkson, *Impolicy of the Slave Trade*, pp. 53–9; C. M. MacInnes, "Bristol and the Slave Trade," in Patrick McGrath, ed., *Bristol in the Eighteenth Century* (Bristol, 1972), p. 174.

34   See the evidence of William James and the "Answers, &c. from the Collector and Comptroller of the Customs," Liverpool, 13 November 1788, in *Privy Council Report* (1789), pt. II.

and sent on board the tender, like a negro to a slave-ship." Writing the same year that Parliament's inquiry into slavery and the slave trade began, a reform-minded ex-officer in the Royal Navy called a legislator's attention to the "perfect air of slavery" inherent in such practices as impressment.[35]

The actions of individual sailors provide further evidence that they may have viewed themselves at least partially as slaves. The early history of the British settlement at Sierra Leone, located adjacent to a busy slave trading area on the West African coast, furnishes a striking example. Among the other problems faced by the fledgling settlement, founded in 1787 as a refuge for ex-slaves from America and London's "Black Poor," was the temptation it posed for British seamen also looking to escape the oppression of the slave trade. "We are and have been frequently much pestered by renegade seamen, quitting ships employed in the Slave Trade, and refuging here," reported a British traveler in Freetown in 1792. Deserters easily found local employment, often stranding ships ready to sail for the West Indies for lack of crew. Pressure from merchants and captains to apprehend deserters from the slave ships created "an aukward situation" for Governor John Clarkson, whose orders called upon him to "protect every man" seeking a new life in the colony. In the end, Clarkson, despite his misgivings about the slave trade, instructed constables to seize deserters and return them to their ships.[36]

The movement to abolish the slave trade made more concrete the common political interest of these eyewitnesses to the slave trade and the trade's African victims. In England, issues surrounding British seamen figured prominently in the widening debate over slavery and the slave trade. Thomas Clarkson discovered the depth of resentment

---

35   [James Aspinall], *Liverpool a Few Years Since, by an Old Stager* (Liverpool, 1869), p. 8; Robert Nation, *A Letter to a Member of Parliament: proposing a Plan of Regulations for the Better and More Compleat Manning the Navy* (London, 1788), p. 6.

36   [Anna Maria Falconbridge], *Narrative of Two Voyages to the River Sierra Leone, during the Years 1791–1793, performed by A. M. Falconbridge*, 2nd ed. (London, 1802), pp. 171–2. A substantial number of black ex-sailors discharged from His Majesty's fleet after the American Revolution also settled in Sierra Leone.

among former seamen in the slave trade, and the evidence which he gathered on the docks of Bristol and Liverpool in the summer of 1787 on the treatment of sailors in the trade boosted the abolitionist cause immeasurably by destroying the myth that the trade was a "nursery" for seamen. After his initial informants, mostly respectable merchants and sea captains, had deserted him, Clarkson to his surprise was approached by scores of common seamen willing to share damaging testimony regarding the treatment of sailors in the slave trade. In addition, Clarkson himself, sometimes disguised as a sailor, communicated with seamen arriving in slave ships and found them "always forward to speak to me, and to tell me their grievances, if it were only with the hope of being able to get redress." It was largely through this evidence that Wilberforce was able to assert in his historic 1789 speech against the slave trade that "instead of being a benefit to our sailors, as some have ignorantly argued, I do assert that it is their grave."[37]

In the West Indies, sailors also actively protested conditions in the slave trade. "There is scarcely a Vessel in that Trade that calls at Barbadoes," reported Governor Parry in 1788, "from which I have not a Complaint made to me, either by the Master or the Seamen, but more frequently (and generally with greater Reason) by the latter, who are often shamefully used."[38] In St. Vincent in 1786, after sailors refused to carry out the captain's orders "till they received some Refreshment" after a long voyage, local magistrates committed "Three of the best Men" to jail and the remainder of the "discontented Seamen rowed on Shore, forfeiting their Wages, and leaving Part of the Clothes behind."[39] By the time of the parliamentary inquiry, abuses of sailors had become so commonplace at St. Vincent that officials called upon Parliament to "attend to the Protection of the Mariners,

---

37   Anstey, *Atlantic Slave Trade*, pp. 264–5; Clarkson, *Abolition of the Slave Trade*, I, p. 314; James Currie to William Wilberforce, 31 December 1787, reprinted in *Memoir of the Life, Writings, and Correspondence of James Currie*, 2 vols. (London, 1831), I, p. 122; John Debrett, ed., *The Parliamentary Register, or History of the Proceedings and Debates of the House of Commons*, 45 vols. (London, 1781–96), XXVI, p. 143.

38   "Extract of Letter from Governor Parry to Lord Sydney," 13 May 1788, *Privy Council Report* (1789), pt. III (Barbados).

39   Evidence of James Arnold, *Privy Council Report* (1789), pt. II.

who are frequently so ill treated during the latter Part of the Voyage, that they are induced to run away from their Ships, and thus to forfeit their Wages become due to them by the Time of their Arrival here."[40] In addition to the many who deserted in the islands, others who were discharged against their will may also have been interested in reforming the slave trade's practices. Consider the case of William Dineley, a surgeon aboard the Bristol slaver *Fame*, which arrived at Jamaica in 1791. After clashing with the captain over the unhealthy conditions and the treatment of the slaves and seamen during the passage from Africa to the islands, Dineley was locked out of his vessel by the captain's orders and remained stranded in Jamaica after the vessel's departure. As he desperately searched for a berth aboard another vessel bound to his home port, Dineley asked for the help of the ship's owner, vowing that "Sh'd I ever sail out again to Africa, I will ... have nothing to do with a Cap't. [as] they are a sort of over bearing men."[41]

If discontented whites like Dineley had reason to identify with the abolitionist campaign, black sailors carried their knowledge back and forth across the Atlantic, making direct contributions to the effort to end the slave trade. News from West Indian seamen like Olaudah Equiano proved invaluable to Granville Sharp, William Wilberforce, and others in England searching for ways to rally popular opposition to the trade. Equiano, who had experienced life aboard slavers both as a captive below deck and as a sailor, met frequently with Sharp while in London, sharing personal insights into Caribbean slavery and relating stories he learned through connections with incoming sailors. Sharp credited Equiano, for example, with informing him of a 1781 incident in which "one hundred and thirty Negroes [were] thrown alive into the sea, from on board an English slave ship" off Jamaica. Kept alive in the oral tradition of black seamen for two years,

---

40 "Extract of a Letter from Mr. Chief Justice Ottley to Sir William Young. Dated St. Vincent, August 6, 1788," *Privy Council Report* (1789), pt. III (St. Vincent).

41 William Dineley to James Rogers, 10 September 1791 (photostats of PRO originals in James Rogers Papers, Duke University Library). Dineley was unsuccessful in his appeals, and later "died in Kingston, leaving a disconsolate widow and Six helpless Children." Alex Kent (Kemp?) to James Rogers, 16 April 1793, Rogers Papers.

the case of the *Zong* received wide publicity beginning in 1783, and the public discussion of the grisly details of this affair signaled a major shift in British public opinion. Contacts between black mariners and prominent abolitionists in England continued into the 1790s. As late as 1795, "a poor Negro, from on board one of His Majesty's Ships lately returned from the West Indies" sought out Sharp with accounts of the mistreatment of people of color taken off French vessels as prisoners of war.[42]

The slave trade question headed for and comfortably survived a second vote on the floor of the House of Commons in April 1791. News of the outcome of the vote reached Jamaica in mid-June, where one official reported not "the least apprehension of any insurrection or disturbance amongst the slaves," but added that a vote against the slave trade may very well have produced a different outcome.[43] Through the summer and into the fall, Lord Effingham, Jamaica's new governor, and Adam Williamson, recently arrived commander of the island's military force, watched closely for signs of unrest related to the slave trade but found none. Still, they proceeded with extreme caution lest their public actions lend credence to the rumors around them. Suspecting from having been in England during the early stages of the slave trade debate that "Disturbances might arise here," Governor Effingham quietly shored up the island's military preparedness while trying "to avoid such appearance of preparation as might put mischief into peoples' heads." But just as the first notices of a revolutionary outbreak in neighboring Saint-Domingue were arriving, he confessed that all was not within his control: "What the Gossiping of Idle Folks may produce," Effingham intimated to the Secretary of State, "I can't tell."[44]

42   Prince Hoare, ed., *Memoirs of Granville Sharp. Esq., Composed from his own Manuscripts and other Authentic Documents in the Possession of his Family and of the African Institution* (London, 1820), p. 236; James Walvin, *The Black Presence; A Documentary History of the Negro in England, 1555–1860* (London, 1971), 209n.; Granville Sharp to William Wilberforce, 4 June 1795, William Wilberforce Papers, Duke University Library, box 1.

43   Grenville to Adam Williamson and Lord Effingham, 21 April 1791, Williamson to Grenville, 4 July 1791, C.O. 137/89, FRO.

44   Effingham to Grenville, 6 August 1791, Effingham to Henry Dundas, 17 September 1791, C.O. 137/89, PRO.

Reports from other segments of the white population of Jamaica from the end of the year, however, present a very different picture from that which emerges in official dispatches. Wilberforce's birthday provided the occasion for a massive celebration of slaves in Westmoreland parish, some "100 Miles," noted a private letter of early November, "from any of the quarters where Regular Troops are stationed." The assembled slaves, estimated to number 3,000, ate and drank but were dispersed "before their liquor had produced much effect." This incident was but "one proof," the correspondent concluded, "how greatly Mr. W____'s intentions are misrepresented to the Slaves."[45] Meeting at Spanish Town the same day as the arrival of this report from across the island, the Assembly made its strongest public statement calling for an immediate end to further consideration of the slave trade:

> It is vain to urge, that the Trade alone, and not the Situation of our Slaves, is the Object of Deliberation. Our Negroes cannot, or will not, make any such Distinction—They are taught to believe, and do most certainly believe, that they are held in a Condition of Servitude which is reprobated in the Mother Country: and that the ultimate Aim of those Gentlemen, whom they call their Friends, in England, is to place them on a footing with the civilized Part of this Community; an opinion which, in their present Ideas of Right and Wrong, can tend only to involve them in one common Destruction with ourselves.[46]

The added drama of the Haitian Revolution clearly sharpened the concern of the Jamaican legislature in the closing weeks of 1791; early reports of the rebellion only intensified for white colonists the "dangerous and distressing state of suspense during the months of agitation in Parliament, which has been the case for these two years past."[47] Even after the Haitian Revolution erupted next door in late August of 1791, reports concerning the slave trade debates in Parliament continued to influence the political climate in Jamaica. In June of 1792, Kingston

---

45   "Extract of a Letter dated Spanish Town Jamaica, 5th Novr. 1791," FLB.

46   Members of the Assembly to Stephen Fuller, 5 November 1791, extract reprinted in *Petition of Stephen Fuller*, 30 March 1792, NLJ.

47   Fuller to Effingham, 7 December 1791, FLB.

officials observed a disturbing "air of insolence" among blacks in that city shortly after the arrival of a premature report that Parliament had voted to abolish the slave trade.[48] The next year, as if to emphasize that the threat of abolition was as strong as that of republican radicalism, whites in Kingston burned Wilberforce and Tom Paine in effigy side by side.[49]

Though by November of 1791 the slaves did not yet betray "Symptoms of the same Phrenzy which rages a few Leagues distant," the revolutions in the French islands would in the weeks to come gradually supercede the slave trade agitation, both in England and in the colonies, as the major news item.[50] Wilberforce and his party in England would continue to push for Parliament to end the slave trade through the 1790s, but for the present, in England and in the colonies as well, the attention of all those with some stake in West Indian affairs would shift to the French Revolution in the Caribbean.

As the British debated the future of the slave trade in the late 1780s, producing a "state of suspense" in the British Caribbean, similar developments were taking place elsewhere in Europe. At the Spanish Court, cabinet ministers, anticipating that Caracas, Cuba, and the Spanish colony on Hispaniola were about to blossom finally into full-blown plantation economies, codified and tried to put into effect a set of strict guidelines under which they would expect slaves and masters to operate as the number of slave laborers expanded. Next to the movement to abolish the slave trade in the British Empire, the Spanish reform effort seems quiet, private, and official; these measures did not generate a public debate in Spain over the slave trade, officials gathered no evidence from disaffected witnesses, nor did word of dramatic speeches reach the Spanish colonies to stimulate the hopes of

48   Williamson to Dundas, 17 June 1792, C.O. 137/90, PRO. Not until the fall did Governor Williamson receive official confirmation that the earlier reports of Parliament having abolished the slave trade effective in 1796 were false. See Dundas to Williamson, 6 September 1792, C.O. 137/90, PRO.

49   [Falconbridge], *Two Voyages*, pp. 234–5.

50   Address of the Council (Jamaica Assembly) to Williamson, [29 November 1791], C.O. 137/90, PRO.

slaves. All the concern centered around one specific document and its application. Yet the resulting excitement and uncertainty involved elements of rumor, suspicion, and underground activity which proved strikingly similar to the dynamics that affected the British colonies during the parliamentary debates. The reaction to Charles IV's real *cédula* of 21 May 1789 "concerning the Education, Treatment, and Occupation of Slaves" in the Indies exposed the racial and class tensions in the Spanish colonies and showed again the awesome power of uncontrolled news and ideas in Afro-America in the years prior to the outbreak of the Haitian Revolution.

In February 1789, the Council of the Indies enacted what its ministers hoped would be one of the most far-reaching of its reforms, allowing free trade in slaves to selected ports in Venezuela, Cuba, Hispaniola, and Puerto Rico. By loosening age-old restrictions on the foreign slave trade, the Bourbon reformers hoped to accomplish an economic miracle similar to the one which had made French Saint-Domingue the envy of every colonial power. But at the same time they anticipated a transformation in the economic fortunes of their colonies, members of the Spanish cabinet had no intention of surrendering control to a new and powerful class of slaveowners. In addition, they recognized the dangers which a rapidly expanding black population posed to the security of the colonies. Mindful of both these considerations, the court agreed upon the need to spell out a series of specific policies to control the growth of their slave colonies. Immediately after finalizing the free slave trade provisions, the Council charged Minister of Grace and Justice Antonio Porlier with drawing up regulations for governing the thousands of slaves about to arrive as a result of free trade. Following the Council's instruction, Porlier determined the efficacy of present laws and proposed new measures to control insofar as possible the "abuses" which had already resulted from the absolute power of slaveowners over their "unfortunate" workers.[51]

Designed in the interest of making slavery compatible with "public tranquillity," Porlier's decree envisioned a carefully monitored system

---

51 "Junta Suprema de Estado de 27 de abril de 1789" (report of Eugenio Llaguno), AGI, Indiferente General, leg. 802.

of reciprocal obligations in which the state would jealously guard certain rights of the slaves in return for their labor.[52] Of course, Porlier expected slaves to "obey and respect" their overseers and owners, and to "venerate them like fathers" in faithfully carrying out their prescribed duties. He obliged slaveowners and overseers, on the other hand, to instruct their slaves in the Catholic religion in preparation for baptism, to provide food and clothing in amounts dictated by local working conditions, to take direct responsibility for the old and infirm, and to allow and encourage marriages among slaves, even if they lived on distant estates. In addition, the code of 1789 exempted slaves from working before sunrise, past sunset, or on any of the Catholic holy days, and entitled them to receive a two-hour break from regular duty each day to work on their own provision grounds. It enjoined owners from employing Africans under the age of seventeen or after they reached sixty. Other rules obliged overseers to demarcate clearly male from female work, reserving the more strenuous tasks for men only, and even to provide a salary, though a small one, to women involved in domestic service.

The code also limited the range of punishment available to employers of slaves. For failing to work without good reason and for running away or other common "crimes," slaves faced confinement in prison or with shackles and chains, but the lash was to be used sparingly: the state would allow no more than twenty-five lashes, administered with a "soft instrument" so as not to "cause serious contusions or any effusion of blood." Porlier allowed owners and the overseers they employed to administer only minor punishments, leaving the disposition of crimes of a more serious nature to the local authorities.

Finally, the code proposed by Porlier and approved by the Council of the Indies outlined arrangements by which local governments would detect and punish transgressions of the rights of slaves. While relying on government officials to keep an eye on estates near cities, the Council called for special methods in order to ensure the compliance of the owners of outlying haciendas. First, the regulations

---

52   The *cédula* of 21 May 1789 has been reprinted in Richard Konetzke, *Colección de documentos para la historia de la formación social de Hispanoamérica*, 3 vols. (Madrid, 1953–62), III, t. 2, pp. 643–52.

delegated priests who traveled from estate to estate to say mass to act as roving observers and report instances of overwork or bad treatment secretly to the nearest *procurador síndico* (city attorney), who, "as the protector of slaves," must investigate such allegations. In addition, Porlier directed town councils to appoint "a person or persons of character" to visit local *haciendas* three times a year to determine possible violators, who faced punishments ranging from fines to criminal proceedings. In all court cases, slaves bringing complaints enjoyed the same rights before the bar as free people.

In mid-August, 200 or so copies of the ordinance of 31 May 1789 were loaded among other official dispatches and shipped out to officials in the Indies, where they began to arrive late in October. Predictably, slaveowners in Spanish America raised an immediate and unanimous outcry. Even before local officials had fully digested the contents of the document, or indeed made them public, the new provisions became the subject of anxious concern among employers, buyers, and sellers of slaves, all of whom eagerly awaited the start of a new spirit in the slave economy. On behalf of the slaveowners, governors at New Orleans, Santo Domingo, and the city of Tocaima in New Grenada fiercely resisted the *cédula* and disclosed that pressure from local creoles had forced them to delay publication of the decree.[53] Meanwhile, slaves and free people of color, equally aware of the ominous signs of an incipient slave boom, showed just as much concern. They soon applied their own understanding of the significance of the *código* to the public discussion. So the reaction of the privileged few told only half the story.

When two of Havana's *comisarios* (municipal commissioners) approached interim governor Domingo Cabello and entreated him to suspend enforcement, they feared the immediate danger that making the regulations public might "move the slaves" to revolt. Such

---

53 See the index of documents comprising an *expediente* (the documents are not enclosed) in AGI, Caracas, leg. 180; the *resumen* of the dispatch of Louisiana Governor Miró, Nueva Orleans, 10 September 1790, AGI, Indiferente General, leg. 802; and José Torre Revello, "Origen y aplicación del Código Negrero en la América española (1788–1794)," *Boletín del Instituto de Investigaciones Históricas* (Buenos Aires) 15, no. 53 (julio–septiembre de 1932), p. 45.

rebellions were "regular occurrences," explained Cabello in justify-
ing to his superiors his decision to suppress the document.[54] But later
reports revealed that despite official secrecy, or perhaps as a result
of it, the mysterious *cédula* soon became a topic of public speculation in which Havana slaves were active participants. "Just with the
rumors which have spread that there exists a Royal *Cédula* favoring
the Negroes, they are already halfway in revolt," reported Havana's
ayuntamiento (town council) early in 1790, citing as evidence a recent
uprising among slaves working one of the island's largest sugar mills.

Moreover, word of the royal dispensations had intertwined with
other rumors of a violent uprising of slaves in one of the French colonies. While this ominous admixture of foreign and domestic news
had not yet catalyzed a mass rebellion, it had clearly been "sufficient
to keep [the slaves] of this island in [a state of] expectation."[55] The
Council was forced to take these alarmist reports more seriously
when, two days after the arrival of Cabello's dispatches from Havana,
the mail brought a letter from a man identifying himself as a Havana
slave. "We have seen the royal order in favor of the Ethiopian slaves
thwarted by greed," wrote Diego de Jesús. The existence and contents
of the document, he continued, had "reached the notice of the slaves,"
who understood, even if their owners did not, that the king's wish was
that they be "treated as Individuals of the human race."[56]

In Caracas, where landowners and merchants had been among
the most active in the Spanish Caribbean in promoting and buying
into the boom mentality in the Americas, separate constituencies
reacted strongly. Since 1783, more Africans had arrived in the province as slaves than at any previous time in the area's short history as a
settled Spanish colony. Notwithstanding the recent signs of imminent
change, masterless people of color continued to outnumber heavily

---

54   Domingo Cabello to Antonio Porlier, La Habana, 14 December 1789, AGI,
Indiferente General, leg. 802.

55   Petition of the *ayuntamiento*, La Habana, 15 January 1790, AGI, Santo
Domingo, leg. 1253; Cabello to Porlier, La Habana, 14 December 1789, AGI,
Indiferente General, leg. 802.

56   *Resumen*, Cabello to Porlier, 14 December 1789, AGI, Indiferente General,
leg. 802; Torre Revello, "Origen y aplicación," p. 47.

both whites and slaves, comprising forty percent of the inhabitants of the city of Caracas and more than forty-eight percent of the population of the entire colony.[57] Against this backdrop, the wave of street discussion and speculation which attended the arrival of the king's decree in October of 1789, writes one historian of the incident, was reminiscent of modern Caracas, where even "the most secret news spreads without anyone knowing how or by what means such a [grapevine] succeeds."[58]

Official efforts to keep the *cédula* of 1789 a secret in Caracas failed to keep the public from becoming surprisingly well informed almost immediately. In a matter of days, the *audiencia* sitting at Caracas reported strong reactions among both slaves and *hacendados*. Powerful rumors heralding an impending end to slavery engulfed the capital city. "Since the arrival of the last mail," reported Francisco García de Quintana, one of the *regidores* (councilors) of the Caracas *cabildo* a week to ten days later, "it is said publicly in the City that we have received a Royal *Cédula* concerning the governing and treatment of slaves." Since García had "already observed a certain [air of] expectation and insolence among the slaves," he moved that publication of the document be postponed until the council could examine in detail its possible impact.[59] Other governmental bodies acknowledged that word had somehow leaked into the streets and expressed concern that such uncontrolled intelligence might inspire slaves to entertain "the idea of liberation."[60]

The provisions of the king's order remained a carefully guarded official secret through November, and the governor still had not issued it in early December when the Caracas elite called upon city attorney Juan José Echenique to summon the *audiencia* into session.

---

57   See the figures from 1787 in Ildefonso Leal, "La aristocracia criolla venezolana y el Código Negrero de 1789," *Revista de historia* (Caracas) 6 (febrero de 1961), p. 66. Leal's article provides an excellent overview of the impact of the *cédula* of 1789 in Venezuela.

58   Leal, "La aristocracia criolla," p. 71.

59   See García's testimony in a session called by the *síndico procurador general* of Caracas, 12 December 1789, AGI, Caracas, leg. 168.

60   Real Audiencia of Caracas to Porlier, Caracas, 29 June 1790, AGI, Indiferente General, leg. 802.

They wanted officials to discuss the local uproar which the rumored decree regarding the slaves was causing. Echenique, who despite his official status still discounted news of the king's order as little more than an irresponsible rumor, traced the reports to the black and brown communities of Caracas, adding that "this is not the first time" that these residents of the capital city had created news to suit their own interests. Perhaps Echenique knew about the abortive rebellion of 1749, but probably he had more recent developments in mind. Just a year before the 1789 *cédula*, the Caracas *cabildo* had met to discuss how to suppress rumors circulated by local free blacks (*pardos*) that the king had granted their men rights to enter sacred orders and to contract marriages with white women of the commoner class.[61] Even as Echenique dismissed news of royal dispensations for the black and colored residents of Caracas as a figment of hopeful imaginations, the city's slaves were already moving to assert their new rights. At the meeting of 12 December 1789, testimony surfaced that slave-owners were "finding themselves insulted by their Slaves, with such boldness that they chide and threaten them face to face in various ways," even to the point of citing "the different Chapters which they say are contained in the alleged *Cédula*." These slaves asserted—and quite accurately—that the new regulations called for a shorter work day with "hours of rest." Like Echenique, confused owners wondered whether the slaves had advance knowledge of regulations about to go into effect, or had simply "invented" these reports.[62]

Over the next few months, as Caracas officials waited for the king to rule on their request to rescind the new provisions, local pressure on them from opposite directions mounted steadily. Early in May, after they awoke one morning to discover several menacing posters referring specifically to the as yet unpublished code plastered in public places in two areas of Caracas, the alarm of the city's white residents increased. The posters warned that local slaves knew about the *cédula* itself and about those local whites guilty of suppressing its letter and intent. If officials would not put the articles into effect of their own

61 Pedro M. Arcaya U., *El cabildo de Caracas* [Caracas, 1965], p. 117.

62 See the testimony of Juan José Echenique, Caracas, 12 December 1789, AGI, Caracas, leg. 168.

volition, the posters went on to say, perhaps force would persuade them. Beneath the lines of text loomed an even stronger statement— a rough drawing of a dark-skinned man wielding a raised machete apparently about to cut the throat of a white man.[63]

This startling discovery led Caracas officials to convene a second series of meetings in the spring of 1790 and take further testimony regarding black sedition in the city and its surrounding area. Once again, reports indicated slaves openly challenging overseers with the belief that "His Majesty has made them free" and in some cases laying down their implements and refusing to work. In Caracas itself, ripples of discontent among domestic slaves surprised employers. Moreover, officials now faced not only the problem of controlling the spread of ideas between slaves but also the difficulty of containing rising interest in the *cédula* among Caracas's extensive masterless population. They feared the "vagrant and malicious" citydwellers intent on fomenting "discord and disturbance," as well as the bandits from the surrounding plains who, after preying on highway travelers by day, slipped into the city under the cover of night. In order to control such nocturnal activity as "idle conversation, men gathering at all hours on street-corners, [people hanging] posters, and all the [other] symptoms which [portend] serious uprisings," the governor issued orders requiring all individuals and groups of more than "six or eight" to burn lanterns on city streets after ten o'clock or spend the night in jail. In such an atmosphere of tension, unrest, and repression, whites in Caracas felt dangerously close to an outbreak of violence, especially after authorities dispatched a substantial militia detachment to nearby La Guaira, the port of Caracas, following an attempt of some "low life persons" to force a powder magazine. In at least one instance, the suppression of the *cédula* did result in the eruption of violence. Slaves from the plantation of one Fernando Ascario attacked and killed their overseer, "all believing," according to reports received by the *audiencia*, "that His Majesty had given them freedom, or at least had granted them equal status with free people." By late June, members of the *audiencia*

---

63   "Carta original que queda en el Archivo Secreto de esta Real Audiencia," Caracas, 8 May 1790, AGI, Indiferente General, leg. 802. One of the original posters has been preserved in AGI, Pasquines y Loas, 4.

could report that, despite their efforts, knowledge of the contents of the document had extended so widely that "it can be assured that all free people and slaves are informed [both] in this city and in the Province."[64]

In 1794, with their reform energies dampened both by the determined resistance of the creole elite in the colonies and, more importantly, by the challenge of the French Revolution, Spanish ministers chose to allow the *código* of 1789 to die quietly. Yet the memory of the *cédula* and the brief hopes which it engendered remained alive in the culture of opposition among Spanish slaves. Some six years after residents of the colonies first learned of the *cédula* of 31 May 1789, the document resurfaced as a central issue in two separate instances of black resistance in Spanish America. In 1795, slaves in Buenos Aires mounted a brief general strike protesting the suppression of the code.[65] In the same year, a group of slaves, free blacks, and people of "mixed blood" living near the western coastal city of Coro in the captaincy-general of Caracas attempted to establish an independent government by organizing the largest revolt of its kind in Venezuelan history. Official inquiries found one of the roots of the Coro insurrection in the agitation of 1789–90 surrounding the king's order and the still prevalent belief that the rights of black and brown people to liberty and equality were being wrongfully withheld by local whites. Two mobile masterless men were instrumental in bringing word of the king's blocked intent to the people of the Coro region. An "idler" known as Cocofio "occupied himself living from *hacienda* to *hacienda* under the specious pretext of [being a] healer," and told slaves about the supposed royal emancipation order and how whites had suppressed the will of the king by keeping them enslaved. After the death of Cocofio, José Caridad González, a Spanish-speaking runaway from nearby Curaçao and the key figure in the revolt of 1795, continued to make use of this theme as he organized an armed rebellion against

64   "Copia del acuerdo original que queda en el archivo secreto de esta Real Audiencia," Real Audiencia to Porlier, 29 June 1790, AGI, Indiferente General, leg. 802.

65   Leslie B. Rout, Jr., *The African Experience in Spanish America: 1502 to the Present Day* (Cambridge, London, New York, and Melbourne, 1976), p. 120.

local Spanish authorities.[66] However, by this time, the black revolution in Saint-Domingue exercised the strongest influence on the imaginations of dissident Spanish slaves.

Though British abolitionism and Spanish reformism challenged the future of colonial slavery in the late 1780s, only the French Revolution exerted the overwhelming social and ideological pressure which would lead eventually to black freedom in the Americas. A revolution which pitted class against class in a struggle over the ideals of "liberty, equality, and fraternity" presented obvious problems for societies based upon white solidarity and slavery. So even before the fall of the Bastille signaled the final days of the *ancien régime* in France, officials began to take measures to assure that the spirit of inquiry and change alive in Europe did not affect the French Caribbean. As early as the fall of 1788, the Crown issued orders "to abolish every press" in Saint-Domingue "in order to keep the flame of liberty from spreading to the Colonies," a move which led to an effective news blackout lasting at least "several weeks." The preface speaks of General A. N. de la Salle. Confronted with a group of enthusiastic recruits ready to sail from France to Saint-Domingue in 1792, he took a different approach. Aware of the explosive potential of the watchwords and rituals of the French Revolution if applied in the colonies, the general instructed his charges to alter their banners and caps, which displayed the slogan "Live Free or Die," to read "The Nation, the Law, the King." La Salle also rejected the soldiers' plan to plant liberty trees upon their arrival in Saint-Domingue, suggesting instead that they plant "a tree of peace."[67]

General La Salle's dilemma was the same one facing the colonial lobby in France and the plantocracy in the colonies, and his fragile solution likewise reflected the larger strategy of planters, merchants, and shipowners as they came to terms with the French Revolution.

---

66 "Testimonio ... sobre la sublevación de los negros, sambos, mulatos Esclavos y libres de la Jurisdicción de Coro," Caracas, 23 March 1797, AGI, Caracas, leg. 426, folios 24, 84.

67 *Savanna-la-Mar Gazette*, 9 September 1788; La Salle to Desparbés, 11 July 1792, in Corre, *Papiers du Général de la Salle*, pp. 26–7.

Unlike the creole elites in the British and Spanish colonies who fought all apparent new departures in colonial policy in the late 1780s, the richer and more powerful French planters welcomed the disruption of the Revolution at home and hoped to take advantage of the weakness of French colonial administration in order to increase their power. Just as La Salle attempted to disentangle the republican meaning from the popular rituals associated with the Revolution, however, the planters and the commercial bourgeoisie undertook the similar task of supporting the Revolution while at the same time working to keep the social forces which it unleashed from spilling over into the colonies. But as was clearly evident by the time La Salle's troops cleared La Rochelle for the revolutionary world of Saint-Domingue, neither careful military commanders nor vigilant planters could hope to hold in check the irrepressible force of the French Revolution, especially when ritual and symbol—banners and cap slogans, for example—could communicate its currents as effectively as pamphlets and broadsides.

When Louis XVI called the Estates-General in 1787, the planters of Saint-Domingue, influenced in part by the recent example of North American independence, took the lead in pressing the claims of the French Caribbean slavocracy. Even before the architects of the new system of estates had ruled upon what their place would be, the French planters elected deputies to represent them in the Assembly and agents to coordinate lobbying efforts on their behalf. By June of 1789, the colonial deputies sided with the Third Estate in its struggle against the Crown and the aristocrats, but refused to endorse the Declaration of the Rights of Man and quickly organized to keep the Revolution out of the colonies. Through the voice of the influential Society of French Colonists, known from its meeting place in a Paris hotel as the Club Massiac, the absentee planters and their representatives and sympathizers stood firm in their demand that the Assembly leave social and economic policy in the colonies to them, even in the face of eroding support for their position both within the Third Estate and among the colonial ministers.[68]

---

68   Mitchell Bennett Garrett, *The French Colonial Question, 1789–1791* (Ann

Along with absentee planters, other Parisians expressed an active interest in questions of colonial governance in the early stages of the Revolution. The city's community of free people of color organized its own Society of American Colonists, seeking to use the Revolution to rid the colonies of the disabilities which free nonwhites suffered, and which had increased in intensity since the 1770s. In fact, the free mulattoes of Saint-Domingue anticipated by four years the actions of the colony's planters by having sent Julien Raimond to France in 1784 to lobby for equal rights for Saint-Domingue's propertied free people of color. Every bit as determined as the planters to win representation in the Constituent Assembly, the *gens de couleur* encountered greater obstacles in getting their voice heard, and their disillusionment presaged the coming revolution in the colonies.[69] In addition, the British abolition movement had inspired a small group of French humanitarians to found in 1788 the Société des Amis des Noirs (Society of Friends of the Blacks), modeled along the lines of the London Committee founded the previous year. The Société des Amis had not made the strides in either organization or constituency-building of its London counterpart, nor did it wield the influence of the Club Massiac in French politics, but writings produced by its members proved quite influential in creating support for the cause of antislavery. For that reason, proslavery lobbyists made the Amis a constant target for attacks, fearing the impact which their published ideas might have in the colonies.[70]

While the earthshaking events of the summer and fall of 1789 in Paris focused the attention of all of Europe, residents of the French capital, and their compatriots on the other side of the Atlantic, struggled to separate fact from rumor as they speculated on what the changes in France might mean for the colonial regime. British

---

Arbor, 1916), pp. 4–22.

69 Gabriel Debien, "Gens de couleur libres et colons de Saint-Domingue devant la Constituante (1789–mars 1790)," *Revue d'histoire de l'Amérique française* 4 (décembre 1950), pp. 398–9; Shelby T. McCloy, *The Negro in France* (Lexington, 1960), p. 65.

70 See Daniel P. Resnick, "The *Société des Amis des Noirs* and the Abolition of Slavery," *French Historical Studies* 7 (Fall 1972), pp. 558–69.

abolitionist Thomas Clarkson, whose study of the slave trade brought him to Paris that eventful summer, stumbled into the charged atmosphere unaware of the intense struggle between competing factions over questions of rights for free people of color and slavery. Soon after his arrival, a story appeared in "the public prints" accusing the Amis of promoting black insurrection by shipping out some 12,000 muskets to the colonies. "Reports equally unfounded and wicked were spread also in the same papers relative to myself," remembered Clarkson years later. Some accounts accused him of being a British spy, others asserted that he had been banished from Britain for his radical views.[71] The same absentee planters who attacked Clarkson's presence generated other alarmist reports warning their constituents in the Caribbean of the "imminent danger" that some Frenchmen "drunk with liberty" were about to depart for the colonies and intended to spark a slave uprising.[72] A wave of rumor about events in the West Indies, including unsubstantiated accounts of violent slave uprisings in Martinique and Guadeloupe, gripped Paris in the fall. "Alarmed by the very unfortunate rumors," members of the Club Massiac asked Minister of the Marine La Luzerne to confirm or deny the reports. La Luzerne replied helplessly that he had received no dispatches from administrators on the scene for two months; he apparently knew less about the situation in the colonies than the Club's membership.[73]

Residents of the colonies experienced equal difficulty in piecing together the situation in France. In the absence of direct information through official channels, both tension and uncontrolled speculation ran high. A trade depression which severely limited the number of French merchant vessels arriving in colonial ports only exacerbated matters. No news from Paris reached Saint-Pierre, Martinique,

71   Clarkson, *History of the Abolition of the Slave-Trade*, II, pp. 129–30, 154.

72   *Correspondence secrète des colons deputes à l'Assemblée Constituante, servant à faire connaître l'esprit des colons en général, sur la Révolution* (Paris, [1793]), pp. 9–10, reprinted in *La Révolution française et l'abolition de l'esclavage: Textes et documents*, 12 tomes (Paris, [1968]), VIII.

73   Société des Colons-Français to Minister of the Marine, 26 November 1789, Minister to Société, 27 November 1789, reprinted in *Extrait particulier des registres de délibérations et de correspondence de la Société des Colons-Français réunis à Paris* (Paris, 1790), pp. 12–14, RSD.

during the months of August and September, 1789, igniting interrelated rumors regarding what was happening in France and, inevitably, the future of slavery in the Caribbean. Copies of British newspapers had filtered into the island, and the accounts of Parliament's agitation of the slave trade spawned local suspicion that the English might be spreading such reports in order to create excitement among the slaves. And what, curious colonists asked, was the significance of this tricolored cockade which adorned the caps of travelers and seamen?[74]

Farther west in Saint-Domingue, where more French ships called, correspondents possessed a greater supply of information, but much of it seemed confused or uncertain, and powerful rumors flowed in every direction. "We have been minutely instructed about all the rumors circulating in Europe," wrote a resident of Cap Français in October, adding that these second- and third-hand accounts had "contributed in no small measure to occasioning rumors here." From the smaller coastal cities to the west and south came reports that the Assembly was about to abolish slavery—news which had already reached the ears of some slaves on inland plantations. Other rumors had taken root in the port town itself. Like the residents of rural France whose "Great Fear" of rumored attacks by bandits had spread rapidly through the countryside just months earlier, whites at the Cap lived in daily fear by the end of the year that upwards of 20,000 slaves stood in readiness to take advantage of the current confusion and descend from the surrounding highlands to join secret allies and take control of the city.[75]

Reflecting the individual effort of General La Salle on a broader scale, planters in the French Caribbean and their representatives and sympathizers in France collaborated on a series of measures designed to control the movement of people and ideas from the revolutionary metropole to the expectant colonies. In France, this policy fell with

74 Henry Lémery, *La Révolution française à la Martinique* (Paris, 1936), pp. 21–2.

75 Letter quoted in Debien, *Études antillaises*, p. 119; *Gazette Nationale ou le Moniteur Universel* (Paris), 12 janvier, 6 février 1790. For the Great Fear in France, see Georges Lefebvre, *The Great Fear of 1789: Rural Panic in Revolutionary France*, trans. Joan White (New York, 1973).

special force upon free blacks and *gens de couleur*, as the Club Massiac moved to restrict their access to the sea lanes. Since the middle of the century black and brown mobility between France and the colonies had caused concern and comment. Suspicions were most often directed against slaves who returned to the islands in the company of itinerant owners after sojourns in the mother country. From Martinique in 1753 a typical complaint found Negroes returning from France "insolent" and blamed their contact with humble whites for their new attitudes. In 1777 a royal decree echoed that "when they return to the Colonies, they take with them the spirit of independence and intractability and become more harmful than useful."[76] Nevertheless, the policy of Louis XVI ran so strongly against the presence of blacks in France that police rounded up "scores" of black residents—slaves, runaways, and free people alike—and transported them to the colonies between 1777 and 1789 over the objections of colonial officials.[77]

The onset of the Revolution and the obvious interest which France's free blacks and coloreds showed in its progress sparked the colonial lobby to seek an immediate reversal of the policy of transportation as a way of keeping news of the events in Paris from reaching the slaves overseas. After La Luzerne rejected an early request for a new law banning blacks and browns from boarding vessels bound for the Caribbean, the Club Massiac enlisted directly the support of the chambers of commerce and shipowners of France's major transatlantic ports. The port authorities honored these wishes in large measure, though they sometimes looked the other way.[78]

Across the Atlantic, self-appointed committees of safety in the port cities took similar precautions on their end and placed themselves on

---

76   Peytraud, *L'esclavage aux Antilles françaises*, p. 385; "Declaration du Roi pour la police des noirs, donnée à Versailles le 9 août 1777," reprinted in Maurice Besson, "La police des noirs sous Louis XVI en France," *Revue de l'histoire des colonies françaises* 21 (juillet–août 1928), pp. 436–41.

77   McCloy, *Negro in France*, pp. 55–6.

78   Garrett, *French Colonial Question*, p. 23; Françoise Thésée, *Négociants bordelais et colons de Saint-Domingue; "Liaisons d'habitations"; La maison Henry Romberg, Bapst et Cie., 1783–1793* (Paris, 1972), pp. 127–9.

the lookout for seditious characters of all descriptions. By late October 1789, reported one correspondent, "the harbors and the wharves are so well guarded that it [will be] practically impossible for any evangelists to carry out their plans."[79] Later in the year and into 1790, assemblies of planters in the north and the west continued to make security along the docks a top priority. The public safety committee of the Permanent Provincial Assembly of the North, sitting at Cap Français, applauded the policy of city commissioners to take the names, ages, and descriptions of all arriving passengers, but soon moved beyond these measures by authorizing close inspection of all arriving ships and placing armed guards aboard each of them to assure that no one could land before such an inspection had taken place. Passengers unable to give a satisfactory account of their reason for coming to the Cap were "immediately arrested and placed in jail, in order to be shipped back to France at the first opportunity."[80] In January 1790, the government at Port-au-Prince called for on-board visits and searches, and ordered the seizure of such dangerous cargo as "slaves coming from France, unknown passengers, ... papers, books, engravings and other objects capable of fomenting trouble."[81] Equally stringent measures controlled the presence of foreigners, who, according to a Spanish report, risked arrest and detention upon disembarking in Saint-Domingue, even if in possession of legitimate passports.[82]

Tight security measures, however, only heightened interest and anticipation, and no such regulations could ever prove totally effective. No sooner had the tricolored cockade appeared in the French

79   Letter quoted in Debien, *Études antillaises*, p. 162.

80   Minutes of 26 November 1789, *Journal de l'Assemblée Provinciale Permanente de la Partie du Nord de Saint-Domingue*, no. 8, pp. 66–7; minutes of 30 November 1789, *Journal*, no. 9, p. 69; minutes of 9 December 1789, *Journal*, no. 12, p. 94, copies enclosed with the printed material from Saint-Domingue in AGI, Santo Domingo, leg. 1027.

81   *Nouvelles diverses* (Port-au-Prince), 30 Janvier 1790, copy in AGI, Santo Domingo, leg. 1027. For further evidence of the measures taken at Port-au-Prince, see "Extrait des registres de l'Assemblée générale de la partie française de Saint-Domingue, séance de vingt mai 1790," RSD.

82   Archbishop of Santo Domingo to Porlier, Santo Domingo, 24 January 1790, AGI, Santo Domingo, leg. 1110.

colonies than slaves began to piece together its meaning. Passing along reports of slave unrest near Cap Français, colonial officials reported in October 1789 that a "multitude of printed materials" had apprised the population of developments in Paris. Despite careful precautions, "all that is done or written, particularly on the issue of the emancipation of the blacks" made its way past dockside police. Not surprisingly, blacks at the Cap soon understood that the tricolored cockade symbolized the newly won emancipation of the whites from their "masters" in France.[83] In Martinique, "several slaves" in the capital city donned cockades soon after their meaning became clear in the fall of 1789, so local officials issued strict prohibitions against the use of the cockade by blacks and *gens de couleur*. But some blacks stubbornly insisted on participating in the local political struggle anyway. A riot ensued in the summer of 1790 after a slave playing drums in a militia parade sported a cockade on his cap in defiance of the ordinances. Black rebels in Saint-Domingue continued to identify with what the tricolored cockade represented months after the outbreak of the rebellion of August 1791. Among the demands made by outlying groups of armed slaves near Port-au-Prince in 1792 was the right to wear the red, white, and blue symbol of the French Revolution.[84]

The stream of merchant seamen who frequented island taverns and grogshops while their ships were in port provided a constant, if considerably delayed, source of news on the French Revolution for Caribbean towns. One former colonist accused sailors of being little more than "the agents of the negrophiles" in France. Not only did sailors prove instrumental in introducing outlawed printed materials, he accused, but they even furnished blacks with gunpowder and other explosives. However, the greatest disservice which the merchant marine did the planter class involved not the exchange of tangible articles but the simple sharing of words. As French sailors and local slaves were "always together" loading and unloading vessels or performing other tasks, the waterfront soon became a "cauldron of insurrection,"

---

83   Letters cited in De Vassière, *Saint-Domingue*, p. 368.

84   See the letter of the "Free Men of Color of Martinique" reprinted in *St. George's Chronicle and New Grenada Gazette*, 27 August 1790; Corre, *Papiers du Général de la Salle*, p. 37.

in which sailors, "well fed on the burning slogans of the clubs, [and] friends of the constitution" shared the excitement of the revolution in France with their black co-workers.[85]

Finally, efforts to close the borders and ports of the French colonies to seditious outsiders proved ineffective. Occasionally, characters whom the planters and merchants recognized as clearly dangerous managed to elude authorities and remain at large in the colonies. Among the runaway slaves absent in the vicinity of Cap Français during the spring and summer of 1790 was Jean-Louis, well known in the city for having sold charcoal for his owner's account. According to the local newspaper, Jean-Louis possessed special talents and wide experience. He had formerly lived in France and could speak Spanish, Dutch, English, and *"le jargon creole"* in addition to French.[86] But the most dramatic case of a known colored incendiary slipping the net set for him occurred in the spring of 1790, when mulatto insurgent Vincent Ogé left France for Saint-Domingue, where he led an abortive rebellion of free people of color and some armed slaves. As one of the most vocal members of the Parisian community of *gens de couleur* during the early French Revolution, Ogé attracted the close attention of the members of the Club Massiac.

By early April 1790, after the Constituent Assembly rebuffed the demands of the propertied mulattoes, the committee of correspondence representing the planters in Saint-Domingue received a report that a vessel was about to depart Le Havre carrying a group of whites and mulattoes bent on bringing revolution to the slaves in the colony, with Ogé at their head. In order to aid colonial officials in apprehending the would-be rebels, the committee sent ahead an engraved likeness of Ogé which officials posted in all of Saint-Domingue's major ports. Meanwhile, Ogé departed Paris not for Saint-Domingue as expected but for London, where after six weeks he secured a berth aboard a vessel bound for Charleston. After a short stay in the North American port, where he very likely purchased weapons, Ogé slipped into Cap

---

85   [Félix Carteau], *Soirées bermudiennes, ou entretiens sur les événemens oui ont opéré la ruine de la partie française de l'isle Saint-Domingue* (Bordeaux, 1802), pp. 75–8.

86   *Affiches américaines* (Supplément), 7 juillet 1790, RSD.

Français in disguise, possibly as an American seaman, on 16 October. Within a month he led a corps of brown and black rebels in an unsuccessful yet historically important strike against Saint-Domingue's planter class. While Ogé never espoused freedom for the slaves during his lifetime, his capture and brutal execution early in 1791 galvanized public opinion in France and made a lasting impression on the future revolutionaries in Saint-Domingue, ironically advancing the cause of antislavery.[87]

At the time of Ogé's revolt in 1790, the intensity of public discussion and speculation over the future of slavery in the Caribbean had reached an unprecedented level in the history of the Americas. Slaves and free people of color in each of the three major empires had ample reason to expect a change in their status and therefore paid close attention to the currents of information around them. In this environment of anticipation and suspense, news of developments in Europe and rumors of an end to slavery spread extensively. The inability of colonial officials, lobbyists, and planters to suppress this news and smother public agitation demonstrates the virtual impossibility of keeping such urgent matters a secret. While colonial authorities succeeded in denying their black and brown subjects equal access to most material resources, slaves and free people of color nevertheless proved adept at obtaining, manipulating, and transmitting information to suit their interests.

Of course, news did not arrive only from overseas. Because of the close relations among the American territories, information also flowed across New World imperial and geographic boundaries. While residents of French and Spanish colonies watched with interest the movement for the abolition of the British slave trade and gauged its effect on their economies, the British worried about how the French Revolution might affect slavery in their Caribbean colonies. By the time French authorities in Cap Français executed Ogé and his

---

87   *Lettre de la Société Correspondante des Colons Français réunis à Paris, aux Assemblées Provinciales à Saint-Domingue* (Paris, 1790), p. 10, RSD; *Observations de la Société Correspondante ...* (Paris, 1790), p. 26, RSD; "Diario," in the testimony of Ogé before Spanish authorities in Santo Domingo, 1790, AGI, Santo Domingo, leg. 1028.

lieutenants early in 1791, however, it had become clear throughout the Americas that the ideas he represented carried the potential to catalyze black and brown revolutionaries in all of the American slave societies.

4

"Ideas of Liberty Have Sunk So Deep"

Communication and Revolution, 1789–93

If the transatlantic news pipeline seemed especially busy in the years leading up to the Haitian Revolution, the regional network of communication—the "common wind" which bound together the societies of Afro-America proved even more active. In the late 1780s and early 1790s, the currents of revolution touched all areas of the Caribbean. Along the many avenues of intercolonial contact, rumors and reports from English, Spanish, and French sources intermingled and fed upon each other, strengthening the idea that emancipation was near at hand, and finally leading to armed uprisings in both British and French colonies. By 1793, the continuing rebellion of blacks and people of color in Saint-Domingue provided a rallying point for would-be revolutionaries in other areas, and curtailing the movement of people and ideas had become a paramount issue for the rulers in English- and Spanish-speaking territories.

Studies of commerce and trade are integral to the historiography of eighteenth-century America, yet without exception these studies overlook one of the most important items of exchange which was constantly changing hands—information. In fact, Americans throughout the hemisphere depended as heavily on their neighbors for news as for the other commodities which arrived aboard ships. Not surprisingly, word that war was approaching traveled great distances with particular speed. The rumor of an impending war between England and Spain, for example, occupied a vast space stretching from Virginia to Venezuela between July 1790 and February 1791. When

British officials revived the press gangs in the islands of the eastern Caribbean in anticipation of war, English-speaking seamen as far north as Norfolk got wind of the rumors and scrambled off ships to safety on land.[1] Taking advantage of the greater efficiency with which the English supplied their colonies with transatlantic news, residents of the Spanish territories followed these developments through their commercial links with British America. Cubans learned of this alarming rumor not through official dispatches from the home government but from the small vessels trading in re-exported slaves from Jamaica under the *comercio libre* regulations. Captains arriving in Santiago de Cuba brought British newspapers, whose reports kept fear of war alive in the Spanish island until the end of January 1791. At the same time, inhabitants of New Spain tried to stay informed through London newspapers.[2] From Caracas, officials reported that early in July 1790 "rumors began to spread and be heard about an impending break between our court and that of London." Like the accounts arriving in Cuba and New Spain, the Caracas reports could be traced to a foreign source: an English broadside printed in St. Kitts and brought to the mainland aboard a vessel trading to the coast from the tiny Swedish island of St. Bartholomew.[3]

Through these same channels, expectations and fears relative to emancipation of slaves and equal rights for free people of color passed from territory to territory. Just as residents of all the colonies had to keep abreast of their neighbors' preparations for war, they could ill afford to ignore other political and social developments, especially as they touched the issue of slavery. In the tense months following the first reports of Britain's debate over the slave trade, therefore, liberation rumors naturally assumed a regional dimension. Even before

---

1   James Baillie to James Rogers, Richard Martin to Rogers, 14 December 1790, Moses Myers to Rogers, 10 January 1791, Rogers Papers.

2   Juan Baptista Vaillant to Luis de las Casas, Cuba, 3 July 1790, 22 December 1790, 24 December 1790, 26 January 1791, AGI, Cuba, leg. 1434; Lucas de Galvez to Conde del Campo de Alange, Mérida de Yucatán, 8 February 1791, AGI, Sección de Gobierno, Audiencia de México, leg. 3024.

3   Juan Guillelmi to Pedro de Lerena, Caracas, 29 September 1790, AGI, Caracas, leg. 907.

white colonists in Saint-Domingue connected developments in France with slavery in the colonies, some of them feared that Britain's tampering with the trade boded ill for the opulent French colony. Moreau de Saint-Méry remembered vividly "the tremendous sensation" in April and May of 1788 caused by the arrival at Cap Français of several French gazettes "giving details and comment" on the British debate over the slave trade.[4]

Beginning in 1789, however, officials in the Spanish and British colonies detected a more serious threat in political developments in the French Caribbean. News of the events in France and their ominous repercussions in the colonies of the revolutionary nation traveled to Spanish territory on the same ships which brought slaves and rumors of war from foreign colonies. As concern crested, news accounts from the French Caribbean steadily increased in value, and after Spanish prohibitions against French shipping began late in 1789, cutting off direct communication with the island colonies, these accounts reached a premium. As the civil war between royalists and renegade planters widened in Saint-Domingue, the highest level of the colonial government in nearby Cuba found itself obliged to seek out the testimony of small-time traders and even "transient travelers."[5]

The disorders in the French colonies justified Spanish fears and strengthened resolve to limit contact with French islands and to keep out of French affairs. When officials at Martinique requested military aid from the governor of Cuba late in 1789 because residents of the French colony were "at the point of revolt as a result of the confusion in France," Spanish officials cautiously refused such aid, as they would again the following year.[6]

By 1790, officials in all the Spanish colonies were taking decisive precautions to prevent the currents of the French Revolution from

---

4   Cited in Stoddard, *French Revolution in San Domingo*, pp. 72–3.

5   Las Casas to Campo de Alange, La Habana, 20 September 1790, AGI, Santo Domingo, leg. 1253. Royal orders of 23 and 24 September 1789 and of May 1790 prohibited the "introduction of any and all French people regardless of station." See Las Casas to Campo de Alange, La Habana, 16 November 1791, AGI, Cuba, leg. 1486.

6   Las Casas to Campo de Alange, La Habana, 17 August 1790, AGI, Santo Domingo, leg. 1253.

spilling across their borders or entering their ports. Prior to the ministers in Spain turning full attention to the French Revolution in the colonies, local rulers took action which in effect reversed the very commercial dispensations which they had welcomed only months before. Before the end of 1789, British ships trading to the Main returned to Jamaica reporting that customs officials at Cartagena were prohibiting all foreign vessels from docking at that mainland port, "the Troubles in France having excited their fears and Jealousies."[7] A French naval captain named Bruny received the same treatment at Havana two months later. He lodged an official complaint after the interim governor departed radically from accepted practice and refused to allow either the crew or the captain himself to land. Moreover, Spanish seamen on nearby ships in the harbor subjected the French sailors to loud jibes "insulting to [France]." Their epithets, echoing the hostility of Spanish officialdom toward the French Revolution, also illustrated that news of events in France circulated on Spanish ships in Cuba despite official policy.[8] Such vigilance sharpened as the divisions among whites in Saint-Domingue deepened. By the summer of 1790, off the coast of Caracas as well as in Cuba, Santo Domingo, and Puerto Rico, even foreign fishing vessels were not above suspicion. The next year, the colonial ministers directed authorities to search incoming cargoes for jewelry, tobacco boxes, and coins bearing revolutionary inscriptions.[9]

Despite all these precautions, the Spanish who shared the island of Hispaniola with the French were confronted in a very direct way with the issue of racial revolt when Vincent Ogé and fifteen lieutenants arrived at the border separating French and Spanish territory in the aftermath of the abortive rebellion of 1790. The Ogé incident shows how much recent events in Saint-Domingue had affected the views

---

7   Philip Affleck to Philip Stephens, 28 December 1789, ADM 1/244, PRO.

8   Domingo Cabello to Antonio Valdés, La Habana, 25 February 1790, AGI, Santo Domingo, leg. 1254.

9   Joaquín García to Antonio Porlier, Santo Domingo, 25 July 1790, AGI, Santo Domingo, leg. 953; Las Casas to Porlier, La Habana, 30 July 1790, AGI, Santo Domingo, leg. 1253; García to Lerena, Santo Domingo, 3 August 1791, AGI, Santo Domingo, leg. 954.

of Spanish officials. From the earliest days of the troubles in Saint-Domingue, Spanish authorities on the opposite side of the island began to express concern about the frequent desertion of slaves back and forth across the border. And they took seriously the suggestion of the French commander at Cap Français in May of 1790 that the Spanish colony might plausibly become a staging area for a group of Parisian radicals to mount a revolt to "overturn the [French] Colony and obtain complete equality between the people of Color and the whites."[10] So by the time Ogé's band of rebels arrived in search of protection six months later, Spanish territory was no longer the sanctuary which it had been in less politically charged times. The Spanish government never considered Ogé's request for asylum; instead a Spanish border patrol arrested the insurgents and brought them across the island to the city of Santo Domingo under heavy guard. Satisfied after examining the rebels that Ogé and his followers harbored no hostile intentions toward the Spanish, Ogé's Spanish captors turned him over to French authorities. After a trial lasting two months, officials in Cap Français executed Ogé and more than twenty others in early 1791, first breaking the rebels upon the wheel and then decapitating them. Ogé's defeat began a wave of repression against mulattoes and free blacks throughout Saint-Domingue.[11]

Though the Spanish escaped a direct attack, the Ogé incident provoked serious reconsiderations which spread to other parts of Spain's American empire. Marathon meetings of the *audiencia* in the city of Santo Domingo considered the possibility that "innumerable mulattos of the same condition and mode of thinking as Ogé, and perhaps also many discontented whites with depraved hidden ideas" might enter Spanish territory as a result of the conflicts in Saint-Domingue. Officials immediately dispatched troops to guard the winding and fluid border. The following year, troops from Spain and Puerto Rico were imported to "form a Cordon to prevent any communication whatever between the French and Spanish part of the Island."[12]

---

10   García to Valdés, Santo Domingo, 25 May 1790, AGI, Santo Domingo, leg. 953.

11   James, *Black Jacobins*, pp. 74–5.

12   Joseph Antonio Vrizar to Porlier, Santo Domingo, 25 November, 25

The earliest accounts of the French Revolution threatened whites in British Jamaica less than their Spanish neighbors. Unlike Spain, England possessed no dynastic ties to the French Crown, and at least in the western Caribbean, no British colony shared a physical space with the French. So before the fall of the Bastille, newspapers in the British islands reported news of the French Revolution with surprising enthusiasm. In the summer of 1788 a Jamaican newspaper, in language which seemed subversive only a short time later, could support the struggle of the Third Estate: "The great body of the people, are generously determined to resist, by every means in their power, the high and arbitrary measures of the Court, and protect from oppression all ranks of their fellow-subjects." Reader demand for news from France apparently grew even as British support for the French revolutionaries waned. After 1789, the progress of the revolution continued to command bold front-page headlines in British Caribbean papers both east and west.[13]

As the effects of the Revolution on the neighboring French colonies became evident, British officials, like their counterparts in Cuba and Santo Domingo, watched intently. As early as September of 1789, British warships heading to and from the naval station at Jamaica "looked into" Cap Français and over the succeeding months brought back detailed reports of Saint-Domingue's "distressed state" to the island's naval commanders and governor.[14] As the busiest commercial hub of the western Caribbean, Jamaica served as an important clearinghouse for news from a variety of sources. Because French ships invariably rode at anchor in the harbors, printed materials reflecting the deep social conflicts in Saint-Domingue circulated freely in the British island. French merchants and other persons "of the first consequence" discussed events with British officials over meals and drinks, while sailors from their vessels refreshed themselves in the taverns of Port Royal and Kingston.[15]

December 1790, AGI, Santo Domingo, leg. 1027; Adam Williamson to Lord Grenville, 4 July 1791, C.O. 137/89, PRO.

13   *Savanna-la-Mar Gazette*, 29 July, 5 August 1788; *St. George's Chronicle and New Grenada Gazette* (St. George's, Grenada), 8 October 1790, file in AAS.

14   Affleck to Stephens, 14 September 1789, 12 September 1790, ADM 1/244, PRO.

15   Williamson to Grenville, 5 August 1791, C.O. 137/89, PRO. So much

Through such channels, Jamaica's dockside streets soon overflowed with graphic reports, many of which would have been of particular interest to the island's black and brown population. For instance, Jamaicans quickly learned of Ogé's rebellion and its bloody aftermath. In January 1791, Kingston newspapers reported that the backlash against equality had grown so virulent in Saint-Domingue that "it is scarcely safe for a man of colour to appear in public." Perhaps the brutal crushing of Ogé's uprising in Saint-Domingue was partially responsible for one Jamaican official's observation that "every thing is perfectly quiet" just two weeks before Saint-Domingue's slaves rose to complete what the mulatto rebel had started.[16]

Everything was not so quiet in the eastern Caribbean, where the events of 1789 and 1790 activated overlapping networks of Afro-American communication. Partly owing to geography and partly to the unique history of European colonization in this region, contact among British, French, and Spanish subjects occurred more frequently and intensely here than in other Caribbean subregions. Between 1789 and 1791, slaves and free people of color moving from place to place helped to communicate the liberation rumors currently brewing in each empire, kindling the spirit of open rebellion in the eastern islands.

The string of stepping-stone islands known as the Windwards—stretching from Guadeloupe in the north to Grenada in the south—had witnessed much of the action during the Anglo-French wars of the eighteenth century. Commercial and social contact continued in peacetime. Two former French islands, Dominica and Grenada, had only recently come under British control, and each retained many of its French inhabitants and customs. Just south of Grenada lay the Spanish-controlled island of Trinidad, which linked the eastern archipelago to the mainland, but which maintained close ties to the British and French islands as well.

---

information changed hands at Jamaica during the early French Revolution that Cuba's trade in small vessels proved to be the Spanish island's most reliable source of intelligence about developments in Saint-Domingue and in Europe.

16 *Kingston Daily Advertiser*, 12 January 1791, AAS; Williamson to Grenville, 5 August 1791, C.O. 137/89, PRO.

Ironically, the incessant maneuvering for imperial advantage which characterized this region brought the British, French, and Spanish closer together. In order to attract foreign trade, especially French, the British gave newly acquired Dominica two free ports under the act of 1766.[17] Likewise, the Spanish scheme for peopling and developing Trinidad hinged upon attracting foreigners. A royal *cédula* of 1783 openly invited discontented French settlers, promised special dispensations for those bringing slaves with them, and even granted land to free blacks and people of color who immigrated to the Spanish island. By 1784, according to one nineteenth-century source, "Trinidad was a French colony in all but name."[18] Trinidad's open door policy attracted all types, "the knave and the fraudulent debtor," French- and English-speaking free Negroes, and runaway slaves. When these various deserters returned to their former places of residence as sailors, traders, or visitors, authorities accused them of tempting slaves to follow their example. By the 1790s, officials in nearby British and French islands watched Trinidadian seafarers closely, and sometimes even went so far as to restrict their landing. While the British in Dominica "suffered" the presence of a small group of Spanish "*renegados*," obliging them only to pay fees and take periodic oaths of allegiance to the King of England, Grenada required Trinidadians entering the island to post a prohibitive bond of 1,000 pounds sterling or be jailed as vagabonds, "without any other proof than that of usual or frequent residence in Trinidad."[19]

In the eastern Caribbean, with French, English, and Spanish territories coexisting uneasily in close proximity, attentive slaves quickly caught wind of exciting developments in all three empires during the era of the French Revolution. Late in 1789, for example, Trinidad became the source of some dramatic news for slave communities

---

17   Armytage, *Free Port System*, pp. 36–46.

18   E. L. Joseph, *History of Trinidad* (Trinidad, London, and Glasgow, [1838]), pp. 161–6. Joseph reported that even in his day, forty years after the British annexation of Trinidad in 1797, "creole French is more the language of the people here than either English or Spanish."

19   Thomas Atwood, *History of the Island of Dominica* (London, 1791), p. 218; Joseph, *History of Trinidad*, pp. 166–7.

up and down the eastern archipelago. Even as the Spanish ministers debated the sweeping reforms which would soon become issues of contention in Caracas and elsewhere, a royal *cédula* dated 14 April 1789 instructed Spanish colonies to welcome runaway French and British slaves who could show a "legitimate" claim to freedom and protect them from their former owners. In August, José María Chacon, governor of Trinidad, publicized the decree. Reaction through the eastern Caribbean was immediate. Calling Trinidad "the common Asylum for Fugitives of every description," absentee British planters and merchants meeting in London made public anxious letters from Caribbean correspondents. By early 1790, they reported,

> the French Government has taken the alarm for its own Colonies, and …
> in Grenada, the Inhabitants have found it necessary to keep regular
> Night Guards on the Sea Side, and to support the heavy expence of two
> armed Vessels constantly cruising round the Coast, as the only effectual
> means of preventing a ruinous Emigration of their Slaves.[20]

Even with these measures, slaves in Grenada and other islands close to Trinidad slipped through the net and found their way to the Spanish island. Notices regarding escapees headed for Spanish territory crop up in newspapers as late as the fall of 1790. A French mulatto whom the English called "La Pierre" disappeared from Grenada in mid-September and was said to be "contriving to carry along with him a number of Negroes in a large canoe." In mid-August, two male slaves from the tiny island of Carriacou near Grenada absconded in a canoe headed for Spanish territory, but, "as the canoe was too small to carry them to the main," likely ended up in Grenada. Even less fortunate was Antoine, who was apprehended hiding aboard a Frenchman's sloop "with an intent to get away to Trinidad."[21]

Close examination of these descriptions of runaways to Trinidad reveals other important facets of Afro-American culture in the eastern

---

20   Minutes of WIPM, 23 March, 1 April, 6 April 1790, reel 3. For the *cédula* of 14 April 1789, see AGI, Indiferente General, leg. 2787.

21   *St. George's Chronicle and New Grenada Gazette*, 27 August, 10 September, 15 September 1790.

Caribbean in 1790. Clearly some of the region's slaves and free people of color, both in British and French areas, possessed special communication skills. A group of black men who absconded from Grenada in a "small schooner" in October 1790 included Hector, an African-born mason who spoke English and French "fluently," and John, a native of Grenada who had also mastered both languages, though he preferred French. Other notices for runaway slaves in the latter half of 1790 furnish dozens of additional examples. Bilingual black runaways at large in this region in the fall of 1790 included Dominica-born Cellestine, whose owner warned ship captains at Grenada of her likely intention to board an outgoing ship; Kitty, a seller of goods around St. George; and a missing "sailor Negro" called King John.[22] Able to speak French and English, yet responding to an invitation from Spanish territory, these runaways of 1790 had access to policies toward slavery in three colonial empires and could therefore play a vital role in bringing together and transmitting the politics of each.

But the world around them was changing rapidly, as these slaves on the move soon discovered. Just as in Santo Domingo, political events in the eastern region, especially the news of growing unrest among slaves and free coloreds in the French colonies, influenced Spanish policymakers to erect barriers to hinder black and brown mobility and short circuit any communication taking place between blacks in Spanish colonies and outsiders. It did not take long, therefore, for the Crown to decide to reverse its policy granting rights of refuge for black fugitives from slavery in foreign territories. In force for only a brief time, the Spanish edict which attracted so many runaway slaves to Trinidad in 1790 was revoked as suddenly as it had appeared.

In fact, by the time Governor Chacon issued the *cédula*, practices in Trinidad had already fallen out of step with those in other areas in the Spanish orbit. While slaves from British and French islands struggled to make their way to Trinidad, Caracas governor Juan Guillelmi anxiously reported the arrival of a number of French-speaking blacks on the mainland. According to Guillelmi, incoming cargoes of slaves

22   *St. George's Chronicle and New Grenada Gazette*, 20 August, 22 October, 29 October, 11 November 1790. For more cases, see ibid., 13 August, 27 August, and 15 October 1790.

often included people who "had spent considerable time in French colonies." In addition, masterless French-speaking runaways arrived regularly in Caracas via Trinidad, and Guillelmi feared that "many more may come ... infected with the dangerous ideas they have seen triumph" in the rebellious French territories.[23]

Moreover, Chacon's action even contradicted new policies which the Crown had ordered months before. The earliest reports from the French colonies prompted an order of 17 May 1790 stipulating that fugitive slaves from foreign colonies would no longer be welcome in the Spanish dominions. Four days later followed a second, more specific order which instructed that Spanish officials no longer admit "Negroes purchased or deserted from French colonies," nor "any other person of color (*casta*)" who might import seditious "maxims" into the colonies.[24] When they finally learned of the new stipulations in early fall and put them into effect, colonial officials like Guillelmi were relieved and confident that news of the change in policy would "spread very quickly to the foreign colonies and put an end to the transmigration" of slaves. Guillelmi took matters a step further by calling for the expulsion of all "foreign" slaves, though nothing indicates action upon his decree.[25] In the British colonies, officials printed Chacon's letter of retraction in a prominent place in island newspapers with similar hopes that word would circulate among slaves and stem the tide of fugitives to Spanish territory.[26]

Other items besides the Trinidad edict and its revocation made news among all classes throughout the eastern archipelago in 1790. With so many French territories in such close proximity to English and Spanish islands, a great deal of popular interest all over

23   Letters quoted in William J. Callahan, Jr., "La propaganda, la sedición y la Revolución Francesa en la Capitanía General de Venezuela (1789–1796)," *Boletín histórico* (Caracas) 14 (mayo de 1967), pp. 200, 201–2.

24   Porlier to Lerena, Aranjuez, 14 June 1790, AGI, Indiferente General, leg. 2787; Las Casas to Porlier, La Habana, 7 August, 12 August 1790, AGI, Santo Domingo, leg. 1253.

25   Guillelmi to Lerena, Caracas, 29 September 1790, AGI, Caracas, leg. 115.

26   See, for example, *St. George's Chronicle and New Grenada Gazette*, 17 September 1790.

the subregion focused upon the French Revolution. Within a short time, satisfying reader demand for information on the latest developments both in France and the colonies grew to become something of a minor industry. In the resulting debate which engulfed British and Spanish colonies as well as French, slaves and free people of color found ways to assert themselves.

With its political fluidity and extensive intercolonial communication, the eastern Caribbean provides further evidence for the distribution of news as a regionally shared commodity. Non-English residents, for instance, sometimes chafed at their dependence on the British press for foreign intelligence. One French colonist observed (in a newspaper published in British Grenada, appropriately) that "the English news papers come in so great a number" that street conversation inevitably took a British slant. Locally, editors of papers in the British islands recognized their broad readership and published their stories in both English and French, a fact that further contributed to the development of bilingualism at all levels.[27]

The French Revolution, however, inspired editors in the French islands to acquire presses that soon gave birth to a new breed of political gazette. Printed exclusively in French, these papers specialized in coverage of the French Revolution and its effect in the French colonies in America, reprinting the proceedings of the Paris Assembly as well as those of the new colonial assemblies. They enjoyed wide distribution and provided crucial sources of information for residents and officials in British islands.[28] The excitement of the French Revolution even stimulated French residents of British colonies to publish journals which vied with the old-line papers. These upstart gazettes also competed with each other in political terms, some hewing to the "aristocratical" line, others openly supporting the Third Estate.[29]

27 St. George's Chronicle and New Grenada Gazette, 22 October 1790. The Chronicle appeared in both English and French, as did a Dominican paper, Gallagher's Weekly Journal Extraordinary (Roseau, Dominica). See the copy dated 21 December 1790 in C.O. 71/18, PRO.

28 Many copies of such gazettes from Martinique, Guadeloupe, and Sainte-Lucie are collected in C.O. 71/20, PRO.

29 St. George's Chronicle and New Grenada Gazette, 15 October 1790, for example, refers to an "aristocratical" French paper published in Dominica.

As they passed back and forth between French and English islands, copies of these French newspapers and broadsides also leaked into the Spanish colonies. In Caracas and its provinces, officials reported some success in stemming the flow of "foreign" printed materials, much of it concerning the French Revolution, between December of 1789 and March of the following year. During this same period, however, French residents of Trinidad directly challenged age-old Spanish restrictions on the press. The appearance in Spanish territory of an independent voice sympathetic to the French called forth swift and decisive official action. Early in 1790, Trinidad's governor moved to stop the activity of one Jean Viloux, a French immigrant who edited a weekly newspaper which included extensive coverage of events in France and featured long reprints of debates and resolutions of the National Assembly. Governor Chacon suspended the sale of Viloux's sheet, closed down his printing press, and rounded up all extant copies. But because such an instance of overt suppression might arouse discussion of matters "better kept quiet," Chacon invented a spurious—and undoubtedly transparent—pretext for banishing Viloux from Spanish territory.[30]

Both the printed and the spoken word triggered rumors regarding slavery which exercised a powerful influence on politics in the eastern Caribbean between 1789 and 1791. In the late summer of 1789, copies of British newspapers reporting Parliament's agitation of the slave trade question filtered into Martinique and spawned local suspicion that the English might be spreading such reports in order to create unrest among the slaves. Whether or not this charge carries weight, news from some source of the moves in Parliament evidently reached the slave grapevine in Martinique before larger news of the French Revolution arrived. By early September, as slaves in the nearby English colonies contemplated the prospect of a parliamentary act outlawing slavery, evidence of discontent surfaced among French slaves at Martinique. Black workers began to desert plantations in the French island, and, according to one report, "the reason they give is

---

30   José Maria Chacon to Porlier, Trinidad, 27 January 1790, AGI, Caracas, leg. 153; Guillelmi to Valdés, Caracas, 2 March 1790, AGI, Caracas, leg. 115.

that as all the English Negros are to be made free they have a right to be the same."[31]

Soon the winds would blow in a different direction. An abortive uprising of slaves and free people of color in British Dominica in January 1791 shows that slaves in British areas could pay close attention to news from the French colonies. While some historians have argued that the Dominica incident "owed very little" to the influence of events in or ideas from the nearby French colonies, considerable evidence suggests a fluid situation in which rumors originating in French and British—and possibly even Spanish—territories intertwined and reinforced one another.[32] Indeed, given Dominica's many and varied connections with her non-British neighbors, it would be surprising if such an interchange had not occurred. Located halfway between Martinique and Guadeloupe, Dominica lay at a distance of just twenty-five miles from each of the French islands. With the many mobile groups which inhabited Dominica in 1791, all the preconditions for a rapid and effective transfer of news and information existed on this formerly French island.

Dominica appears to have been a particularly difficult island to govern. In the late 1780s officials often registered their frustrations in controlling the movements of their subjects both at home and abroad. First, the geography of the island invited deserters from sugar plantations. Dominica's dense forest and rugged terrain sheltered runaway slaves from the earliest days of plantation agriculture, and runaways from neighboring islands such as Guadeloupe to the north and Martinique to the south often managed to settle in the island's backcountry. Early in 1788, the Dominica Privy Council lamented that despite determined recent efforts to eliminate groups of outlying slaves, many remained at large and continued to hold "Considerable Correspondence with the Estates."[33]

---

31   Lémery, *Révolution française à la Martinique*, pp. 21–2; James Bruce to Lord Grenville, 8 September 1789, C.O. 71/16, PRO.

32   For a different interpretation than the one presented here, see Michael Craton, *Testing the Chains: Resistance to Slavery in the British West Indies* (Ithaca and London, 1982), pp. 224–5.

33   Minutes of the Privy Council, 22 February 1788, C.O. 71/15, PRO.

The shape of Dominica's commerce, which brought residents into regular contact with foreign colonies and people, provided another avenue of mobility and communication. As one of Britain's free ports, Dominica played the same role in the imperial scheme in the eastern Caribbean as Jamaica played in the west. After 1763, foreign trade became the mainstay of Dominica's commerce. By 1788, French, Spanish, and other non-British vessels made up fully sixty-three percent of the ships which registered with customs at the local port of Roseau.[34] Likewise, Dominican seamen frequently traveled aboard merchant ships to French ports, where they witnessed firsthand the evolution of French politics from the *ancien régime* through the Revolution. As graphic depositions on Governor Orde's desk in 1788 attest, imprisonment, impressment, and loss of wages were common experiences for British sailors in the French islands. But equally vivid episodes after 1789 foreshadowed the fundamental changes which were just over the horizon. In December 1790, an armed French ship "navigated by Whites and coloured People free and Slaves" detained a British merchant ship trading at Martinique. For the one black mariner aboard the British ship, "a Servant to the owner of the Vessel," the three nights of temporary captivity represented a world turned upside down. He alone was allowed to move about freely, while the captain and crew were kept in irons.[35]

Alongside Dominica's system of legal foreign trade flourished a strong black market counterculture. Just as the rough terrain of the island's hinterland aided runaway slaves, miles of unguarded coastline helped illegal traders escape detection. Governor John Orde constantly complained of the "disposition of many here to carry on illicit Trade" with the French and Spanish and lamented the enormous amount of French sugar which smugglers brought to the island. This unlawful trade had become a part of the accepted order of things in Dominica, much as it had been in New England several decades

34 Orde to Sydney, 10 May 1788, 1 September 1788, C.O. 71/14, PRO; Orde to Sydney, 13 December 1788, 22 January 1789, C.O. 71/15, PRO.

35 Orde to Sydney and enclosed depositions, 29 May 1788, C.O. 71/14, PRO; "Statement of the Case of the Captain & Crew of the Schooner Union of Barbados," 31 December 1790, C.O. 71/18, PRO.

earlier. So in April 1790, when someone informed customs officials about prohibited goods being landed, a "mob" gathered in the streets of Roseau and accused one John Blair, whom they proceeded to tar and feather and then beat within an inch of his life.[36]

Significantly, the ships and boats which plied inter-island routes, both legally and illegally, carried many free people of color from the French islands. Their numbers included sailors and travelers as well as more permanent settlers. In a history of Dominica published in 1791, Thomas Atwood estimated that more than half of that island's 500 free people of color—a "very idle and insolent" lot—had migrated from French islands.[37] As revolts in the French islands gathered steam after 1789, white residents of the British islands like Atwood cast watchful eyes on these mobile free coloreds. Following the first anniversary of the fall of the Bastille, a Grenada weekly called attention to the "great number of coloured people lately arrived here from the French colonies" and expressed the prevalent concern that locals might be "misled" by the ideas of "those vagabonds who have lately made their appearance here in such a questionable shape." Later in the year the same paper lamented the reappearance of "Mulatto Balls—those scenes of amusement for the idle and dissolute" which seemed to have become nightly occurrences "in almost every street."[38]

Dominica's white citizens assumed by January 1791 that free people of color arriving from Martinique and Guadeloupe imported the seditious ideas which had already affected the French islands. In Martinique, the civil struggle had shifted momentarily in favor of the blacks and mulattoes, and word reached Governor Orde's desk that the slaves on that island had for the first time begun to express publicly

---

36   Orde to Sydney, 13 April 1788, C.O. 71/14, PRO; Bruce to Grenville, 15 April 1790, C.O. 71/16, PRO; Minutes of the Privy Council, 27 March 1790, C.O. 71/17, PRO; Orde to Grenville, 8 January 1791, C.O. 71/18, PRO.

37   Atwood, *History of the Island of Dominica*, pp. 219–20. According to official estimates, these free coloreds made up only about 3 percent of the island's population in 1791, compared to 2,000 whites (11 percent) and 15,400 black slaves (86 percent). See "Return of White People, Free People of Colour & Blacks," 14 February 1791, C.O. 71/20, PRO.

38   *St. George's Chronicle and New Grenada Gazette*, 16 July, 26 November 1790.

the idea that "a general Emancipation" was "their end and aim."[39] Four days later, a French planter in Dominica warned Governor Orde that the "continual arrival of free People of Color as well as slaves from Martinique" had already planted similar "illusory notions" and "false ideas" in the minds of his and other slaves. Returning from errands in the capital, slaves brought back word to the estates in his district that Governor Orde had published an order granting them three days per week to work for themselves without supervision and stipulating that they would be paid for any work performed for planters. In ordinary times slaves might have quietly ignored such a rumor or dismissed it as preposterous. But with neighboring revolutions growing in intensity and with agitation of the slave trade and slavery in the air in both British and Spanish colonies, such a manufactured spark could fall upon ready tinder. Within a matter of hours, slaves deserted some estates and simply refused to work on others.[40]

During an uneasy standoff of several days, British officials and planters attempted to dispel the rumors and negotiated with the slaves to return to work. Then, suddenly, a different sector of the island—an area "commonly called the French Quarter"—erupted into violence. A group of slaves "headed by some Free Mulattoes" took up arms, killing one white man and threatening "other acts of Violence and Hostility."[41] But a military detachment quickly controlled the incipient revolt, and those not captured immediately were eventually apprehended from their hideouts in the woods.

The details of the Dominica uprising of 1791 offer a revealing look at networks of Afro-American communication. After quelling the revolt, Dominican officials assigned the highest blame to the "constant and Improper intercourse of Foreign Vesells" with unguarded

---

39   Orde to Grenville, 8 January 1791, C.O. 71/18, PRO.

40   B. Blanc to Orde, 12 January 1791, Renault Briollard to Orde, 13 January 1791, C.O. 71/19, PRO. The ideas that slaves would be given days to work on their own and would be paid bear some striking similarities to rumors current in the Spanish slave colonies at the same time. Given the recent Trinidad episode, the *código negrero* of 1789 might have influenced these reports. See Chapter Three.

41   Minutes of the Privy Council, 20 January 1791, Orde to Grenville, 3 February 1791, C.O. 71/19, PRO.

stretches of coast, in the course of which "persons were frequently landed and taken off … for Suspicious purposes." Not only had the "first Symptoms of the Disturbance" shown themselves in places adjacent to the familiar haunts of the interlopers and illegal traders, but one of the rebel leaders along with thirty of his followers attempted to escape by the same route. In order to close off these channels, Orde called for armed warships to cruise the windward side of the island to "prevent all Communication between this Island and the Foreign Islands."[42] Other measures attempted to control networks of communication internal to the island itself. New laws ordered tavern keepers in town to clear the blacks from their establishments at the appointed time; they provided that "Dances and Assemblies" would be more closely monitored; and they reinstituted the moribund system of tickets for public porters and other slaves whose jobs took them away from plantations.[43]

Finally, Orde, echoing Governor Chacon in nearby Trinidad, suggested the "checking by Wholesome and moderate Laws, the Licentiousness of Printers."[44] The governor did not have in mind Dominica's pro-planter/merchant press, though it often criticized him and the colonial government, but rather one of the region's newly established newspapers, a popular sheet published in French under the intriguing title *L'Ami de la Liberté, l'Enemi de la Licence* (*The Friend of Liberty, the Enemy of License*). For once, both the governor and his critics in the island's proslavery press could agree upon the subversive nature of this infamous "French gazette" published in Guadeloupe. Like other gazettes of its type, *L'Ami* featured reprints of speeches and debates, but beyond that the paper maintained a strong editorial policy, under the anonymous pen of "XYZ," which attracted the particular attention of Dominicans on both sides of the slavery issue. A competing English language paper attacked the editor of *L'Ami* as "a

---

42   Minutes of the Privy Council, 17, 20 January 1791, Orde to Laforcy, 20 January, 28 January 1791, C.O. 71/19, PRO.

43   Orde to Magistrates and Planters, 15 January 1791, Council Minutes, 24 January 1791, C.O. 71/19, PRO.

44   Orde to President of the Council and Speaker of the Assembly, 21 January 1791, C.O. 71/19, PRO.

Mulatto Fellow of no Character or principle," but conceded that the paper had won an extensive and eager following in Dominica. "It was not only read with avidity by free People of colour," wrote Thomas Anketell, editor of *The Charibbean Register*, "but Negro Slaves were Subscribers to it, and it is well known that Negroes on a Sunday have frequently clubbed together a quarter dollar to purchase it, in order to have it read to them." Dominica's Privy Council echoed Anketell, denouncing the open "encouragement … given to slaves and opinions promulgated in their favor" by *L'Ami*.[45]

Like Jean Viloux's paper in Trinidad a year earlier, *L'Ami* could not survive indefinitely in the face of such opposition. Before long the controversial editor apparently had to make an escape. But a month after a series of grisly public executions signaled the end of the insurrection at Dominica, "XYZ" and his newspaper surfaced again in—of all places—Trinidad. In the breezy journalistic style which had become so familiar to readers throughout this region of the Caribbean, he taunted Anketell and other opponents. Though pursued by detractors in both Martinique and Dominica, the nameless editor had arrived "healthy and safe" on the Spanish island. But his experience had only strengthened his resolve to take up his pen in the cause of liberty. Soon he and the ideas he espoused would be "on the way up again."[46]

In Saint-Domingue, the execution of Ogé occurred just weeks after the suppression of the brief Dominica uprising in January 1791. In subsequent months, divisions among whites in the French colony widened, as did the conflict between the colonists and legislators in Paris. News of Ogé's violent death at the hands of white colonists prompted the National Assembly in France to pass on 15 May 1791 a measure which enfranchised a small percentage of free mulattoes and blacks and took the bolder step of asserting the right of the Assembly to legislate upon "the status of persons" in the colonies. Word of the

---

45   *The Charibbean Register, or Ancient and Original Dominica Gazette*, 26 March 1791, copy in C.O. 71/20, PRO; Minutes of the Privy Council, 29 January 1791, C.O. 71/19, PRO.

46   *L'Ami de la Liberté, l'Enemi de la Licence* (Port of Spain), 22 février 1791, copy in AAS. Unfortunately, this is the only known copy of this paper still extant.

May Decree arrived in Saint-Domingue on 30 June, and, according to one member of the elite, "no words can describe the rage and indignation which immediately spread throughout the colony." Propertied colonists reacted to what they perceived as a dangerous intrusion into colonial affairs by resurrecting local and regional assemblies to resist the authority of the Assembly in France. In the succeeding months, violent attacks against free blacks and mulattoes who dared to speak out in defense of their newly granted rights increased dramatically. Planters and merchants began to talk openly of total independence from France. This turbulent political situation created an opening for slaves to entertain ideas of independence as well. While whites and mulattoes debated among themselves, sporadic reports from both the North and West provinces as early as July described a sudden wave of slave uprisings. Preoccupied with other concerns, however, the planter class ignored these warning signs of the massive rebellion to come.[47]

On the night of 22 August 1791, even as planter deputies made their way toward Cap Français to convene a regional assembly, slaves in the rich northern plain encircling the Cap began their rebellion. For weeks black leaders had spread word of the intended uprising, and when the moment arrived, the widespread and well-planned nature of the rebellion caught whites defenseless. Within hours after slaves first rose on an estate located nine miles from the Cap, as many as 100,000 slaves learned about and joined the revolt, setting fire to plantations and cane fields and mercilessly attacking slaveowners and their families. Immediately officials in the Cap sent delegations to Cuba, Jamaica, and the United States to request assistance in fighting the black rebels, but they received only half-hearted cooperation. To compound their problem, just days after the rebellion in the northern provinces mulattoes and blacks in the west triggered a second wave of armed uprisings. Pitched battles between government troops and poorly armed insurgents resulted in thousands of deaths on the rebel side, but these defeats failed to subdue outlying groups who continued to raid and destroy plantations. They even threatened to invade

---

47 Garrett, *French Colonial Question*, pp. 97–117; Edwards, *History, Civil and Commercial*, III, pp. 68–9; Stoddard, *French Revolution in San Domingo*, p. 129.

the cities, now crowded with white refugees. Two months after the uprising in the north, French officials estimated that more than 2,000 whites had lost their lives, and that the rebels had destroyed 180 sugar plantations and more than 900 other estates specializing in coffee, cotton, and indigo production.[48]

News of the unprecedented happenings in Saint-Domingue in August 1791 passed quickly to all parts of the Americas, but these events naturally held special interest for residents of other plantation societies. Never in the history of New World slavery had blacks struck so violent a blow against their oppressors, and by the middle of 1792 observers in all parts of the Americas recognized that the rebels of Saint-Domingue would not soon allow the French to end the revolution which had begun.

Through their extensive commercial connections, substantial numbers of North Americans had intimate concerns over the revolution in Saint-Domingue from its very beginnings. In the years leading up to and following the slave rebellion of 1791, ships representing all the major ports of the new nation frequented the harbors of the French colony. Besides furnishing the flour, lumber, and other goods which the French desperately needed during the trade depression of the early 1790s, United States merchantmen kept residents of the thirteen states as well as residents of the Caribbean abreast of developments in Saint-Domingue.

When the disruptions in France beginning in 1789 restricted the number of ships arriving from Europe, vessels from the United States materialized to supply the needs of the French colony. By late 1790, North American ships represented a vital lifeline for an uncertain economy. Without the Americans to furnish flour and provisions, wrote one French colonist during this time of scarcity and high prices, "we would find ourselves in the most extreme circumstances." He did not exaggerate the significance of United States traders in the months leading up to the slave rebellion. In a typical week from late August

---

48   Thomas O. Ott, *The Haitian Revolution, 1791–1804* (Knoxville, 1973), pp. 47–52; James, *Black Jacobins*, pp. 85–90; Edwards, *History, Civil and Commercial*, III, p. 83.

to early September 1790, ships from New London, Newburyport, Boston, Philadelphia, Baltimore, Hampton, and Charleston registered at Port-au-Prince, and at Cayes vessels arrived from Salem, Boston, and Norfolk. During the same period, ships departed these Saint-Domingue ports for Baltimore, New Bern, Boston, Philadelphia, and New York.[49] At Cap Français, Saint-Domingue's largest port and the most accessible to southbound shipping, American commercial agents and captains reported "about fifty Sail of american Vessels … and others arriving daily" in February 1790 and "a great number of Americans" at anchor a year later.[50]

After the outbreak of the rebellion at the Cap in August 1791, vessels from the United States were instrumental in spreading word of the insurrection to other parts of the Americas. North American merchantmen headed for their home ports furnished a great deal of valuable information to Spanish authorities, and presumably other interested inhabitants, during stopovers in Cuba. Their vivid and detailed reports imply that captains and crews alike realized that they had witnessed history in the making. In a period of eight weeks in the late summer and fall of 1791, captain John Davison of the *Charming Sally* viewed battles between black insurgents and government troops in both Cap Français and Port-au-Prince. Davison even recounted a startling example of the rebels exercising their newly acquired power, having seen a delegation of armed black rebels enter the latter city "demanding the freedom of Man otherwise they would lay the town in Ashes." By 1793, American slavers engaged in the re-export trade of Africans from Caribbean islands to the North American states had replaced their Spanish and French rivals as Cuba's main suppliers of both slaves and information from Saint-Domingue. Ships headed to and from Charleston seem to have been especially busy at this time.[51]

---

49 Letter quoted in Deschamps, *Colonies pendant la Révolution*, p. 84. For arrivals and departures at Port-au-Prince and Cayes, see *Affiches américaines*, 11 septembre 1790, RSD.

50 Benjamin Bailey to Christopher Champlin, 13 February 1790, Samuel Lawton to Christopher and George Champlin, 18 February 1791, reprinted in *Commerce of Rhode Island, 1726–1800*, 2 vols. (Boston, 1915), II, pp. 409–10, 432–3.

51 Las Casas to Campo de Alange, La Habana, 9 November 1791, AGI, Cuba,

The North Americans who engaged in this trade to Saint-Domingue during the early years of the slave revolution made up a diverse group representing all points on the political spectrum. In United States ports, organizations of sailors like Charleston's Marine Anti-Britannic Society supported the French Revolution, and Yankee seamen in Saint-Domingue often joined the locals in drinking toasts to the continued health of the Republic.[52] While welcoming the trade of the Yankee vessels, French officials complained that the Americans tended to trade with all of the competing factions in the colony. In 1792, a French admiral feared the consequences of a slackening in American trade with desperate white colonists, but the next year another naval official requested that a frigate or warship be stationed off Port-au-Prince to intercept North American "interlopers," with the implication that the Americans were trading with the rebels.[53] After declarations of war against France in 1793 encouraged the English and Spanish to invade the rebellious colony from opposite directions in simultaneous attempts to annex it, North American trade fortified the occupation forces of both nations.[54]

News of developments in Saint-Domingue quickly reached the United States aboard these merchant vessels. By the time Vincent Ogé

leg. 1486. For other examples, see the observations of Nicholas Thorndike (Salem) and William Newton (Charleston), with Las Casas to Ministro de Guerra, La Habana, 8 February 1792, AGI, Cuba, leg. 1486; Las Casas to Campo de Alange, La Habana, 7 May, 11 July 1793, AGI, Santo Domingo, leg. 1261.

52   Eugene Perry Link, *Democratic-Republican Societies, 1790–1800* (Morningside Heights, N.Y., 1942), pp. 26–7, 95–6; "Lista de los Franceses que se aprendieron el 18 de mayo," La Habana, 8 July 1794, AGI, Cuba, leg. 1474. As late as the 1830s, some white working-class organizations continued to drink toasts to Tom Paine and to the "pure Republicanism" of the Haitian government at the same gatherings. See Eric Foner, *Politics and Ideology in the Age of the Civil War* (Oxford, New York, Toronto, and Melbourne, 1980), p. 61.

53   Vicomte Henri de Grimouärd, *L'Amiral de Grimouärd au Port-au-Prince d'après sa correspondence et son journal de bord (mars 1791–juillet 1792)* (Paris, 1937), p. 58; La Salle to Sonthonax, 24 February [1793], reprinted in Corre, *Papiers du Général de la Salle*, pp. 148–9.

54   A "List of all Ships & Vessels that have clear'd Outwards at the Port of Jeremie in the Island of St. Domingo since the Commencement of the British Governement 20th September to the 9th Novr. 1793," C.O. 137/92, PRO; Vrizar to Gardoqui, Santo Domingo, 25 February 1794, AGI, Santo Domingo, leg. 957.

arrived in Charleston late in 1790, newspapers in the South Carolina port city had been using the reports of sea captains to cover the factional and racial struggles in the French Caribbean for some eight months; by the next year, Charleston papers regularly reprinted translated dispatches from colonial assemblies in the French Caribbean and significant European documents such as the Declaration of the Rights of Man.[55]

Not surprisingly, accounts of the dramatic occurrences in Saint-Domingue made for good copy, and they furnished widely printed and discussed news items along the eastern seaboard in the late weeks of 1791. As soon as they could confirm verbal reports, newspaper editors did not delay in printing stories about the black rebellion for their readers. First word of the revolt did not arrive in Philadelphia until the middle of September 1791, but by the time careful publishers had corroborated these earliest accounts, rival papers from New England to South Carolina had already rushed into print with lengthy and lurid tales of the happenings of the night of 22 August.[56]

As whites devoured these accounts of the insurrection in Saint-Domingue, they soon detected the first indications this news had reached the ears of blackNorth Americans. Reports of mounting unrest among slaves along the coast forced officials to devise ways to dismantle the networks of communication which slaves utilized to keep informed about events in other parts of the Atlantic basin. The Virginia legislature, for example, undertook several measures to suppress public discussion of foreign affairs during the early stages of the revolutions in France and Saint-Domingue. During the spring of 1792, signs of an impending general uprising of slaves appeared in tidewater Virginia. Examining officials blamed "the example of the West Indies" for local conspiracies of slaves in Northampton and

---

55   George D. Terry, "A Study of the Impact of the French Revolution and the Insurrections in Saint-Domingue upon South Carolina: 1790–1805" (M.A. thesis, University of South Carolina, 1975), pp. 11–12, 38–9.

56   P. Bond to Lord Grenville, 2 October 1791, Foreign Office Records, class 4/ vol. 11, PRO; Mary Treudley, "The United States and Santo Domingo, 1789–1866," *Journal of Race Development* 7 (July 1916), pp. 103–4; Alfred Nathaniel Hunt, "The Influence of Haiti on the Antebellum South" (Ph.D. dissertation, University of Texas at Austin, 1975), 221n.

Norfolk, discoveries which prompted the state's General Assembly to revise its entire slave code and tighten restrictions against meetings of slaves for whatever purpose. By the end of the year, worried magistrates resorted to more sweeping steps to curb the spread of political excitement and uncertainty in the Old Dominion, both among slaves and within the population at large. An act of December 1792 reveals the extent to which Virginia's rulers feared the consequences of the uncontrolled passing of information and ideas while it betrays their sense of powerlessness to control it. Citing the many "idle & busy-headed people" in the state who "forge & divulge false rumors & reports," civil authorities imposed an "Act against divulgers of false news" which remained in effect for most of the decade.[57]

I n Jamaica, the sugar-producing colony whose economy and demography most closely resembled Saint-Domingue, word of the nearby rebellion had profound and lasting effect. Less than two weeks elapsed between the night of 22 August and the initial indications that white Jamaicans were discussing the revolt and circulating news of the event among themselves, and news of the uprising may have reached the island's black majority even sooner. On 7 September, Governor Effingham reported to the Secretary of State the "Terrible Insurrection of the Negroes," accounts of which he gathered from emissaries sent from the French colony to "crave Assistance" from the Jamaica Assembly. But by this time the insurrection had certainly become common knowledge in the streets of Spanish Town and Kingston. On 10 September, William Dineley, a "Guinea surgeon" who had been to Africa in the slave trade and who was spending a great deal of time around the docks trying to secure a return passage to England, wrote to Bristol merchant James Rogers of "a rebellion … in some of the French Settlements," adding that "the Negroes has killed a great many white people."[58]

---

57   Thomas Boyd, *Light-horse Harry Lee* (New York and London, 1931), pp. 206–207; Richard R. Beeman, *The Old Dominion and the New Nation, 1788–1801* (Lexington, 1972), pp. 95–96; Daniel Bedinger to Henry Bedinger, 19 September 1797, Bedinger-Dandridge Family Papers, Duke University Library.

58   Effingham to Dundas, 7 September 1791, C.O. 137/89, PRO; William

While government officials like Effingham and private citizens like Dineley voiced urgent concern in their sealed letters, publicly there appears to have been an effort on the part of Jamaican whites to suppress discussion of the growing revolution next door. One searches in vain, for example, for any accounts from the French colony in the pages of Jamaica's most informative weekly newspaper. From October 1791 through the end of the year, only one brief and colorless reference appears to the "late troubles in Hispaniola" in Kingston's *Royal Gazette*—and this fully three months after the rebellion began.[59] The official conspiracy of silence—a familiar device intended to limit the fears of whites and the hopes of blacks with respect to nearby slave revolts—persisted even as government resorted to the most public defensive measures. A member of the Methodist congregation in Kingston added an ironic note to her lengthy and detailed description of Jamaica's turbulent "political situation" late in 1791. Though rumors of slave unrest abounded, militia units trained night and day, and people talked openly of the possibility of martial law, she wrote, "the Motives for all this are endeavour'd to be kept Secret."[60] Aware that even privately shared written communication ran unnecessary risks in this world where news of interest to the black majority could spread quickly and uncontrollably, individual white observers practiced the ultimate in self-censorship. One correspondent's assessment of the same tense situation referred obliquely to some "*particular circumstances, which we think at present improper to commit to paper.*"[61]

In contrast to this careful silence among free whites, their slaves quickly showed avid interest in the rebellion in Saint-Domingue, an interest which sometimes became public enough for whites to notice and record. The commander of the island's military forces observed that Jamaican slaves were "immediately informed of every kind of news that arrives," and knew "perfectly well every transaction at Cape Francois." By mid-September, already the revolt of the

Dineley to Rogers, 10 September 1791, Rogers Papers.

59   *Royal Gazette*, 26 November 1791.

60   Mary Smith to William Hammet, 29 November 1791, William and Benjamin Hammet Papers, Duke University Library.

61   Letter quoted in Fuller to Dundas, 2 January 1792, FLB.

French slaves had found expression in the oral culture of the slaves: traditional songs now included new stanzas describing "the Negroes having made a rebellion at Hispaniola."[62] As the end of the year drew closer, reports coming in from various parts of the island, both city and country, echoed these observations. By November, Kingston slaves were said to be "perfectly acquainted with every thing that has been doing at Hispaniola." Centrally located Clarendon parish magistrates detained several "head Negroes of some of the Plantations" for speaking "very unreservedly about the Rebellion in Hispaniola." Besides celebrating vicariously the resistance of the "'Negroes in the French Country' (such is their expression)," the prisoners confessed to "expressing also their hope that a similar revolt would soon take place in Jamaica."[63] Though this hope was never realized, the revolt of the slaves in Saint-Domingue cast a long shadow over the British island, as it did throughout the New World, and it remained central to regional politics for a generation.

Jamaicans had hardly begun to adjust to the reality of Saint-Domingue before strong winds and currents and the short distance from the French colony to Jamaican shores brought the neighboring revolution closer. Blacks from Saint-Domingue began to arrive in Jamaica shortly after the uprisings of August and September 1791. Many of these eyewitnesses to revolution remained slaves in the custody of their emigrating owners, while others had taken advantage of the disorganization of the planters in order to escape slavery. Jamaican officials immediately expressed concern about both kinds of black immigrants from the French colony. In mid-September,

62   Williamson to Dundas, 18 September, 6 November 1791, C.O. 137/89, PRO. For an example of a Trinidad folk song based in part on the Saint-Domingue slave revolt, see David Lowenthal, West Indian Societies (London, New York, and Toronto, 1972), p. 45. The chant may in fact have some Jamaican origins; the black population in Trinidad in 1807, the year in which some resident of the island heard and made note of the song, included several hundred French Negroes shipped there from Jamaica after the British annexed the island in 1797.

63   "Extract of a Letter from Jamaica dated Kingston 18th Novr. 1791," C.O. 137/89, PRO; "Extract of a Letter dated Spanish Town Jamaica 5th Ncvr. 1791," FLB.

after the first wave of white refugees appeared, Governor Effingham issued orders designed to "prevent their Negroes from coming to mix with Ours." These measures prohibited the landing of blacks "without particular permission," and banned every incoming "male Negro" altogether. Controlling the arrival of masterless black and brown immigrants, however, presented a greater problem. Even as Effingham's orders went into effect, "several Canoes had arrived at the East End of Jamaica with Negroes from St. Domingo."[64]

Between 1791 and 1793, the fear that any "French Negro," whether slave or masterless, could communicate the spirit of rebellion to blacks in Jamaica shaped official policy. While the earliest laws did not strictly prohibit the landing of nonwhites from Saint-Domingue, they did set some limits. A royal proclamation issued in December 1791 prohibited "free people of color and free negroes" from settling in Jamaica before "two substantial housekeepers (white persons)" had testified to their good character before the chief magistrate of the parish. The Assembly made periodic checks by calling for returns of the names, addresses, and official clearances of all French-speaking free mulattoes and blacks living in Jamaica. Upon the arrival of a second wave of immigrants from Saint-Domingue after the first of the year, including black domestics, newly appointed governor Adam Williamson reiterated Effingham's earlier instructions that local magistrates should be "very Watchfull that there is no communication between the french servants, and the English slaves."[65]

Citing the necessity of preventing "communication between the slaves of this island, and slaves ... brought from the island of St. Domingo," the Assembly passed a law in May 1792 which set strict guidelines for the employment of "foreign" slaves in Jamaica. By its provisions, no one could "purchase, hire, or employ" any slave brought to the island after August 23, 1791—the day following the initial outbreak of the rebellion in Saint-Domingue. But in order to accommodate the French refugees, most of whom had settled in Kingston,

---

64   Effingham to Dundas, 17 September 1791, C.O. 137/89, PRO; Stephen Fuller to Dundas, 30 October 1791, FLB.

65   *Journals of the Assembly of Jamaica*, IX, pp. 50, 82, 85; Williamson to Dundas, 12 February 1792, C.O. 137/90, PRO.

such slaves might lawfully be employed in "sea-port towns," with the provision that they never be permitted "to go into the country."[66]

No sooner had this law gone into effect, however, than officials encountered several layers of resistance to their efforts to monitor the activities of French slaves working in Jamaica. Because owners and employers in urban areas refused to register their foreign slaves with local magistrates, the Assembly found it impossible to keep track of the number of French slaves working on the island. Other employers of black labor chose to ignore the "foreign slave" law altogether. Nathaniel Bayly, proprietor of several estates near the northeastern coast, found nothing wrong in importing French Negroes. At least two ships trading to Saint-Domingue from Port Maria, a small port on Jamaica's north coast, actively engaged in bringing whole gangs of French- and creole-speaking slaves intact to work Bayly's sugar plantations. Parish examiners discovered to their further horror that more than a few of these undocumented workers were "of improved capacity, and speak both English and French." As white observers recognized, the ability to translate French words and ideas into English posed an inherent threat. But this was amplified by the fact that many enslaved Africans could still communicate in their ancestral languages. "Although our negroes do not understand French," warned Jamaica's *Royal Gazette*, "yet they all know *their own country*."[67]

In the towns, the web of contacts basic to the urban milieu soon brought the new arrivals from Saint-Domingue together with the locals. It also furnished opportunities for black and brown immigrants to establish their own networks of support. From the middle of 1792, workhouses in Kingston and Spanish Town confined a steady stream of French-speaking, mostly female runaways—domestics owned by white refugees from the revolution in Saint-Domingue—with the usual diverse cast of local deserters. Ability to communicate in English may have predisposed certain of these trusted slaves to grasp for freedom in this new place. One French settler lost two members of her household between 1792 and 1793. Hairdresser Charmant

---

66   *Journals of the Assembly of Jamaica*, IX, p. 115; *Royal Gazette*, 26 May 1792.
67   *Journals of the Assembly of Jamaica*, IX, pp. 319, 332; *Royal Gazette*, 28 July 1792.

absconded in August 1792 in order to follow his occupation independently in Kingston. Daphne, who left Mrs. Espent's employ the
following March, was suspected of hiding herself in Kingston "with
some of those mulattoes that escaped their merited punishment at St.
Domingo." Both Charmant and Daphne spoke English and French.[68]

As they sought to control the lives of French slaves who came to
Jamaica with their owners, officials also paid close attention to blacks
who came to the island without masters. Reacting to the early reports
of canoe arrivals on Jamaica's sparsely settled and vulnerable eastern
shore, the governor worked with naval officials and port authorities
to keep seaborne French Negroes from reaching Jamaica undetected.
Separated from Saint-Domingue by a channel barely one hundred
miles wide at its narrowest point, Jamaica lay well within range of even
the smallest undecked vessels departing western Hispaniola, and the
prevailing westward winds made for a smooth and swift passage. The
admiral at Port Royal quickly shifted the vessels under his command
into position along the northern and eastern coasts. By June 1792
naval officials had charged one warship cruising the channel between
Jamaica and Saint-Domingue with the specific task of "intercepting
vessels with fugitive Negroes" from the French colony.[69] In addition,
they directed captains at the free ports to "take account" of black and
brown people aboard all incoming foreign ships and to make certain
that nonwhite sailors departed on the vessels in which they arrived.[70]

Even such careful precautions failed to keep out of Jamaica an
informed and varied array of black travelers from Saint-Domingue.
Many arrived in a manner reminiscent of English and French slaves
heading for Trinidad a couple of years earlier: they eluded patrolling

---

68   *Royal Gazette*, 25 August 1792, 13 April 1793. For other examples of runaway
domestics from Saint-Domingue in Jamaica during this period, including bilingual
ones (at least in terms of European languages), see *Royal Gazette*, 28 July, 4 August,
10 November 1792, and 9 March, 17 August, 28 September 1793.

69   Affleck to Stephens, 5 November 1791, "A List of His Majesty's Ships &
Vessels on the Jamaica Station, and upon what Services employed," 17 June 1792,
ADM 1/244, PRO.

70   By the end of the year, however, the Assembly voted to abandon these measures, finding them both too costly and injurious to the island's precious trade with
foreigners. *Journals of the Assembly of Jamaica*, IX, pp. 90, 139–40, 173.

warships and made Jamaica in canoes and other open vessels designed for fishing and coastal commerce. Vague early reports of canoe arrivals with runaways aboard sharpened as weeks of rebellion turned to months. Robert Bartlett, captain of Kingston's town guard, reported that he apprehended eight "dangerous negroes," six men and two women, who had "come in an open boat, and landed at the west end of town" in September 1793. The following month the city's clerk of the peace disclosed that five more "free persons of color" who had arrived by the same means were apprehended, jailed, and later deported.[71]

Some of the passengers aboard these canoes were actually former residents of Jamaica who had been sold or transported and were using the dislocation of the revolution in Saint-Domingue to return to families and friends in the English colony. One prisoner at the workhouse in St. James parish in April of 1792 told authorities that he had been transported, but "made his escape from Hispaniola about six months ago, with three others, in a canoe." A United States vessel picked him up at sea and brought him to Jamaica. While steering a course from the north coast to Kingston, the crew of a small British sloop "discovered a Canoe" making its way toward Jamaica. Upon being picked up, the seven black men aboard reported—in English—that "they were slaves to certain Frenchmen in the island of Saint Domingo who had formerly purchased them from persons in this Island."[72]

Black and brown emigrés from Saint-Domingue arrived aboard larger vessels as well. Early in 1792, Kingston's Town Guard arrested "upwards of twenty foreign negroes, from Aux Cayes, Jeremie, and

---

71   *Journals of the Assembly of Jamaica*, IX, pp. 218, 235. Though the dates do not coincide exactly, a newspaper report of the arrival and arrest of "a mulatto man, five negro men, and two women [who] came down here in an open boat … from Port-au-Prince" probably refers to the same incident reported by Bartlett. See *Royal Gazette*, 31 August 1793.

72   *Royal Gazette*, 21 April 1792; examination of James Ball, 30 October 1794, papers of the prize "7 Negro Slaves" (1794), Records of the High Court of Vice-Admiralty (Kingston, Jamaica), Jamaica Archives, Spanish Town (hereinafter JHCVA Papers, JA). See also the case of John McArthur, a mulatto who returned to Jamaica after once being sold to a Frenchman in Saint-Domingue, *Royal Gazette*, 1 December 1792.

other ports of Hispaniola" at a private home in the city's wharf district. Having been "landed at different times from vessels trading to this port," most of these "stout fellows" spoke English and some had been living in Jamaica secretly for as long as three months.[73] In May, authorities apprehended more speedily "a negro man named Ferror," an English-speaking native of St. Kitts. Two days after his arrival at Port Royal aboard an English vessel from Saint-Marc, a port city in western Saint-Domingue, they committed Ferror to the Kingston workhouse for having played "a very active part in the late dreadful outrages in the vicinity of St. Marc."[74] That same week, a man taking an evening stroll along the shore "beheld, to his great astonishment, upwards of forty foreign people of colour and negroes, uniformly dressed, walking up from the seaside, where they had just, apparently, landed" from a vessel arrived at Port Royal.[75]

Throughout 1792 and into the following year, reports of the latest developments in Saint-Domingue constantly arrived aboard the vessels which maintained a steady trade between the British and French colonies. Virtually every issue of the *Royal Gazette*, however lacking in direct news of the slaves' rebellion in Saint-Domingue, contained notices of arrivals and departures of vessels both French and British engaged in an active though modest commerce between the two colonies. Incoming vessels not only brought news in the form of broadsides and other printed material, but also opened some possibility of human contact between blacks working in sea-going occupations from both shores. Even with the strictest policies in effect regarding the landing of French slaves and mulattoes and nonwhite seamen, still an occasional French-speaking black mariner wandered at liberty in the streets of Kingston and Spanish Town.[76] In January 1793 a pair of enslaved black sailors from a French schooner deserted their ship and disappeared into the underground of Spanish Town only to be apprehended three days later. Apparently their brief incarceration had little or no deterrent effect; the same twosome

---

73   *Royal Gazette*, 18 February 1792.
74   *Royal Gazette*, 12 May 1792.
75   *Royal Gazette*, 19 May 1792.
76   See, for example, the case of Adjo, *Royal Gazette*, 1 December 1792.

soon ended up in the workhouse again on a subsequent trip to Jamaica.[77]

Significantly, but not surprisingly, bits of evidence exist regarding black and colored Jamaican seamen seeking to travel in the other direction and witness, or even join, the rebellion in Saint-Domingue. At least two mulatto sailors exhibited an active interest in making the trip over to the French colony as the revolution there continued. In May 1792 one free colored man "said to be employed in a small vessel that trades from Port-Royal to Hispaniola" attacked the naval officer who refused to allow him to clear port, presumably for Saint-Domingue. The next year another mulatto aboard a schooner bound for Curaçao murdered his captain at sea, "took command of the vessel, and ran her into the French part of St. Domingo."[78]

In the minds of Jamaican whites, the issue of mobility during the early years of the Haitian Revolution reflected a larger concern about the powerful example which the black rebellion represented. In the months following August 1791, many white observers detected undercurrents of resistance among Jamaican slaves which they connected to the news from Saint-Domingue. Jamaican slaves showed more than a detached interest and knowledge regarding the transactions in the French colony, wrote one member of the white minority in November 1791. Already news from Saint-Domingue, he noticed, had made the black workers "so different a people from what they were." He surmised from recent events that "the Ideas of Liberty have sunk so deep in the Minds of all the Negroes, that wherever the greatest Precautions are not taken, they will rise."[79]

As officials predicted from the outset, slave unrest and rumors of revolt ignited by news of the beginnings of the Haitian Revolution showed up with particular force along the north coast of the island. Not only was Jamaica's long coast within easy reach of foreign colonies and attractive to foreign vessels, but island defenses were concentrated

---

77   *Royal Gazette*, 19 January, 9 February, 13 April 1793.

78   *Royal Gazette*, 19 May 1792, 3 August 1793.

79   "Extract of a Letter from Jamaica, dated Kingston 18th Novr 1791," C.O. 137/89, PRO.

in the southeastern corner of the island near Port Royal, Kingston, and the capital of Spanish Town. Throughout Jamaica's history as a British slave colony, the north side had always been the center for insurrection, and the winter of 1791–92 came close to replaying earlier scenes of violent insurrection. While coastal slaves drew upon the reports of revolt next door to reactivate "Ideas of Liberty," white residents of northern parishes prepared themselves for the possibility of a similar rebellion in Jamaica. Their careful observations provide a valuable window into communication and politics in this region between 1791 and 1793.

In the late weeks of 1791, north coast planters did not delay in organizing themselves. Meetings of freeholders in each parish nominated "committees of secrecy and safety" charged with gathering all information relative to local slave activity and keeping open lines of inter-parish communication. Although some of the "alarm" seemed overblown to officials writing from the safety of Spanish Town, by late November committees of safety near the island's opposite coast, in the parishes of St. James, Trelawny, and St. Ann, reported "great reason to apprehend an Insurrection at the North Side."[80] The "defensive reaction" of Jamaican whites assumed several shapes. Every town put newly raised militia units through their paces after a nine-year hiatus. The Assembly petitioned London for arms, soldiers, and warships. With the approach of the Christmas season, traditionally the most difficult time of the year to enforce discipline, the governor and the Assembly instituted martial law throughout the island effective 10 December.[81]

News of the Haitian Revolution figured prominently, even centrally, in the atmosphere of tension, excitement, and fear along the north coast both before and after the imposition of martial law. The committee of safety of St. James parish, for example, uncovered and reported several incidents confirming that accounts of the Saint-Domingue revolt were spreading through slave communities in the region. In

---

80   London *Morning Chronicle*, 2 February 1792, copy in FLB; Williamson to Dundas, 27 November 1791, C.O. 137/90, PRO; Smith to Hammet, 29 November 1791, Hammet Papers.

81   David Geggus, "Jamaica and the Saint Domingue Slave Revolt, 1791–1793," *The Americas* 38 (October 1981), pp. 219–21.

Montego Bay a young man named Guy, described as a "waiting boy ...
extremely artful," learned from "the Negroes to windward" that "Saint
Domingo had risen killed the Boccaras [white persons] and taken the
Country." Guy and his friend Congo Jack may have been instrumental
in conveying this news from the east to correspondents farther west.
Under examination, he confessed that he and his friend "were carriers
of intelligence and held an intercourse with Negroes on some Estates
in Westmoreland." Reports from plantations dotting the mountainous countryside overlooking Montego Bay described slaves as "well
aware of what has happened abroad." Ignoring injunctions "to keep
the affairs of St. Domingo a secret," an attorney working on the Green
Pond estate in St. James proceeded to discuss the situation in Saint-
Domingue with the slaves. To his surprise, the driver "was already
fully apprized thereof," and even added details of planned rebellions
in other parishes of which the lawyer had no idea.[82]

Committee members traced these reports back to the coast, specifically to small-time foreign traders and sailors who had come to
Jamaica in connection with the Free Port Act. In mid-November a
white employee on one estate "overheard a Sensible Negro tell some
others he had been at [Montego] Bay ... and some Spaniards told him
that the Negroes at Hispaniola were now free and enjoyed the rights of
white men." J. L. Winn, the Quaker merchant from Montego Bay who
headed the St. James committee of safety, revealed that some Spanish-
inspired reports played upon a now familiar theme. Not only had the
"French negroes ... obtained their entire liberty," but the same was
due the British slaves; only the opposition of the local planters stood
in the way of the King of England's wish that they be free. Accusations
against the Spanish by prominent Jamaicans did not end here. Besides
holding the Spanish presence responsible for the circulation of "exaggerated accounts" of the slave rebellion on Saint-Domingue, Winn
and his associates accused them of aiding north coast slaves to secure
arms as black Jamaicans organized to follow the example set by the
French-speaking rebels.[83]

---

82   All illustrations are taken from the "Minutes of the proceedings of the
Committee of Secrecy and Safety in the Parish of St. James's, Jamaica," C.O. 137/90, PRO.
83   In addition to "Minutes," ibid., see Winn's letter in the London *Morning*

These findings provided the justification for a series of measures taken in the northern parishes designed to inhibit communication between local slaves and the foreigners who frequently passed along their knowledge of current events. In St. James as elsewhere, these precautions fell heavily upon local Spaniards, including respectable traders and those who worked for them. They had settled on the coast to pursue a profitable trade in slaves, livestock, and other articles which by now had been legal for a generation. At Montego Bay, the committee of safety began to enforce new rules in mid-November which called for foreign sailors to be aboard their vessels by eight o'clock in the evening and restricted departures and arrivals to the daylight hours. Within days, tougher acts mandated the immediate departure of a great number of Spanish "vagrants"—though only about thirty such people were ever expelled—and a simultaneous effort to prevent other suspicious Spaniards "from concealing themselves in the Country." While this housecleaning "met with the sentiment of the Spanish Traders themselves" according to Winn, many cooperated reluctantly, if at all. One captain refused to carry any of the prisoners back to Cuba as "they were all Murderers and Robbers who had flown from justice, and would rise on his crew and seize his vessel."[84]

Significantly, the troublesome "Spaniards" of Jamaica's north coast in the early 1790s included many people of color. One of the settlers whom the law pursued in November 1791 was a "Spanish negro" named Philip. Late that month, Philip landed in jail after attempting unsuccessfully to purchase gunpowder at several stores in Montego Bay. The profile of Philip's life outlined in the report of the St. James committee of safety provides a stunning portrait of the kind of masterless and mobile individual who might play a pivotal role in communication during periods of political unrest. "Remarkable for

Chronicle, 2 February 1792, FLB. French accusations that the Spanish in Santo Domingo aided the slave rebels further bolstered the case against Spaniards in Jamaica. See Royal Gazette, 7 April 1792.

84   "Minutes ... of the Committee of Secrecy and Safety," C.O. 137/90, PRO. Winn's cover letter indicates that Hanover parish undertook similar measures against Spanish residents. In 1793, however, "seven-eighths" of the eighty foreigners who complied with an order to turn out in Montego Bay were Spanish. See Royal Gazette, 27 April 1793.

his intelligence, his designing disposition, his idle course of Life, his gambling and the extent of his connections," Philip had migrated to Jamaica from his native Cuba sometime in the spring of 1788. During the next three years, he made the necessary cultural adjustments, learning English and marrying a Jamaican slave. Though he had not worked for about three months at the time of his arrest, Philip had been "generally employed in the Coast Trade" and had undoubtedly developed his wide experience and extensive contacts during his years as a sailor. Philip's "dangerous and mischievous" friend Jack, himself a former dock worker, proved equally well connected and mobile. Recently Jack had deserted his owner and hired himself to a Jewish merchant in order to "Peddle thro the Country for a Commission." In the course of his travels Jack covered a wide area which included St. James as well as the adjoining parishes of Trelawny and Hanover; he had acquaintances from Montego Bay to Lucea, some twenty-four miles distant. Though their final fates remain unknown, Philip and Jack may very well have been among the number of "vagrants" transported to Cuba. One can only speculate as to what form their resistance may have taken in later years.[85]

So planters everywhere, like those of Jamaica's north coast, quickly put up their guard against foreign masterless people. Figures like Philip and Jack could be found all over the Caribbean playing important roles in communication during the early phases of the revolution in Saint-Domingue. Besides such individuals, however, many other sources of information and ideas became available for slaves attempting to understand the world around them. If the black rebellion on Saint-Domingue carried an immediate special meaning for slaves, other developments suggested the larger ideological currents which engulfed the French colony and were spreading to other parts of the Americas. Like the frenzied military preparations which Jamaica's planters and officials hoped in vain would remain secret, the debate over the ideas and politics of the French Revolution rapidly assumed an irrepressible public dimension in the early 1790s.

Even before the execution of Louis XVI in Paris and the National

---

85   "Minutes ... of the Committee of Secrecy and Safety," C.O. 137/90, PRO.

Convention's declaration of war against Britain, Spain, and Holland, these nations readied themselves for the likely prospect of a military struggle against the French. In the British colonies, as in England, preparation for the coming war took on an ideological as well as a military dimension. By early 1793, counter-revolutionary rituals already prominent in England first appeared in the British colonies, where enemies of the French Revolution and the doctrine of the Rights of Man used public occasions in carefully managed ways to check the spread of egalitarian ideas. Barbadians already felt the "great expectation of war" in January, when a crowd in Bridgetown hoisted aloft an effigy of Tom Paine clutching "his Rights of Man" and then burned it in the streets of the island's capital. A similar scene occurred in nearby Grenada a month later. This time Paine's effigy was first displayed "one day upon a gibbet" before being burned "amid the shouts of a great number of people."[86]

In April 1793, this practice reached Jamaica. The island had been unusually busy since the last days of March, when British ships returning from Saint-Domingue and the packet from England simultaneously confirmed the outbreak of war between Britain and France. On April 3, the governor issued a proclamation limiting severely the freedom of movement of foreigners by requiring them to carry a "special license" in order to step outside a five-mile radius of Kingston. Meanwhile the navy offered merchant seamen bounties for signing aboard His Majesty's warships, and an office opened to receive and administer republican prisoners of war.[87] In the succeeding weeks, the war brought the French Revolution uncomfortably close. Not only did captured French soldiers brought to Jamaica manage to escape their ramshackle place of confinement, but their officers on parole "had the impudence" to walk through the streets of Kingston "bedecked … with National Cockades," brandishing sidearms and singing "their rebellious song of Ça Ira."[88]

Against this colorful backdrop, Jamaican planters and officials conducted a public effort to discredit the French and their ideas between

86   *Royal Gazette*, 2 February, 9 March 1793.
87   *Royal Gazette*, 30 March, 6 April, 13 April 1793.
88   *Royal Gazette*, 25 May, 22 June, 14 September 1793.

April and June 1793. Anti-Paine bonfires provided the main attraction in twin celebrations in Lucea and Montego Bay marking the eleventh anniversary of Admiral Rodney's historic victory over the French fleet in the Caribbean during the American Revolution. The persistence of the French threat and its dangerous present form composed the central themes in the Montego Bay demonstration: Paine burned alongside the Duke of Orleans, dubbed "Mons. Egalité," before a gathering said to represent "the greatest number of people ever assembled here before."[89]

In mid-May, the first official English translation of the French Convention's Declaration of the Rights of Man made the front page of the island's most widely read newspaper. As if in response to this effort to address an English-speaking audience, succeeding Paine effigy burnings in Jamaica grew more elaborate, and they attacked indigenous protest more sharply. In Savanna-la-Mar in early June, Paine's effigy swung ominously back and forth before the face of one Thomas Bullman, recently "convicted … of making use of seditious expressions" and confined in a pillory. Paine's appearance on this occasion was designed to transmit a clear message to Bullman and the crowd of interested onlookers:

> The scoundrel had on the red bonnet (the distinguishing cap of the Jacobins), on the front of which was written, in black characters, "Brissot—Marat—Roberspierre (*sic*)—Egalite," and underneath, "False Philosophy—Massacre—Plunder—Fraud—Perjury." In his right hand he held a paper, with the following words as a title page: "Rights of Man, alias Rights to pillage"; under his left arm was an old pair of stays.

As a band played "God Save the King," Paine's body, filled with gunpowder, was set alight and "soon went off in a great explosion, to the great entertainment of a vast number of spectators." The following month a similar gathering reminded Kingston residents of Paine's antislavery background. In July 1793, the English radical whose career as a pamphleteer began with tracts attacking slavery and the slave

---

89   *Royal Gazette*, 20 April, 27 April 1793.

trade was symbolically hanged and burned in Kingston next to an effigy representing the best-known of latter-day antislavery crusaders, William Wilberforce.[90]

Though newspaper reports present a detailed and suggestive picture of the structure of these counter-revolutionary celebrations and refer to "vast" crowds, broader questions concerning the role of popular (and anti-popular) politics in slave societies in the Age of Revolution remain. What was the popular reaction to this concerted effort to discredit Paine and the French revolutionaries? To what extent did the dynamics of slave societies affect or alter the character and meaning of such political rituals? Did blacks see themselves as active participants in the politics of revolution and counter-revolution or were such things as effigy burnings simply confusing and peripheral to their concerns?

While it may not be possible to answer these crucial questions completely, the form and frequency of anti-French bonfires in Jamaica and other British islands suggest that, like Paine's effigy at Savanna-la-Mar, discussions of the French Revolution and its ideology had literally burst into the open by the middle of 1793. And in societies split decisively along class and race lines, public demonstrations sponsored by local elites may have been something of a two-edged sword. If they intimidated and promoted conformity, these appeals to public channels also highlighted and underscored vividly the firm challenge which the French Revolution posed to the slavocracy.[91] Even if the urban slaves, free blacks, and others who witnessed Paine, Wilberforce, and the Rights of Man under the torch had not followed the progress of the French Revolution and its Caribbean counterpart beforehand, they likely came away with a sense of the issues which conflicted with the

---

90 *Royal Gazette*, 8 June 1793; [Falconbridge], *Narrative of Two Voyages*, p. 234.

91 In England, notes E. P. Thompson, "each bonfire of the effigy of Paine served to light up, in an unintended way, the difference between the Constitution of the gentry and the rights of the people." At least one of Paine's English followers found "more good to the cause than the most substantial arguments" in the effigy burnings, crediting them for igniting "the spirit of enquiry that is gone abroad; scarcely an old woman but is talking politics." E. P. Thompson, *The Making of the English Working Class* (New York, 1964), pp. 113, 122.

intentions of the sponsors. Barely had the smoke from the burnings of Paine and Wilberforce cleared on the eve of Bastille Day 1793 when authorities in neighboring Spanish Town examined four recently captured "French negroes" detained in the workhouse. In what was either an amazing example of blind coincidence or a telling political statement, one of the prisoners identified himself as "John Paine."[92]

---

92   *Royal Gazette*, 13 July 1793. This black Paine was the only one of the French speakers credited with a last name. The "number of marks on his breast" suggest that he had been something of a troublesome property in passing from owner to owner.

5.

"Know Your True Interests"

Saint-Domingue and the Americas, 1793–1800

While John Paine remained confined in a Jamaica prison, else-where in the greater Caribbean region Afro-American people were learning about and responding in a positive way to the politics and ideas of the French Revolution, even where their governments strongly opposed its currents. By early 1794, Havana's Governor Luis de las Casas could see that the eight-month-old war against the French involved a struggle for hearts and minds as much as a military contest. Unlike opponents in earlier conflicts, he observed, the present enemies of the Spanish were "less fearsome for their weapons than for their words and for the contagion of the spirit of sedition and anarchy which they seek to inspire."[1]

For almost four years, Las Casas had witnessed a succession of measures designed to contain the "contagion" of French republican-ism. Initially the Spanish colonies attempted to protect themselves by simply staying out of the affairs of the French. In November 1791, when first news of the slave rebellion on Hispaniola reached the min-isters in Spain, they urged colonial authorities to exercise "perfect neutrality" in the conflict. Such a policy, of course, ran counter to the entire logic of regional interaction which had come to characterize life in the Caribbean. Since that time, events had forced Spanish authori-ties to take a more active, if shifting, stance. At various times since the

---

1   Luis de las Casas to Conde del Campo de Alange, La Habana, 20 February 1794, AGI, Cuba, leg. 1488.

Saint-Domingue uprising, Cuban governors had refused settlement to white French colonists; admitted French colonists but prohibited their bringing slaves; expelled French colonists after they had settled; made efforts to keep out books and other printed materials alluding to French politics; and refused French ships and merchants from landing cargoes of African slaves on the island.[2]

Despite these efforts, in recent months the wide appeal of the ideas and example of the French Revolution had been demonstrated repeatedly both in Cuba and throughout the Spanish Caribbean, where some residents seemed as eager to import the revolution as the French were to export it. In New Orleans in 1793 as in Caracas a year later, apothecaries, ship captains, and militia officers were among those involved in local conspiracies to translate and circulate a pamphlet from the National Convention calling upon "citizens of all nations" to resist "the tyrants united against the French Republic." All parties were said to be active in "adopting and celebrating [French] slogans."[3]

Much of the inspiration for this kind of activity came directly from Saint-Domingue. Late in 1793, merchants in Santiago de Cuba implicated a longtime French resident of that city as a key source of local intelligence from Cap Français. Not only did this notorious contrabandist communicate on a regular basis with radical members of the colonial assembly in the French colony, he made liberal use of the "detestable maxims" of the French in encouraging his friends to resist the Spanish yoke. In other parts of the Spanish empire, likeminded French-speaking traders in contraband were plotting to use the Cap as a base of operations for a proposed attack on the port of Vera Cruz in New Spain.[4]

---

2   Juan Baptista Vaillant to Las Casas, Cuba, 27 July 1793, 3 October 1793, AGI, Cuba, leg. 1434; Las Casas to Conde de Lerena, La Habana, 30 March 1792, Josef Pablo Valiente to Lerena, La Habana, 28 March 1792, AGI, Indiferente General, leg. 2822. For the doctrine of "perfect neutrality," see Conde de Floridablanca to Las Casas, San Lorenzo, 26 November 1791, reprinted in José Luciano Franco, ed., *Documentos para la historia de Haiti en el Archivo Nacional* (La Habana, 1954), p. 67.

3   Barón de Carondelet to Las Casas, Nueva Orleans, 28 October 1793, AGI, Estado, leg. 14, doc. 54; Pedro Carbonell to Duque de Alcudia, Caracas, 31 August 1794, AGI, Estado, leg. 65, doc. 20.

4   Vaillant to Alcudia, Cuba, 29 October 1793, AGI, Estado, leg. 14, doc. 53;

If the Saint-Domingue revolution inspired discontented traders to mount their own rebellions, the state of affairs in the French colony provided an even stronger example for slaves. By 1794, the progress of French antislavery focused the attention of slaves and defenders of the slave system alike. In the two-and-a-half years since the outbreak of the slave rebellion in the French colony, the radicals in the French government had gradually steered metropolitan policy toward the idea of emancipating the slaves as a way to restore order in the colonies and defend them against British and French designs. As early as 1792, when a Jacobin named Leger Felicité Sonthonax and two other Civil Commissioners arrived to assume the reins of government in Saint-Domingue, rumors surfaced in Cuba and elsewhere that their real mission included placing Saint-Domingue under the command of the people of color, setting free the slaves, and igniting a chain reaction of violent slave uprisings which would spread throughout the New World.[5] In late June 1793, a small canoe carrying several British prisoners of war who had just escaped the Cap landed near Baracoa in eastern Cuba with dramatic news which bore out the apprehension of neighboring Spanish planters and officials: not only had black rebels taken over Cap Français, but the notorious Sonthonax, the Commissioner in charge of the northern district, had liberated those slaves rallying to the cause of the French against Spain and England. Like the Spanish in Cuba, the British in Jamaica now looked out for a possible landing of "a body of Mulattoes & Blacks … in different parts on the north side of this Island, [to] endeavor to spirit up the Slaves to Rebellion."[6]

Beginning in late June 1793, thousands of people fleeing the rebellion in Saint-Domingue boarded North American and other vessels destined for ports all over America, where they recounted the events

John Rydjord, *Foreign Interest in the Independence of New Spain: An Introduction to the War for Independence* (Durham, 1935), pp. 133–6.

5   Joaquín García to Acuña, Santo Domingo, 13 January 1793, AGI, Santo Domingo, leg. 956. See also the "Noticias" enclosed with Vaillant to Campo de Alange, Cuba, 3 May 1793, AGI, Santo Domingo, leg. 1260.

6   Vaillant to Campo de Alange, Cuba, 30 June 1793, AGI, Santo Domingo, leg. 1260; Adam Williamson to Henry Dundas, 13 July 1793, C.O. 137/91, PRO.

leading to the rebel victory in the Cap. Ten thousand emigrants departed on the morning of 22 June alone.[7] This mass exodus was by no means confined to whites. One French official who witnessed the bustle and confusion as one wave of emigrants boarded vessels in the harbor commented upon "the quantity of whites, yellows, and blacks who took the benefit of this little Flotilla to quit the Cape."[8] Like Jamaica, Cuba received its share of French immigrants, with many of the new arrivals congregating in Las Casas's jurisdiction in the area of Havana.[9]

If the presence of French refugees in Cuba and elsewhere did not ensure the diffusion of ideas of liberty and equality, political events taking place would soon pose further challenges. Even as Las Casas recorded his observations, the Convention in Paris was in the process of hammering out an historic decree ratifying Sonthonax's order and bringing slavery in the French possessions to an end. Learning of the Convention's open avowal of the antislavery cause, Stephen Fuller in London expressed the concern which would eventually make its way across the Atlantic, calling the decree "the worst political stroke that the French have struck since the Revolution," and asking whether enslaved blacks living in areas adjacent to French territories would "bear the continuance in slavery, when in a neighbouring island … the Negroes are all free?"[10] The following year, while planters in the islands resorted to repressive measures to ensure that slaves did not follow the example of Saint-Domingue, British and Spanish reformers alike responded to the challenge of the French example by proposing "modifications" in their systems of slave labor "so as to prevent any violent rising on their part to claim their independence."[11]

---

7   Stoddard, *French Revolution in San Domingo*, p. 220.

8   "Treasurer Paymaster of the Colony of St. Domingo to Bizouard his predecessor," [Port Républicain], 8 [September?] 1793, in papers of *Rising Sun* (1793), JHCVA Papers, JA.

9   Gabriel Debien, "Les colons de Saint-Domingue réfugiés à Cuba (1793–1815)," *Revista de Indias* 13 (octubre–diciembre de 1953), pp. 562–5.

10   Stephen Fuller to Committee of Correspondence (Jamaica), 20 February 1794, Fuller to Williamson, 8 March 1794, FLB.

11   *Considerations on the Present Crisis of Affairs, as it respects the West-India Colonies, And the probable Effects of the French Decree for Emancipating the Negroes.*

As Las Casas spoke in February 1794, word of the Convention's action had not yet reached the Americas. However, recent developments in the Caribbean itself had energized the culture of expectation and anticipation among slaves. Already the Spanish governor could report that among slaves in his district "the rumor is too widespread that the French desire that there be no slaves, and that [the French] will make all of [the slaves] free."[12]

B ecause Spain's colony abutted that of the French on Hispaniola, Spanish officials commanded a unique vantage point from which to view developments in Saint-Domingue. Not only did the Spanish monitor the progress of the black rebellion in the northern parishes of Saint-Domingue before 1794, but they also watched at close range the movement of people and ideas during this crucial phase of the revolution. During this time, Spanish authorities witnessed and recorded the earliest communications of officials and black rebels in Saint-Domingue with blacks outside the French colony regarding the ending of slavery.

By late 1792, slave unrest and the French army's effort to restore order had pushed steadily westward from Cap Français and had reached the towns of Fort Dauphin, Ouanaminthe, and Vallières, all situated short distances from Spanish territory. French victories and rebel retreats brought the battle front ever closer, exposing border patrols to the dislocation caused by revolution. The shifting fortunes of war complicated Spanish policy. For example, refugees with unclear political loyalties fled battle areas in the French zone and sought protection over the border. Spanish documents describe many of these refugees as mulattoes fleeing "the fury of the [rebel] blacks," but also count black rebels escaping the advances of the

---

Pointing out a Remedy (London, 1795), p. 11. See also the remarkably similar report of Joseph Antonio Vrizar, *regente* of the *audiencia* of Santo Domingo, entitled "Discurso sobre Modificación de la esclavitud," Santo Domingo, 25 June 1795, AGI, Santo Domingo, leg. 1032. Both plans outline ways to maintain the loyalty of slaves in light of the pressures of abolition in the French colonies.

12   Las Casas to Campo de Alange, La Habana, 20 February 1794, AGI, Cuba, leg. 1488.

French army and runaway slaves from French plantations among their numbers.[13]

From the standpoint of Spanish policy toward Saint-Domingue, the most important—and the most troublesome—group of refugees who sought the safety of the Spanish colony were Jean-François, Biassou, Toussaint Louverture, and other leaders of the black rebellion who, like Ogé in 1790, came to the Spanish seeking help in their battle against the French. By late in 1793, these rebels and the troops under their command agreed to fight under the Spanish flag in return for their protection and support. Largely through these "auxiliary" forces, the Spanish made incursions into Saint-Domingue in hopes of bringing the colony into the Spanish orbit. The first Spanish success in this effort to occupy Saint-Domingue occurred in the city of Fort Dauphin, a small but strategically vital port whose French planters capitulated to the Spanish admiral in January of 1794.[14]

Once inside Saint-Domingue the Spanish inherited a host of problems, among them a severe shortage of provisions and the resistance of fractious inhabitants who refused to give up their republican practices or aspirations. The occupation forces met considerable resistance as they attempted to impose a new set of laws upon the French townspeople. Soon after their arrival in Fort Dauphin, Spanish officials collected all broadsides and pamphlets from the Convention and banned use of the tricolored cockade. They also placed strict controls on the activities of printers, prohibited independent meetings, and closed the port to immigration from France.[15] Enforcing these regulations, the Spanish quickly learned of the extent to which ideas and

13 García to Diego de Gardoqui, García to Acuña, Santo Domingo, 25 November 1792, AGI, Santo Domingo, leg. 955; García to Campo de Alange, Santo Domingo, 12 March 1793, AGI, Santo Domingo, leg. 956; Archbishop of Santo Domingo to Acuña, Santo Domingo, 25 May, 25 September 1793, AGI, Santo Domingo, leg. 1110.

14 García to Acuña and enclosures, Bayajá, 5 February 1794, AGI, Santo Domingo, leg. 957. The Spanish called Fort Dauphin "Bayajá."

15 García to Gardoqui, Bayajá, 6 February 1794, AGI, Santo Domingo, leg. 957; "Reglamento para el buen Gobierno ... de las partes conquistadas en la colonia Francesa," n.d., with Vrizar to Alcudia, Santo Domingo, 2 February 1794, AGI, Estado, leg. 13, doc. 3.

rituals associated with the French Revolution had taken hold among the various social classes in the colony. Because of their involvement in such practices, hundreds of the French residents of Fort Dauphin suffered the fate of John Paine. Not prisoners of war in the traditional sense, these unfortunates are more accurately described as political or ideological prisoners, branded as dangerous and condemned to prison for their ideas.

A group of 110 prisoners rounded up in Fort Dauphin and shipped to Havana in May of 1794 consisted entirely of individuals whose recent expressions and actions against the counter-revolutionary Spanish presence were informed by the spirit and language of republicanism. Topping the list were the infamous Flores brothers, Luis and Rafael, whom officials described as "Jews who have vowed to re-establish the Republic" after engineering the ouster of the Spanish. The white prisoners also included such "rabid republicans" and "denouncers of all Royalists" as the head of the city's Jacobin club and one Menier, who "not three days ago, drank a toast to the health of the French Republic" in a local tavern.[16]

People of color, however, made up the majority of the prisoners. These mulatto and black republicans had actively celebrated the ideas of liberty and equality and resisted Spanish authority. The context of their opposition is significant. In Cap Français and Fort Dauphin, as in other cities in Saint-Domingue after the spring of 1793, the flight of large numbers of white colonists and their families left those remaining behind an unprecedented measure of freedom to operate. In September, observers in Santo Domingo received reports— perhaps exaggerated—that no more than 500 whites remained in Cap Français, that all whites who had not fled Port-au-Prince had been imprisoned as royalists, and that Fort Dauphin was "controlled by Mulattoes and some black domestics."[17] In the early weeks of Spanish

---

16   Las Casas to Ministro de Guerra, La Habana, 17 July 1794 and enclosed *relación*, n.d., AGI, Cuba, leg. 1488. For more detailed descriptions of the prisoners, see Joaquín García to Las Casas, Bayajá, 18 May 1794, and "Lista de los Franceses que se aprendieron el 18 de mayo," La Habana, 8 July 1794, AGI, Cuba, leg. 1474.

17   Archbishop to Acuña, Santo Domingo, 25 September 1793, AGI, Santo Domingo, leg. 1110.

occupation, despite official assurances that the free people of color would retain their rights granted by the Convention, many of the city's black and brown residents seemed determined to recapture their elusive freedom from white control. Several of the mulattoes arrested by Spanish authorities were said to be followers of Marco Antonio and Nicoló, who were also detained, the latter for having "held meetings of people of color at his home by night." Adapting the egalitarian ideology of the French Revolution to the racial politics of the Caribbean, a "free Negro" named Delrrival publicly declared himself the "enemy ... of all whites" yet a "good republican." Others were imprisoned for having carried their resistance to the Spanish invasion to the point of taking up arms. In the succeeding weeks, the boatloads of political prisoners shipped out of Saint-Domingue to Cuba for various forms of "evil conduct" included slaves, free blacks and browns, and white men, soldiers and civilians accused of such "crimes" as attempting to raise a rebellion and "maintaining communications and correspondence with our Enemies." By detaining these dangerous characters "in a secure place, in confinement and without communication," Governor Las Casas hoped to keep their ideas from spreading out across Cuba.[18]

As the Spanish on Hispaniola already knew all too well, the mobility of the ideas and images originating in rebel-controlled areas of Saint-Domingue warranted such attentive concern. Even prior to the taking of the Cap by rebel slaves or the Spanish occupation of Fort Dauphin, armed troops and militia spent "a good portion" of their time pursuing masterless "blacks and others, not only runaway slaves, but a multitude of Vagabonds, without trade or occupation" who, "encouraged by the example of the French," roamed between

---

18   "Lista de los Franceses," AGI, Cuba, leg. 1474. In addition, see Las Casas to Campo de Alange, La Habana, 20 February 1794, AGI, Cuba, leg. 1488, and García to Las Casas, Bayajá, 4 June, 18 June 1794, AGI, Cuba, leg. 1474. As for Delrrival's ambiguous republicanism, consider the description of one Monsieur Borel, who left Saint-Domingue for Jamaica in 1793, as among "the most violent Democrats imaginable" yet "an active enemy to the people of Colour [who] never would consent to their having any privileges whatsoever." Williamson to Dundas, 5 September 1793, C.O. 137/91, PRO.

French and Spanish territory raiding plantations and engaging in other "mischief."[19] Members of these mobile bands sometimes proved to be valuable sources of information for Spanish officials, and therefore, they reasoned, might provide the same service for not-so-mobile slaves. One rebel captured in French territory turned out to be a runaway slave of long standing from a plantation on the Spanish side and was brought under heavy guard to the capital for interrogation.[20]

Between 1793 and 1794, this uncontrolled movement became more purposeful, and the Spanish grew ever more dependent on blacks as providers of intelligence on matters relating to the French colony. When the auxiliary troops became the focus of a determined French recruitment effort in the months after the taking of the Cap, the leaders of these black battalions acted in effect as the eyes and ears of the Spanish in Santo Domingo. This dependence in matters of communication reinforced a sense of disquiet among the Spanish by late 1793. In addition, events across the border and the content of the messages transmitted from the Cap constantly tested the loyalty of their black allies. For instance, it was clearly by design that auxiliaries encamped near the border were first to receive copies of Sonthonax's historic proclamation of 29 August 1793. This document affirmed the freedom of the slaves and mapped the guidelines for the shift from slave to free labor in the French colony. Only after one of the black generals passed the document on to Governor García did Spanish officials get their first look at the proclamation.[21]

The French used more than public proclamations to communicate with and recruit the auxiliaries. The same month, messengers from Cap Français bearing letters from Pierrot, an ex-slave now commanding his own unit, slipped into the camp of Jean-François to

---

19   Archbishop to Acuña, Santo Domingo, 25 May 1793, AGI, Santo Domingo, leg. 1110.

20   García to Marques de Bajamar, Santo Domingo, 25 November 1791, AGI, Santo Domingo, leg. 954.

21   García to Acuña, Santo Domingo, 12 September, 22 October 1793, AGI, Santo Domingo, leg. 956. The French plan entitled domestic workers to receive fixed salaries and field workers to one-third of the annual profits of their estates in addition to food and clothing.

urge him to leave the Spanish and join the republican side. Pierrot's letters explained that life for blacks and people of color in the Cap had changed considerably in recent weeks. "Not one white person" remained in power in Saint-Domingue's largest city, he revealed. "The people of color are in control." According to authorities who saw his written communications, Pierrot painted "a grand picture" of racial solidarity in the common struggle against slavery and oppression, calling upon all blacks in the island to put aside current political differences and "unify as brothers" under the French flag against proslavery forces.[22] Soon other leaders of the auxiliaries disclosed that they, too, had received such entreaties from across the border. Not to be outdone, Biassou acknowledged late in 1793 that a "profusion" of written material from the republicans was circulating among his charges. In addition, he had personally entertained various "delegations of the Republic." In bold print, the appeals to Biassou and his troops called upon readers to "*open your eyes and know your true interests*"—to abandon the proslavery Spanish in favor of French antislavery. Like Jean-François, Biassou was also recruited with proposals for military alliances and new systems of agriculture protecting the rights of the workers.[23]

Under such constant political pressure, the auxiliaries would follow separate paths sometime the following spring. While Jean-François and Biassou continued to resist the French pleas to return to the fold, Toussaint Louverture, after learning of the Paris decree of February 1794 outlawing slavery in French colonies, made an abrupt shift in alliance and chose to cast his lot with the French. Because the brilliant leadership which Toussaint displayed in French service after 1794 altered the entire course of events in the Caribbean, his controversial "defection" marks the key turning point in the Haitian

22   García to Acuña, Santo Domingo, 6 September 1793, AGI, Santo Domingo, leg. 956. Such language, strikingly reminiscent of calls for black unity in more recent times, would become a cornerstone of Haitian nationality after independence in 1804. See David Nicholls, *From Dessalines to Duvalier: Race, Colour, and National Independence in Haiti* (Cambridge, 1979), pp. 41–6.

23   See García to Acuña and enclosures, Santo Domingo, 23 November 1793, AGI, Santo Domingo, leg. 956.

Revolution.[24] Besides Toussaint, other rebels shifted their allegiance to the French as a result of the emancipation decree. In 1795, a Spanish official from Santo Domingo confessed that the abolition of slavery by the French Convention "had changed the minds of many blacks who used to take our side" against the French.[25] But the beckoning call of the Haitian revolutionaries, this appealing image of Saint-Domingue as a center of antislavery and black self-determination in the hemisphere, reached a wider audience than simply the French Negroes in the Spanish section of Hispaniola. News of the decisive events of 1793 soon made the revolution in Saint-Domingue an object of identification for Afro-Americans throughout the New World.

Within a one-month period in the spring of 1795, Spanish officials in two widely disparate regions along the outer rim of the Caribbean basin discovered and put down major conspiracies against their governments. In western Venezuela, a group of armed slaves, free blacks, mulattoes, and *zambos* (people of Native American and African ancestry) under the leadership of a runaway slave from nearby Curaçao descended from the highlands overlooking Coro in an attempt to take over the coastal town and establish a multiracial "republic" free of Spanish domination. At the same time, authorities in Louisiana were conducting hearings to unravel the details of a conspiracy of French-speaking slaves working on plantations in heavily black Pointe Coupee parish, a similarly isolated area outside New Orleans. While local factors determined the nature and character of the Coro and Pointe Coupee plots, their timing involved more than coincidence. By 1795, half a decade of agitation related to the French Revolution had greatly affected both regions, as had the news of the emancipation of the slaves in Saint-Domingue. Illustrating dramatically the strains which both French revolutions placed upon

---

24   The precise circumstances surrounding Toussaint's "defection" from the Spanish and his motivations remain subjects of debate. See David Geggus, "From His Host Catholic Majesty to the Godless *République*: The "*Volte-Face*" of Toussaint Louverture and the Ending of Slavery in Saint Domingue," *Revue française d'histoire d'Outre-Mer* 65 (1978), pp. 481–99.

25   Vrizar, "Discurso sobre Modificación de la esclavitud," n.p.

Spanish-American territories in the mid-1790s, these flashpoints also reveal the power, extent, and some of the avenues of regional communication during the revolutionary period.[26]

Initially, official reaction in the captaincy-general of Caracas to the challenge of the French Revolution did not differ markedly from the rest of Spanish America. After 1789 authorities followed the same series of defensive measures as did Cuban officials. They placed strict prohibitions on the settlement of all possible French sympathizers, including foreign slaves and free blacks; banned all printed material concerning the revolutions in Europe or America; and searched incoming cargoes for other expressions of the material culture of the revolutionary era—coins, watches, jewelry, medallions, and other articles alluding to revolutions in Europe and America. But the many connections linking these coastal provinces to the rest of the Caribbean proved impossible to break, and French influence eluded Spanish defenses in a number of ways. Emigrés from Martinique and Guadeloupe journeyed to the continent via Trinidad, and French ships from Hispaniola, which had grown accustomed to trading slaves for horses and other livestock under the provisions of *comercio libre*, continued to arrive in the ports of La Guaira and Puerto Cabello long after the Spanish outlawed this trade. Finally, the deepening involvement of other Spanish colonies in the affairs of Saint-Domingue eroded the ability of Venezuelans to take a neutral stance. Officials in Spanish slave societies located closer to Saint-Domingue fully expected that Venezuelans would identify with their problems after 1791 and contribute to the effort to contain the spread of the slave rebellion. When

---

26 For accounts of the events in Coro and Pointe Coupee, see Pedro M. Arcaya, *Insurrección de los negros de la Serranía de Coro* (Caracas, 1949), and Jack D. L. Holmes, "The Abortive Slave Revolt at Pointe Coupée, Louisiana, 1795," *Louisiana History* 11 (Fall 1970), pp. 352–61. These two revolts represent only a small fraction of the black uprisings of 1795. For rebellions in Cuba, Puerto Rico, Jamaica, and Grenada which occurred the same year, see, respectively, José Luciano Franco, "La conspiración de Morales," in *Ensayos históricos* (La Habana, 1974), pp. 95–100; Guillermo A. Baralt, *Esclavos rebeldes: Conspiraciones y sublevaciones de esclavos en Puerto Rico* (1795–1873) (Río Piedras, 1981), pp. 13–20; A. E. Furness, "The Maroon War of 1795," *Jamaican Historical Review* 5 (November 1965), pp. 30–49; and Cox, *St. Kitts and Grenada*, pp. 76–91.

residents of Spanish Santo Domingo feared an imminent French invasion in 1793, they called upon Caracas officials for aid.[27]

Residents of Venezuela were therefore well aware of political
developments in Europe and their repercussions in America by 1793.
But the Spanish invasion of Saint-Domingue brought Caracas and
the other coastal provinces comprising the colony into sudden and
unexpected direct contact with the revolution in the French colony.
Overwhelmed with the numbers of prisoners captured in campaigns
in Ouanaminthe and Dondon—more than a thousand—and without
a place to keep them securely, Governor García of Santo Domingo
decided in August 1793 to ship a large number of these republican
prisoners to Caracas. Late in the year, hundreds of French prisoners of war and political prisoners began to arrive at La Guaira, the
port which served the capital city. Some 538 prisoners arrived in late
August. Like the prisoners rounded up in Fort Dauphin and sent to
Cuba the following year, these individuals were "for the most part
revolutionary patriots, loyal to the new government of the so-called
Republic of France," according to García. Barely had the excitement
subsided over their arrival when another shipment of 422, more than
half of them blacks, reached La Guaira. García described the black
prisoners in equally cautionary terms; some had been "taken up with
arms in their hands" and others were runaways "of long duration
whose rebellious spirits and conduct during four years of Liberty"
rendered them too troublesome to remain on Hispaniola.[28]

From the time of the arrival of these boatloads of unwelcome guests
until the spring of 1795, officials in the capital wrestled with the difficult questions of how to contain these prisoners physically as well
as keep their ideas from spreading through the colony. Both of these

---

27   Callahan, "Revolución Francesa en Venezuela," pp. 177–9; Sanz Tapia,
Militares emigrados y prisioneros franceses, pp. 41–50; Carbonell to Gardoqui,
Caracas, 30 November 1793, AGI, Caracas, leg. 94; Esteban Fernández de León
to Gardoqui, Caracas, 19 May 1792, AGI, Caracas, leg. 503; Carbonell to Alange,
Caracas, 31 July 1793, AGI, Caracas, leg. 94.

28   García to Gobernador de Caracas, Santo Domingo, 16 August 1793,
AGI, Estado, leg. 58, doc. 4; León to Gardoqui, Caracas, 11 December 1793, AGI,
Caracas, leg. 505; García to Gardoqui, Santo Domingo, 25 October 1793, AGI, Santo
Domingo, leg. 956.

goals proved difficult. Because existing facilities in La Guaira could not possibly accommodate such large numbers, authorities shifted some of the prisoners to Puerto Cabello, a coastal center two days' sail west of La Guaira, transported some up to Caracas, approximately twelve miles away, and confined the blacks in a makeshift prison—the basement of a winery—in La Guaira itself.

Barely two months passed after the arrival of the French prisoners before Spanish authorities in Caracas came together, determined to rid the province of their "irreligious conduct" and "seditious maxims." Official reports cited several alarming recent developments in Caracas, La Guaira, and other parts of Venezuela. Frenchmen had put silver coins with "inscriptions degrading Royal authority" into circulation in Caracas. French officers and others set at liberty refused to attend mass, and those who did attend boldly turned their backs to the altar and in other ways flouted the authority of the Church. Moreover, French sympathizers wandered at large in the countryside as well as the cities. At least one Frenchman traveled from Caracas as far away as Coro, where authorities accused him of spreading sedition and arrested him.[29]

The inordinate interest which slaves and free people of color showed in both the prisoners and what they represented constituted the most ominous sign of trouble. While no reports exist that any of the black rebel prisoners escaped at any time, their very presence, together with the dramatic public actions of white Frenchmen, sparked this interest. Two slaves working in a bakery in La Guaira, where the French Negroes chafed in their winery-prison, spoke in the fall of 1793 of how "within a year they would be free as the blacks of Guarico" and spoke of "throwing off the yoke of the Spanish Just as the Negroes of Guarico had shaken off that of the French." Observers in La Guaira and other cities reported that once-trusted slaves and free coloreds now openly challenged them with ideas of equality and antislavery associated with the French.[30]

---

29   García to Gardoqui, Caracas, 11 December 1793, AGI, Caracas, leg. 505; "Duplicados de las Juntas" [1793], with letter of Carbonell, Caracas, 13 March 1794, AGI, Estado, leg. 58, doc. 4.

30   "Duplicados de las Juntas," AGI, Estado, leg. 58, doc. 4. The Spanish referred to Cap Français and its surrounding area as "Guarico."

For almost two years, even after Caracas officials had emptied the jails of white Frenchmen whom they sent to Europe and elsewhere, the black prisoners and the problem of what to do with them remained. Their continuing presence took on a threatening symbolism for whites as evidence continued to mount that the colony's people of color had a thirst for information about developments in the French world. Early in 1795, authorities discovered that free blacks and browns in Caracas were openly discussing egalitarian ideas. Juan Bautista Olivares, a free black, assured one of the city's mulattoes that the meek would inherit the earth, a view backed up by a printed sermon in Olivares's possession attributed to the Archbishop of Paris. Authorities found this sermon, which Olivares had apparently read and explained to blacks and mulattoes in Caracas on several occasions, "full of the most detestable of liberty and equality." Further evidence of "the flame of insubordination" also resurfaced within the city's corps of mulatto militia. In response, officials rounded up and deported a small number of Frenchmen and arrested Olivares and sent him to Spain, where he landed in a Cádiz jail "without communication." Finally, they prohibited the use of skyrockets in Caracas, noting with alarm that they lit up the night sky "at all hours" and could very well signal "dangerous meetings" involving masterless Frenchmen and "the most numerous body in these provinces," the people of color.[31]

G eographic factors hampered Spanish efforts to rid Venezuela of the influence of the French and the revolutions in their territories. Even if all "dangerous" republicans could be expelled from the colony, its proximity to Saint-Domingue and other French colonies and its long unprotected coastline served to bring those revolutions closer. In terms of sailing time, a vessel from the south coast of

---

31   Antonio López Quintana to Gardoqui, Caracas, 15 February 1795, AGI, Caracas, leg. 472; León to Gardoqui, Caracas, 15 January 1795, AGI, Caracas, leg. 507; *consulta* (Manuel Romero, Juan Gonzalez Bustillo, Jorge Escobedo, Vicente Hora), Madrid, 6 October 1795, AGI, Caracas, leg. 15. About this same time authorities in Philadelphia considered a similar prohibition on the use of skyrockets "because they had been employed as signals in San Domingo." See Thomas Wentworth Higginson, *Travellers and Outlaws: Episodes in American History* (Boston, 1889), p. 208.

Hispaniola enjoyed more ready access to many of Venezuela's coastal cities than these cities had to each other. A merchant ship of average tonnage could travel from Santo Domingo to La Guaira and return in fifteen sailing days, with prevailing easterly winds and currents on the beam during each leg of the voyage. Round trips between La Guaira and Maracaibo or Trinidad, in contrast, required at least a month at sea, for the journey eastward involved tacking endlessly upwind along the coast.[32]

Beginning in 1793, armed French privateers operating out of Saint-Domingue made unauthorized visits to Spanish colonies throughout the region, and they did not overlook Venezuela's vulnerable coast. By 1795, these vessels posed threats to both transatlantic and coastal shipping, and they frequently put ashore their republican crews which included numerous mulattoes and black ex-slaves. From early in the eighteenth century French policy supported the use of blacks as sailors in wartime, but never had the black presence on the sea been as central as it proved to be in this revolutionary war. In the 1790s, the crew lists of French privateers often register large numbers of black sailors, and references to blacks aboard these vessels appear in both British and Spanish documents. One notoriously menacing "republican *corsair*" even boasted a brown captain, and undoubtedly other black and brown officers directed their own vessels.[33]

Like the privateers outfitted by their rivals, these *corsairs* preyed on all types of enemy shipping, but often their violent actions at sea reflected France's opposition to slavery in the colonies. French privateers operating between Cuba and Jamaica, for example, singled

---

32   For sailing times from La Guaira to various ports in Spanish America, see "Reglamento para Transportes de Oficiales de los Puertos de esta Capitanía General para todos los de la Península de Europa, y de unos a otros Puertos en América," Caracas, [1800], AGI, Caracas, leg. 96.

33   Richard Pares, "The Manning of the Navy in the West Indies, 1702–63," *Transactions of the Royal Historical Society*, 4th ser., 20 (1937), pp. 31–2. For examples, see papers of *Le Flibustier* (1795) and *L'Adelaide* (1795), JHCVA Papers, JA, and the *relaciones* of French prisoners enclosed with Juan de Araoz to Las Casas, La Habana, 4 June, 13 June 1795, AGI, Cuba, leg. 1455. For the activities of the mulatto captain see Juan Nepomuceno de Quintana to Las Casas, Cuba, 29 July 1796, AGI, Cuba, leg. 1435.

out Spanish ships carrying slaves for especially harsh treatment. In one case, a French ship seized a Spanish vessel headed for Bayamo in eastern Cuba with a cargo of sixty-eight Africans from Jamaica for sale. After freeing the slaves, the French crew threw the captured sailors overboard for good measure.[34] In addition, Spanish authorities accused French seamen of creating all kinds of mischief ashore, from raiding plantations for provisions and livestock to kidnapping slaves. But Trinidad's governor Chacon, who reported in 1796 that most members of French crews which landed at his island were "Mulattoes and blacks, many of whom have been slaves," offered a more nuanced view of the activities of the colored crews of the republican *corsairs*. He observed that their presence had a profound effect upon the slaves. Inevitably, wrote Chacon, local slaves came into contact with these newly freed French sailors, and "their conversations and discussions, although unsophisticated, are not so much so that they are not effective in perverting the ideas of our [slaves]." The actions of slaves provided some evidence of the content of these conversations. Earlier, Chacon had noted that the black victims of French "kidnappers" in Trinidad turned out to be slaves who had intentionally directed their canoes toward the privateers, where they knew they would be "received and protected."[35]

French privateers hovering near Venezuela affected the political climate in the colony in the mid-1790s. When these ships darted in and out of ports undetected, local residents gained access to crew members and their ideas and experiences. Occasionally, French sailors succeeded in recruiting some of the locals to serve aboard their vessels. Visiting Venezuela in 1799, Alexander von Humboldt

---

34 For this and other attacks against Spanish slavers, see Vaillant to Gardoqui, Cuba, 15 May, 27 May, 9 June 1795, AGI, Santo Domingo, leg. 1263. French ships off the African coast directed even more aggressive assaults against British, Dutch, and Portuguese slavers, burning ships and liberating African captives. See *Courrier de la France et des colonies* (Philadelphia), 15 octobre 1795 (microfilm copy in Yale University Library).

35 Archbishop of Santo Domingo to Príncipe de la Paz, Santo Domingo, 15 October 1796, AGI, Estado, leg. 11-A, doc. 1; José María Chacón to Gardoqui, Trinidad, 17 June 1796, AGI, Indiferente General, leg. 1595; Chacón to Gabriel Aristizábal, Trinidad, 29 December 1795, AGI, Caracas, leg. 153.

and his party had a violent confrontation with an ex-crew member of a Saint-Domingue privateer, a *"zambo"* and native of an Indian village near Maracaibo whose captain had left him in Cumaná after a quarrel at sea. Even when they did not come ashore, however, outlying French vessels maintained a kind of secondhand correspondence with the coast. Through its contact with Danish and other neutral vessels entering and leaving Venezuelan ports, one French privateer captured near the coast in February 1795 had been gathering "up-to-date news of whatever occurred ... in the capital." Presumably, information flowed in the other direction as well.[36]

The presence of French privateers off the unguarded coast of Coro in 1795 encouraged the rebels in that city in their efforts to organize a mass rebellion against the Spanish government. Leaders of the uprising convinced potential followers that the French would support such a strike, and the appearance of French vessels "enabled them to speak with more self-confidence and to investigate" more fully the possibility of a successful revolt.[37]

Besides the emboldening sight of French privateers, an equally important factor linking the actions of the Coro rebels to the revolutionary world of the greater Caribbean was the city's historic connection with the Dutch colony of Curaçao, a tiny island located due south from eastern Hispaniola and lying less than fifty miles from the South American coast. For years officials in Caracas had pointed to the proximity of Curaçao to Venezuela as the key determinant of the volume of contraband trade in the Spanish colony. In 1790, Caracas governor Juan Guillelmi viewed Coro as little more than "an outpost of foreign Colonies, especially the island of Curaçao which is within its sight."[38] Not only did Curaçao offer an ideal base from

36   Alexander von Humboldt, *Personal Narrative of Travels to the Equinoctial Regions of America, during the Years 1799–1804*, trans. and ed. Thomasina Ross, 3 vols. (London, 1881), I, pp. 343–5; Quintana to Gardoqui, Caracas, 19 February 1795, AGI, Caracas, leg. 514.

37   "Testimonio del expediente formado sobre la sublevación de los negros, Sambos, mulatos Esclavos y libres de la Jurisdicción de Coro," Caracas, 23 March 1797, AGI, Caracas, leg. 426.

38   Carbonell quotes his predecessor Guillelmi in a letter to Campo de Alange, Caracas, 13 March 1794, AGI, Caracas, leg. 95.

which foreign ships and crews could penetrate the closed Spanish market, but its accessibility from the mainland made the Dutch island a convenient safe haven for Spanish fugitives fleeing Venezuelan justice and for runaway slaves. Likewise, hundreds of Curaçao's slaves moved in the other direction and settled as free people in Coro and its hinterlands. By the time of the Coro uprising, these fugitives lived in well-established settlements both in the city and throughout the surrounding highlands, and had even developed what Spanish officials called "a formidable ... [self-governing] economy and polity," with local *cabildos* modeled after the town councils of the Spanish which regulated affairs in mountain villages.[39] Besides offering a sanctuary for fugitives from abroad, the overall demographic composition of this region of Venezuela reinforced the masterless outlook of its inhabitants. By the time of the revolt, free black and brown people, locally born as well as immigrants, made up forty-four percent of the population of the district. Whites constituted fourteen percent of the residents, and black slaves about twelve percent.[40]

Appropriately, the leadership of the 1795 rebellion included both a mobile runaway from outside Venezuela and a native of Coro. José Caridad González, the principal figure of the insurrection, belonged to the large contingent of migrants from Curaçao. He organized these communities around local grievances, especially the opposition to the recent imposition of the *alcabala* (sales tax) by the Spanish government. But in addition to emphasizing the injustice of taxation without representation, González inspired the rebels with his vision of a "republic" under "the law of the French," in which there would be no slaves or ethnic hierarchy. These powerful ideas might have come to González from several sources. He could communicate in several languages; he knew Spanish, *papamiento* (the creole language spoken

---

39   León to Lerena, Caracas, 27 February 1792, AGI, Caracas, leg. 503; "Papeles Relativos a los Quejas de los vecinos de Curazao," 28 March 1770, AGI, Indiferente General, leg. 2787; Guillelmi to Antonio Porlier, Caracas, 23 January 1791, AGI, Estado, leg. 58, doc. 2; *informe* of the *ayuntamiento* of Coro, Coro, 21 April 1796, AGI, Caracas, leg. 95.

40   For population figures, see Jorge I. Domínguez, *Insurrection or Loyalty; The Breakdown of the Spanish American Empire* (Cambridge, 1980), p. 56.

on Curaçao), and even "a smattering of French." He was also quite mobile; he had made several trips to Caracas in recent years, where he could have taken part in the discussions of the French Revolution and its ideas that became so public after 1793. In order to reach Caracas, he would also have passed through La Guaira, and he must have known about the plight of the "French Negroes" imprisoned in that city. Jose Leonardo Chirinos, a native *zambo* and co-conspirator, worked for a time with a Coro commercial house. Like González, he had also travelled extensively in the Caribbean, having visited both Saint-Domingue and Curaçao.[41]

The continuing communication with Curaçao made the watchwords of the French Revolution as well as news of the revolution in Saint-Domingue accessible to the people of the Coro region.[42] Both commercially and politically, the revolution in Saint-Domingue profoundly affected the Dutch island. Its neutral shipping provided a lifeline to the rebels, and these ships made extensive use of a large multilingual pool of free black and brown sailors. The designation "brown men from Curaçao" appears often in the records describing the crews of vessels trading to Saint-Domingue in the mid-1790s; English- as well as Spanish-speaking black sailors claimed the Dutch island as their home base.[43]

The ambitious plan for the Coro uprising called for coordinated strikes on two fronts. While González would attempt to organize the residents of the city, Chirinos inherited the responsibility for leading the revolt in outlying areas. The rebellion began on the eve of a popular Catholic holy day in early May 1795. During festivities late that night, slaves from several neighboring *haciendas* located a considerable distance from the capital banded together and began to attack the homes of their owners, killing at least one of them. By morning, two to three

---

41   *Testimonio* of Mariano Ramírez Valderrain, Coro, 23 May 1795, AGI, Caracas, leg. 426; Arcaya, *Insurrección de los negros de Coro*, pp. 34–5.

42   See the *informe* of Manuel de Carrera, Caracas, 26 September 1796, AGI, Caracas, leg. 426.

43   See the examination of Barbados native Michael Brown, n.d., papers of *Speedwell* (1793); examinations of John Domingo and John Francisco, 18 February 1795, papers of *Le Flibustier* (1795); and examination of black ship's master Nicolás Manuel, 26 March 1796, papers of *Trimmer* (1796), in JHCVA Papers, JA.

hundred slaves had joined the rebels, who proceeded to march on the city where they expected the support of their allies under the direction of González. But one of the owners managed to escape and make his way to Coro in time to warn officials about the impending insurgent attack. Local militia units moved quickly, and their preparations discouraged would-be rebels in the city. After securing the capital and killing González, the Spanish troops waited for and surprised the slaves before they could reach Coro, ending the insurrection.[44]

Four months after the ill-fated Coro uprising, a violent slave revolt took place on Curaçao, further suggesting the importance of the links between the Dutch entrepôt and the Spanish mainland. By 1795, events abroad and closer to home had combined to produce self-reinforcing rumors in the slave community in Curaçao which resulted in a late summer rebellion. When the Treaty of the Hague in May brought an end to the state of war between France and Holland, slaves in the Dutch islands expected that French law, including the emancipation decree of the previous year, would extend to them. When freedom in the colonies did not result from the treaty, Curaçao slaves believed that only the resistance of refractory Dutch authorities stood in the way of their liberation.

Like the rebellion in Dominica four-and-a-half years earlier, the Curaçao revolt began as a work stoppage. In mid-August, slaves on one plantation initiated the strike, which they spread to other plantations in the sugar-producing western region of the island. Soon more than one thousand slaves had quit working and joined the rebels in demanding their freedom. A brief skirmish with a small detachment of troops escalated the rebellion into violence. Like the Paris rank and file which stormed the Bastille in 1789, the black crowd of Curaçao directed its rage against slave prisons, freeing the inmates and setting off a wave of attacks on plantations which threatened to engulf the entire island. Once again, the government dispatched troops to contain the rebels, and this time they proved successful in containing the revolt. This turn of events, combined with a government promise of amnesty, convinced hundreds of the insurgents to return to the

---

44   Arcaya, *Insurrección de los negros de Coro*, pp. 37–9; Domínguez, *Insurrection or Loyalty*, pp. 56–7.

plantations. Dutch forces then captured the leaders, turning the execution of twenty-nine of them in the capital into a public spectacle following a speedy trial.

Accounts of French politics and news of the revolution in Saint-Domingue combined to fuel the rebellion on Curaçao. Once the details of the Franco-Dutch treaty of 1795 became known in the Americas, Curaçao's harbor attracted dozens of French privateers with their mixed crews whose presence may have nourished the liberation rumors which led to the revolt. Moreover, Curaçao's connections with Saint-Domingue encouraged slaves in the Dutch entrepôt to attempt to replicate the successes of the French Negroes. Because of the regular communication between the southern provinces of Saint-Domingue and Curaçao, rumors that André Rigaud, the mulatto leader of the rebellion in southern Saint-Domingue, would come to the aid of the rebels in Curaçao provided an added stimulus for the rebellion of 1795. Meanwhile, slaves in Curaçao found ways to identify with the revolt in Saint-Domingue. One student of Dutch slavery notes that many black parents began naming children after Toussaint. While the organizers of the Coro uprising invoked the ideas associated with the Haitian Revolution, leaders in the Curaçao rebellion of 1795 went so far as to invoke the Saint-Domingue rebels themselves. Of the leaders whom Dutch authorities executed after the 1795 revolt, one called himself "Toussaint," and another, whom authorities identified as "Toelo," was popularly known in the island by the nickname "Rigaud."[45]

The province of Louisiana in the Gulf of Mexico shared several characteristics with the island colonies of the eastern Caribbean in the late eighteenth century. Like the so-called "ceded islands" which passed from France to England at the end of the Seven Years' War, French Louisiana changed hands and came under Spanish control in

45   For accounts of these events, see Leo Gershoy, *The French Revolution and Napoleon* (New York, 1964), p. 303; Cornelis Christiaan Goslinga, *Emancipatie en emancipator: de geschiedenis van de slavernij op de Benedenwindse eilanden en van het werk der bevrijding* (Assen, [1956]), pp. 34–40; idem, *A Short History of the Netherlands Antilles and Surinam* (The Hague, Boston, and London, 1979), pp. 113–14.

1763. And just as islands such as Dominica retained French inhabitants, customs, and commercial connections after the transfer of colonial power to England, Louisiana remained strongly tied to the French world by 1789.

In its social composition, the sparsely populated province resembled Trinidad, Spain's perennial "problem" in the eastern Caribbean. After the American Revolution, the difficulties of defending and peopling Louisiana and stimulating its trade provided constant headaches for Spanish policymakers. They instituted one attempt at expanding commerce through a royal *cédula* of 1782 which permitted French ships to trade directly with the Spanish colony, and even allowed Louisianans to trade lawfully with the French Caribbean islands they knew so well in cases of "urgent necessity." Under these and later regulations, trade between Louisiana and Saint-Domingue expanded rapidly after 1785, making the task of increasing the volume of Spanish commerce in Louisiana "utterly impossible," in the words of one exasperated official in Spain. As for population, the Spanish experimented with Trinidad-style inducements to attract settlers, but with even less success. In 1790, minister Diego de Gardoqui lamented that too many of Louisiana's residents were "people expatriated from various kingdom because of irregular misadventures."[46]

The extensive personal network of freewheeling ship's master Jean Pousson indicates that Louisianans had contacts with many distant areas of the New World. A native Frenchman who settled in New Orleans the same year as the *cédula*'s promulgation, Pousson sailed under Spanish colors to various Spanish-American ports like Campeche for the next twelve years, but he also traded frequently in Kingston and Charleston and conducted business in Cap Français as late as October 1792. In fact, Pousson was in Charleston about to depart again for Saint-Domingue in the early summer of 1793 when "Intelligence arrived of the Destruction of Cape Francois." By this

---

46   Arthur Preston Whitaker, ed., *Documents Relating to the Commercial Policy of Spain in the Floridas, with Incidental Reference to Louisiana* (Deland, Fl., 1931), pp. 30–9, 107, 119. Gilbert C. Din, "Proposals and Plans for Colonization in Spanish Louisiana, 1787–1790," *Louisiana History* 11 (Summer 1970), pp. 197–213, covers unsuccessful efforts to spur immigration.

time, Pousson's voyages may have had political as well as commercial purposes. In the earliest years of revolutionary agitation in the French Caribbean, widely traveled ships like his transported letters between New Orleans and Cap Français planning a French takeover of Louisiana and brought "secret enemies" into the province who spread leaflets criticizing the government and even supporting a slave uprising. Later, during the high point of Jacobin influence in Louisiana, Spanish officials in New Orleans arrested Jean Dupuy, a frequent companion of Pousson, for "having made remarks suggestive of a revolution in Louisiana."[47]

The coming of the French Revolution provided French residents in Louisiana a rallying point for focusing resistance to Spanish authority. When the Baron de Carondelet took over the functions of intendant and governor of the province late in 1791, talk of the French Revolution buzzed in every quarter. Jacobin sympathizers existed among militia and infantry officers as well as among the sailors below decks in the naval squadron. At public gatherings French audiences demanded the playing of "La Marseillaise" and the anti-aristocratic verses of "Ça ira" issued forth from grogshops throughout the territory. Encouragement came from various directions. Vessels put into New Orleans with French newspapers and passengers from the colonies, and pamphlets even arrived from the United States urging French residents to "cease being the slaves of a government to which you were shamefully sold." To counteract such provocative activity Governor Carondelet issued early in 1793 a public proclamation outlining a series of new regulations designed to arrest the growing revolutionary sentiment in the province. These laws strictly prohibited reading or speaking in public about French politics; required that government have twenty-four-hour prior notice of any meetings to be held; and, so that sailors and

---

47   Examinations of Jean Pousson, 26 February 1794; George Clark, 27 February 1794; Henry B. Ludlow, 4 April 1794; and Lachlan McNeal, 8 April 1794, papers of *Joseph/St. Joseph* (1794), JHCVA Papers, JA; Carondelet to Las Casas, Nueva Orleans, 14 April 1792, AGI, Cuba, leg. 1446. For the arrest of Dupuy, see Thomas Marc Fiehrer, "The Baron de Carondelet as Agent of Bourbon Reform: A Study of Spanish Colonial Administration in the Years of the French Revolution" (Ph.D. dissertation, Tulane University, 1977), p. 480.

foreigners disembarking in New Orleans could not claim ignorance of the new regulations, directed all shipowners and naval commanders to inform their crews in order to make the law a subject of discussion along the docks.[48]

Carondelet's attempted crackdown only strengthened the very rumors which he hoped to dispel. For instance, many Louisianans whispered that Spain would soon swap the Spanish colony to the French in exchange for Saint-Domingue. As this report suggests, residents of Louisiana saw their destiny tied up with that of the French colony, and they had for some time. Thirty years earlier, officials barred blacks from Saint-Domingue from entering Louisiana because of a recent series of poisonings of slaveowners which they thought might spread to the mainland. Similar regulations were instituted in 1790, but despite strictures against the introduction of slaves or free people of color from French colonies, New Orleans remained the destination for large numbers of people of both descriptions during the Haitian Revolution. White refugees brought trusted slaves with them, or, in some cases, sent them ahead. In addition, free coloreds constituted as many as one-third of the 10,000 refugees from the French West Indies who settled in Louisiana between 1792 and 1808.[49]

The twin influences of the revolutions in France and Saint-Domingue deeply affected the rapidly expanding population of free

---

48   Jack D. L. Holmes, *Honor and Fidelity: The Louisiana Infantry Regiment and the Louisiana Militia Companies, 1766–1821* (Birmingham, Al., 1965), p. 65; Ernest R. Liljegren, "Jacobinism in Spanish Louisiana, 1792–1797," *Louisiana Historical Quarterly* 22 (January 1939), pp. 47–56; Charles Gayarré, *History of Louisiana*, 4 vols. (New Orleans, 1885), III, pp. 327, 337; Las Casas to Alcudia, La Habana, 2 March 1793, Carondelet to Las Casas, Nueva Orleans, 15 February 1793, AGI, Estado, leg. 14, doc. 7. For a Louisiana-bound ship bringing news from Port-au-Prince, see Las Casas to Campo de Alange, La Habana, 2 July 1792 and the enclosed *relación* of the French captain, AGI, Santo Domingo, leg. 1259.

49   Carondelet to Las Casas, Nueva Orleans, 15 February 1793, AGI, Cuba, leg. 1489; Marc de Villiers du Terrage, *The Last Years of French Louisiana*, trans. Hosea Phillips, ed. Carl A. Brasseaux and Glenn R. Conrad (Lafayette, La., 1982), p. 183; Joseph Villars Dubreuil, draft of speech to legislature, n.d., Joseph Villars Dubreuil Papers, Duke University Library; François Barbé-Marois, *The History of Louisiana, Particularly of the Cession of that Colony to the United States of America*, trans. anon. (Philadelphia, 1830), p. 198; Fiehrer, "Carondelet," p. 394.

people of color in New Orleans and other parts of the province, and they participated actively in the feverish plotting and exchanges of ideas taking place around them. Because of their social position and their access to the ideas and plots swirling about them in Louisiana as well as accounts filtering in from abroad in the 1790s, free color-eds represented an invaluable source of information for Governor Carondelet and other Spanish officials. By the middle of 1793, the governor reported to the Minister of State that "it is only through the free people of color that the government is able to obtain any news." The availability of this information aided the authorities in their campaign to round up, imprison, and deport "those who are most daring in their conversations and who attempt to spread their principles," whether speechmakers on soapboxes in the capital, emigrants, or locals who espoused revolutionary principles or seemed partial to the French. Beginning early in 1793, numbers of these dissidents were shipped from New Orleans to Havana and other places where they made up a first wave of political prisoners which would grow after the declaration of war between Spain and France.[50]

One of the prisoners who entered a Cuban *castillo* in 1794 was a free colored militiaman named Pedro (or Pierre) Bailly, a lieutenant in the *pardo* militia unit in New Orleans. An outspoken opponent of the unequal treatment of members of his caste before 1790, Bailly tangled on occasion with local authorities over these questions. In the fall of 1791, soon after the first news of the black uprising reached Louisiana, Spanish officials arrested Bailly and brought him to trial for publicly identifying himself with the revolutionaries in Saint-Domingue. Testimony of fellow militiamen accused the lieutenant of raising the issue of equality with white officers and of "encouraging others to follow the example of the free Mulattos of [Cap Français]." At a ball given by one of New Orleans's free blacks, he restated his support for the Saint-Domingue rebellion. Bailly went on to reveal that he and a circle of friends daily expected the arrival of word from the Cap in anticipation of striking "a blow like Guarico."[51]

50   H. E. Sterkx, *The Free Negro in Ante-Bellum Louisiana* (Rutherford, Madison, and Teaneck, N.J., 1972), pp. 79–83; Fiehrer, "Carondelet," pp. 484, 485.

51   Las Casas to Alcudia, La Habana, 14 May 1794 and enclosed "Testimonio

Though he escaped imprisonment in his 1791 trial, Bailly found himself before the bar once again two years later facing the same charge. This time, however, evidence against him shows the degree to which his views had evolved and deepened in the two years since the revolution in Saint-Domingue first became news. In Bailly's second trial, fellow officer Luis Declonet related that Bailly had approached him at the fort in Plaquemines in November 1793, just as the troops readied themselves for an expected attack of French forces. "Sir," asked Bailly, "what do you think of the news of the enemy?" Dissatisfied with the negative response to his question, Bailly proceeded to lecture his associate. Perhaps the French had gone too far in killing their king, he conceded, but in doing so they had accomplished the greater good of "granting men their rights." According to Declonet, Bailly then applauded at some length the French policy extending the principle of "a general equality among men, [including] us, people of color" to the Americas. His language echoes the imagery which Pierrot employed in his letters to Jean-François written around the same time:

> We have the title of "Citizen" in Saint-Domingue and the other French islands. [There] we may speak openly, just as any white person, and can possess the same rank. And do we have any of this under the present government? No sir—and it is unjust. All of us being human, there should be no differences: color should not differentiate us.

Other evidence cited Bailly's general insubordination within the militia and described several recent verbal confrontations between Bailly and white residents of New Orleans in which Bailly made similar statements. In one case, he and a white man almost came to blows, with Bailly promising his fellow combatant that "they would take him out feet first" if he dared to strike. Governor Carondelet, who found this behavior symptomatic of Bailly's "diabolical ideas of freedom and equality," shipped Bailly to a Havana prison on 24

---

de la Sumaria contra el Mulato libre Pedro Bailly," [Nueva Orleans, 1794], AGI, Estado, leg. 14, doc. 60; Caroline Maude Burson, *The Stewardship of Don Esteban Miró, 1782–1792* (New Orleans, 1940), 123n.

February 1794, where he remained confined with other political prisoners until the end of the war with France.[52]

The deportation of Bailly and a large number of others during the
Jacobin scare of 1793–94 in Louisiana did little to deter the progress
of republican ideas in the colony. The lengthening shadow cast by
the revolt in Saint-Domingue continued to affect profoundly Spanish
(and later French and United States) policy toward slaves and the slave
trade in Louisiana. In addition, blacks in Louisiana drew inspiration
and in some cases direct support from blacks and browns in Saint-
Domingue in attempts to mount an insurrection on the mainland.
In mid-April 1795, officials discovered that blacks in Pointe Coupee
parish, an area located some 150 miles from New Orleans and with
a heavy black majority, had organized a parish-wide conspiracy to
rise against local plantation owners. An intense month-long investigation turned up extensive evidence that the plot had originated among
French-speaking slaves on the plantation of Julien Poydras but had
spread up the Mississippi as far as Natchez. The observations of con-
temporaries show the Saint-Domingue rebellion to have been one of
the influences on the would-be rebels. While one Frenchman asserted
that an emigré from Saint-Domingue had sparked the revolt by having
"represented how happy those [blacks] of San Domingo were," others
blamed prevalent rumors, originating with Jacobin sympathizers,
of an emancipation decree which had been suppressed by planters
and the Spanish government. In the aftermath of the conspiracy, a
Spanish court sent twenty-six blacks to the gallows, sentenced others
to prison terms and hard labor, and transported two people including
Luis Benoit, a free Negro from Saint-Domingue, for their complicity.
Convinced that the presence of foreign blacks like Benoit had helped

52   "Testimonio ... contra el Mulato libre Pedro Bailly," AGI, Estado, leg. 14,
doc. 60; Roland C. McConnell, *Negro Troops of Antebelum Louisiana: A History of
the Battalion of Free Men of Color* (Baton Rouge, 1968), p. 28. Joao de Deus, colored
leader of a conspiracy in Bahia in northeast Brazil in 1798, expressed in quite similar
terms the same egalitarian ideas as Bailly and likewise called for a new society based
on the ideals of French republicanism. See Emilia Viotti da Costa, "The Political
Emancipation of Brazil," in A. J. R. Russell-Wood, ed., *From Colony to Nation: Essays
on the Independence of Brazil* (Baltimore, 1975), pp. 68–9.

to plant the seeds of sedition in Louisiana, Governor Carondelet immediately close the port of New Orleans to slave imports, and officials continued to enforce this ban until Carondelet's successor lifted it in 1799. With Saint-Domingue in mind, he also ordered authorities to crack down on inter-plantation mobility and visitation.[53]

More than fifteen years later, the black rebellion on Hispaniola figured prominently in a second uprising of slaves which came closer to succeeding. After Haiti became independent in 1804, Governor W. C. C. Claiborne, like Carondelet a decade earlier, acted "to prevent the bringing in of Slaves that have been concerned in the insurrections of St. Domingo," but lamented that despite his efforts and those of customs agents, "no effectual stop can at present be put to their introduction." In 1811, in St. John the Baptist and St. Charles parishes, between 200 and 500 rebel slaves marched on New Orleans, setting fire to plantations on the way. Authorities later identified Charles Deslondes, a driver and "free mulatto from St. Domingo," as one of the principal leaders of the uprising. Crushed by militia units under the command of Wade Hampton after repeated skirmishes, most of the rebels were hanged on the spot or beheaded, "their heads … placed on high poles above and below the city, along the [Mississippi] river, as far as the plantation on which the revolt began." While the nineteenth-century revolts of Gabriel, Denmark Vesey, and Nat Turner have overshadowed the Louisiana uprising of 1811, it proved the largest mass rebellion of slaves in the history of the North American continent.[54]

---

53   See the observations of Paul Alliot reprinted in James Alexander Robertson, ed., *Louisiana under the Rule of Spain, France, and the United States, 1785–1807*, 2 vols. (Cleveland, 1911), I, p. 119; Paul F. Lachance, "The Politics of Fear: French Louisianans and the Slave Trade, 1786–1809," *Plantation Society in the Americas* 1 (June 1979), p. 174; and Holmes, "Slave Revolt at Pointe Coupee," pp. 345–9, 352–61. For Carondelet's measures, see United States, Congress, *American State Papers: Documents, Legislative and Executive, of the Congress of the United States, from the First to the Second Session of the Tenth Congress, Inclusive, 1789–1809*, 2 vols. (Washington, 1834), I, pp. 380–1.

54   William C. C. Claiborne to James Madison, 12 July 1804, in Donnan, *Documents Illustrative of the Slave Trade to America*, IV, p. 663; Eugene D. Genovese, *From Rebellion to Revolution: Afro-American Slaves Revolts in the Making of the*

The mass emigration from Saint-Domingue following the black rebels' victory at Cap Français in the spring of 1793 scattered refugees of all descriptions throughout the Caribbean islands, but the ports of the United States received the largest number of any American territory. Visual and dramatic, the sudden arrival of thousands of refugees from the revolution in the French colony communicated a sense of the rebellion which printed accounts could not provide. The influx of the French emigrés made a strong impression on the minds of North American slaves and free blacks as they pieced together the details of the slave uprising in the Caribbean.

Before the events of 1793 forced French colonists to abandon Saint-Domingue, small numbers of people from the French islands decided to come north to escape the growing restlessness in the colonies. Some 200 emigré families reached Philadelphia in 1792. The same year, the Maryland legislature debated whether the "several inhabitants" of Saint-Domingue who had recently entered the state would be allowed to keep the slaves they had brought with them. By October 1792 a group of Saint-Domingue colonists had established a modest settlement along Virginia's Clinch River.[55]

In contrast to the occasional migrations from the French islands to the United States which occurred in 1791 and 1792, the evacuation of Cap Français and other cities the following spring instantly added more than 10,000 residents to the coastal cities of the new nation by late July 1793. The unexpected appearance of literally hundreds of vessels filled with destitute survivors of the attack on the Cap presented an vivid spectacle in ports both north and south. Some "20 odd" ships loaded with French passengers reached Norfolk, a city of

Modern World (Baton Rouge and London, 1979), p. 43; Gayarré, *History of Louisiana*, IV, pp. 266–8.

55   Monroe Fordham, "Nineteenth-Century Black Thought in the United States: Some Influences of the Santo Domingo Revolution," *Journal of Black Studies* 6 (December 1975), p. 116; *Laws of Maryland, Made and Passed at a Session of Assembly* … (Annapolis, 1792), ch. XVI; James Innis to Governor Lee, 27 February 1792, M. de Tubeuf to Governor and Council, 29 October 1792, in William P. Palmer and Sherman McRae, eds., *Calendar of Virginia State Papers and Other Manuscripts Preserved in the Capitol at Richmond*, 11 vols. (Richmond, 1875–93), V, p. 452; VI, pp. 112–13 (hereinafter *CVSP*).

about 4,000, in a two-day period in early July. By the end of the month, a total of 137 ships bringing refugees had dropped anchor in Norfolk, and residents reported the town "crowded with Frenchmen … [and] too many [French] negroes." Untold "hundreds" of black, brown, and white refugees arrived at Charleston during July and August, while in Baltimore, fifty-three ships with about 1,000 white and 500 black and mulatto immigrants aboard arrived between 10 July and 22 July.[56] As many of the French immigrants came with little but their clothes and a few scattered personal articles, the legislatures of Virginia, South Carolina, and Maryland appropriated relief funds in the late summer of 1793. Federal estimates of French-speaking immigrants "in distress" in 1794 found 400 fitting that description in Maryland, 350 in South Carolina and New York, and 290 in Virginia. Even the relatively small port of Wilmington, North Carolina, reported fifty-four whites and thirty mulattoes from Saint-Domingue "in the greatest possible want" in the fall of 1794.[57]

While the Saint-Domingue emigrés found sympathy in some quarters, numerous whites in the new nation viewed them with suspicion. In some measure, this uneasiness stemmed from a larger opposition to the French Revolution itself. But the greatest concern centered upon the lessons which such a visible French presence, either by design or by implication, might hold for North American slaves. Many white observers harbored little doubt that among French refugees and travelers lurked radicals determined to ignite slave rebellions in the South. The emancipation decree of the Civil Commissioners in Saint-Domingue sharpened these fears. In 1793, Jamaicans imprisoned two Frenchmen aboard a captured prize bound "to the American States." Because they were said to be "active Agents in forwarding

---

56 Frances Sergeant Childs, *French Refugee Life in the United States, 1790–1800: An American Chapter of the French Revolution* (Baltimore, 1940), p. 15; Thomas Newton to Governor, 9 July 1793, *CVSP*, VI, p. 443; Tommy L. Bogger, "Slave Resistance in Virginia during the Haitian Revolution, 1791–1804," *Journal of Ethnic Studies* 5 (April 1978), p. 89; Terry, "Impact of the French Revolution," pp. 43–5; Walter Charlton Hartridge, "The Refugees from the Island of St. Domingo in Maryland," *Maryland Historical Magazine* 38 (June 1943), pp. 103–7.

57 Childs, *French Refugee Life in the United States*, pp. 89–90.

the measures of the Civil Commissioners" in Saint-Domingue, Governor Williamson surmised that these characters "did certainly not mean to be idle where they were going."[58] "I should nearly as soon sleeped at the mast head, as among those disagreeable French from St. Domingo," wrote Ebenezer Pettigrew during a voyage from the West Indies to Charleston in the company of a group of passengers from Saint-Domingue. Though he sympathized with the situation of the refugees, Pettigrew nevertheless was "sorry there has flocked such a number into this country, to poison the minds still more of both white and black," and he predicted ominously that "anarchy, rapine, and plunder" would result.[59]

Because of the uncertainties attending the arrival of French speakers from the Caribbean, rumors about the seditious activities of French envoys took hold quickly and spread. Citing a Charleston source, a Boston newspaper reported in November 1793 that South Carolina officials had apprehended some French "emissaries" from Saint-Domingue with papers in their possession outlining "plans for a general insurrection of negroes in the southern states." In response to these allegations, the implicated parties, still angry because of their treatment in Charleston, charged that authorities persecuted them only because of their strong republican credentials and contended that their mysterious packet contained nothing more than routine diplomatic correspondence. "Americans of the South," they assured, "from the French patriots, the true republicans, you have nothing to fear."[60]

South Carolina officials nevertheless continued to cast a watchful eye on French travelers arriving at Charleston harbor. They exercised special vigilance toward blacks from the French colonies. Following a tip in October 1793, the city's committee of public safety arrested a black immigrant who bragged during the voyage from the Cap of "having himself massacred eleven whites" in Saint-Domingue.

58   Williamson to Dundas, 10 August 1793, C.O. 137/91, PRO.

59   Ebenezer Pettigrew to James Iredell, 4 July 1804, James Iredell Papers, Duke University Library.

60   Boston *Independent Chronicle*, 8 November 1793; Baltimore *Daily Intelligencer*, 4 December 1793.

Committeemen immediately turned over the alleged revolutionary to the captain of the vessel, whom they prohibited from re-entering Charleston harbor until he produced a notarized document from Cap Français affirming that he had safely returned his black passenger. Otherwise, South Carolina authorities threatened, the captain might face the gallows. Soon after this incident, Governor Moultrie issued orders calling for the expulsion of all free blacks and people of color from Saint-Domingue within ten days.[61] The following year, South Carolina's legislature made it illegal for any West Indian black to enter the state. Municipal financial accounts which list several entries for "passage of French Negroes" and "confining French Negroes" between 1793 and 1795 imply that blacks from the West Indies continued to arrive in smaller but significant numbers at Charleston harbor after the immense wave of the summer of 1793.[62]

Beginning in 1793, legislatures in states where numbers of "French Negroes" had arrived and settled followed South Carolina's example and passed laws restricting black immigration from the West Indies. A Georgia statute of that year severely limited the importation of blacks. A 1794 South Carolina law extended the ban on blacks from the Caribbean. In 1795, North Carolina's legislature prevented "any person who may emigrate from any of the West-India or Bahama Islands, or the French, Dutch, or Spanish settlements on the Southern coast of America, from bringing slaves into this State." The Maryland legislature adopted a similar provision in 1797. This concern with foreign-born blacks reached as far north as Boston, where in 1800 all black residents not born in the state were threatened with deportation.[63]

---

61   *Journal des Révolutions de la partie française de Saint-Domingue* (Philadelphia), 28 octobre, 9 décembre 1793, RSD.

62   Thomas D. Candy, *A Digest of the Laws of the United States and the State of South Carolina, now of Force, ... for the Government of Slaves and Free Persons of Color* (Charleston, 1830), p. 147; Terry, "Impact of the French Revolution," pp. 63–4.

63   *Digest to the Laws of the State of Georgia, from its Settlement as a British Province, in 1755, to the Session of the General Assembly in 1800, Inclusive* (Savannah, 1802), pp. 442–3; James Iredell, *Laws of the State of North Carolina* (Edenton, 1791), pp. 1–2, 10–11; *Laws of Maryland*, n.p. (1797); Higginson, *Travellers and Outlaws*, p. 208.

While Virginia's legislature passed no such laws, whites in the Old Dominion proved every bit as concerned with the problem of black immigration as their counterparts in other coastal states. In January 1795, officials in Norfolk met to discuss "the peculiar situation of the inhabitants ... on account of the frequent migrations of the negroes and people of colour," and sentiment for mass deportations appeared strong. In April and June Norfolk authorities refused landing rights to vessels from the eastern Caribbean with "French Negroes" aboard, and they expressed fears regarding French ships in the harbor with black sailors aboard. In the countryside, white residents remained unsettled because of the presence of "divers free negroes, who have come from the West Indies Islands and other places ... ranging at large."[64]

Despite such opposition, settlers from Saint-Domingue, including free *gens de couleur* and slaves, established their own community life and, because most of them saw their sojourn in the United States as only temporary, soon established communication with the islands in order to keep up with events as they transpired. The number of newspapers which immigrants from Saint-Domingue established in the United States between 1790 and 1800 specializing in intelligence of interest to French citizens reveals the importance and extent of this communication. Bold headlines promising "fresh news from St. Domingo" guaranteed a quick sale, and the volume of such news reaching North America was sufficient to keep French newspapers in business from Boston to Charleston at steady intervals during the 1790s. In late 1793 and into 1794, these newspapers carried extensive, if often inaccurate, coverage of the Spanish and British occupations of Saint-Domingue. On occasion these stories identify black travelers as sources of the latest accounts.[65]

---

64   "In Council," 14 January 1795; Thomas Newton to Governor, 28 April, 9 June, 11 June, 23 June, 29 June 1795; A. Dunscomb to Lieutenant Governor Wood, 18 September 1795, *CVSP*, VII, p. 475, VIII, pp. 254–6, 260, 274, 277–8, 298.

65   George Parker Winship, "French Newspapers in the United States from 1790 to 1800," *Papers of the Bibliographical Society of America* 14 (1920), pp. 82–91; *The American Star, or, Historical, Political, and Moral Journal* (Philadelphia), 4 February 1794, file in Historical Society of Pennsylvania, Philadelphia (hereinafter HSP).

The French also used the pages of their newspapers to continue their struggle over the issue of slavery. Beginning soon after their arrival in 1793, French emigrés were faced with conflicting accounts of the stance of the National Convention with reference to slavery, and an open debate ensued. By the fall, rumors that the Convention had abolished slavery swept the mid-Atlantic states with such force that a group of "citizens of color of Philadelphia" drafted a letter to the Convention, thanking the members for "breaking our chains" with "the immortal Decree wiping out all traces of slavery in the French colonies" and promising to "tell our descendants of [your] good deeds." But newspapers published in the same city discounted reports of abolition, asserting that "the National Convention has revoked the general liberty granted to the blacks ... [and] annuled its decree for the abolition of the negro trade."[66] While French slaveowners would not admit until May 1794 that the Convention had indeed abolished slavery in February, many slaves belonging to French owners in Pennsylvania, Delaware, Maryland, and other states had already taken matters into their own hands and slipped away from their owners, most likely in response to earlier rumors of the abolition decree. If some of the runaways attempted to return to the Caribbean, others probably found their way into local communities of urban slaves and free blacks.[67]

Centering as it did upon the large port cities of the eastern seaboard, the mass immigration from Saint-Domingue in 1792 and 1793 and the political discussions sparked by their arrival could not fail to attract the notice of black residents of those cities. In fact, this influx of political refugees from black rebellion in the Caribbean coincided with a rapid expansion of the black urban population in North America which took off in the 1790s. From Massachusetts to South Carolina, the increase in the numbers of blacks in the cities

66 *Journal de Révolutions de la partie française de Saint-Domingue*, 6 janvier 1794, file in HSP; "Les citoyens de couleur de Philadelphia à L'Assemblée Nationale," 24 [September] 1793, RSD; *American Star*, 6 February 1794.

67 For runaway notices covering several mid-Atlantic states, see *American Star*, 4 March, 1 April, 10 April, 1 May 1794.

was one of the key demographic trends of the early national period, and this migration carried with it important consequences for Afro-American social and institutional development. After the decline of slavery in Massachusetts, blacks moved to coastal areas in order to test their freedom, and by 1795 black residents of the state were said to "have generally, though not wholly left the country, and resorted to the maritime towns."[68] Philadelphia's black community grew at a rate of 176 percent between 1790 and 1800, compared to a 43 percent rise in white population. Baltimore's black population increased from 1,600 in 1790 to 5,600 ten years later. In Charleston, the number of free blacks tripled between 1790 and 1820, and there was a substantial increase in the slave population as well.[69]

Besides furnishing opportunities for maritime employment, port cities provided black residents the other benefits of access to the sea. One of these advantages was exposure to a wide variety of sources of information and news from abroad. News of particular interest to black urbanites often followed the routes of commerce which led inevitably through the Caribbean. Blacks in Newport for example showed much enthusiasm for the colonization project at Sierra Leone, word of which they received "from Africa, by way of the West Indies." In Charleston, slaves working in the office of Peter Freneau's avowedly republican *City Gazette*, which covered Caribbean news and issues and followed developments in the French West Indies, took for their own use 200 copies of each issue.[70] But neither secondhand accounts

68   "Queries Respecting the Slavery and Emancipation of Negroes in Massachusetts, Proposed by the Hon. Judge Tucker of Virginia, and Answered by the Rev. Dr. Belknap. Williamsburg, Virginia, January 24, 1795," *Collections of the Massachusetts Historical Society*, 1st ser. (1795), p. 206. *Cities, 1790–1825* (Charlottesville, 1967), p. 33; George C. Rogers, Jr., *Charleston in the Age of the Pinckneys* (Norman, 1969), p. 141.

69   W. E. B. DuBois, *The Philadelphia Negro: A Social Study* (Philadelphia, 1899), p. 17; Everett S. Lee and Michael Talli, "Population," in David T. Gilchrist, ed., *The Growth of the Seaport Cities, 1790–1825* (Charlottesville, 1967), p. 33; George C. Rogers, Jr., *Charleston in the Age of the Pinckneys* (Norman, 1969), p. 141.

70   Samuel Hopkins to Granville Sharp, 15 January 1789, in Hoare, ed., *Memoirs of Granville Sharp*, pp. 340–2; E. S. Thomas, *Reminiscences of the Last Sixty-Five Years, Commencing with the Battle of Lexington*, 2 vols. (Hartford, 1840), I, pp. 77–8.

nor newspapers could convey so powerfully the success of the black revolt in Saint-Domingue as the arrival of thousands of destitute refugees during the summer of 1793. In Baltimore, or perhaps in another place, one black observer named Newport Bowers showed a keen interest in the fate of these refugees and the country they left behind.

Even his name suggests that Newport was part of the generation of Afro-North Americans which gravitated toward the port towns in the post-revolutionary period. Born free in Massachusetts, Bowers most likely made a living either as a sailor or as a tradesman in the district of Baltimore's wharves.[71] Within a short period in mid-July 1793, more than fifty of the French ships which left Cap Français for the north loaded with refugees arrived in Baltimore. Precisely at the time of their arrival Bowers apparently decided to travel in the other direction and visit the Cap.

He must have found his new surroundings stimulating. During a residence of six months, Bowers witnessed firsthand the unfolding of freedom in the northern provinces following the rebel victories at the Cap, and he participated in the evolving if unstable self-government about which Pierrot boasted to Jean-François. Even if he arrived after the actual events which brought Saint-Domingue's largest city under rebel control, Bowers was present in October 1793 when Sonthonax issued his proclamation of freedom, the first of its kind in the Americas. He set up a "store" in Cap, from which he apparently engaged in frequent transactions with the sailors of incoming merchant ships, including many from North America. For whatever reason, sometime late in 1793 Bowers decided to return to the States, and made arrangements to travel aboard the *Juno*, a Baltimore vessel returning to that city which departed Cap on 4 December 1793.

In addition to Bowers, at least six other black passengers—French-speaking residents of Saint-Domingue—boarded the *Juno* that December day. While Bowers later described them as "people who had been given free by the Commissary and who had agreed to go with

---

71   Examination of Newport Bowers, 16 December 1793, in papers of *Juno* (1793), JHCVA Papers, JA. The supposition that Bowers resided in Baltimore is based entirely on the fact that he engaged a berth aboard a Baltimore-bound vessel in order to return "home." See below.

[Bowers] to America" and as "free Negroes and not the property of any Person on board," white members of the crew planned to stop over at Havana and sell them (and most likely Bowers as well) for a profit.[72] Neither Bowers's plan nor those of the crew members came to fruition. A British cruiser intercepted the *Juno* soon after its departure, and brought the vessel to Jamaica as a prize of war. Finding in favor of the captors, the vice-admiralty court sold the "French Negroes" for their account. Like John Paine, Pedro Bailly, and untold numbers of other masterless blacks during this period, Newport lost his freedom; the same court relegated him to the Kingston workhouse. He never completed his journey. The following March, a public auction sold off "Sundry old Cloathes belonging to Newport, who died in the Workhouse."[73]

The brief and abortive adventure of Newport Bowers indicates the perils of sea travel for blacks in general as it reflects the larger difficulties of direct long-distance communication in the late eighteenth century. Despite such obstacles, available evidence shows other English-speaking North American blacks were witnesses to the crucial early stages of the revolution in Saint-Domingue. Among a group of more than 200 male slaves transported from Port-au-Prince and presented for sale in Honduras in November 1791 because of their insurrectionary activity was Paul Williams, an English-speaking native of Charleston.[74] In fact, the crew of the very vessel in which Bowers took his final voyage included a cook described as "a Black man ... born upon the Coast of Affrica" who had shipped at the voyage's origination in Baltimore. In addition, Bowers's friend Bridgewater, who ferried him out to the *Juno* and was present at the time of capture, was tentatively identified by one crew member as "an Englishman," but may have been North American as well.[75]

72   See examinations of Bowers; George Parker and Robert Ellis, 14 December 1793; and James Fuller, 17 December 1793, ibid. It is instructive to note that the crew members were confident about making a sale at Havana despite Spanish injunctions against the purchase of "foreign" black creoles.

73   Balance sheet, 25 May 1795, ibid.

74   Entry of 18 November 1791, "Minutes of the proceedings of the Magistrates and Inhabitants of Honduras respecting a Cargo of Slaves from St. Domingo landed and left on English Key," C.O. 137/90, PRO.

75   Examinations of Parker and Fuller, papers of *Juno*, JHCVA Papers, JA. It

Other North American blacks journeyed to Saint-Domingue at the same time as Bowers, experienced the revolution there, and apparently succeeded in returning to their homes to the north to relate their experiences and observations. William Johnson of Philadelphia arrived at Cap Français in July 1793, about the same time as Bowers, as a cook aboard the *Rising Sun*, a Philadelphia vessel hired by two French merchants in that city. After leaving Cap, *Rising Sun* coasted to Port-au-Prince, where Sonthonax himself hired the vessel for the purpose of transporting money and documents. A British passenger testified that rumor in Saint-Domingue had it that the Philadelphia ship "was then and had been on a former voyage in the Employ of Monsieur Santhonax and his agent or agents in America."[76] A black cook from Richmond shipped aboard the *Nancy*, a ship which made at least three voyages to Saint-Domingue in 1792 and 1793. While in Saint-Domingue in the late summer of 1793, the *Nancy* touched at Port-au-Prince and Cayes, where a group of French passengers, including two mulattoes and two blacks, came aboard with intent to travel to North America.[77]

But the most intriguing of the scattered pieces of evidence of Afro-North American presence during 1793 comes from one of many letters among the papers of the *Fox*, a Petersburg, Virginia, ship bound from Cayes in southern Hispaniola to Baltimore in the late summer of 1793. In this letter, a young woman from Charleston informs her mother of her recent travels and experiences. She reports that the "master" to whom she was just recently sold to be "very Kind to me indeed," and that she has found a pleasant companion in "a Girl with the Same Master that Comes from New York." "I want for nothing," the letter continues, "but a letter from you to Know how affairs gos at home." At present, she and her friend are in Saint-Domingue, awaiting their

---

is not clear whether either of these individuals was sold along with the others or imprisoned with Bowers.

76   Examinations of Peter Torris, 25 November 1793, and William Johnson, n.d. [November 1793]; affidavit of James Patterson, 30 November 1793, in papers of *Rising Sun* (1793), JHCVA Papers, JA.

77   Examinations of David Crocker and Howland Powers, 25 October 1793, in papers of *Nancy* (1793), JHCVA Papers, JA.

owner's return to France. "This is a troublesome Country," she reports. "They are obliged to give Liberty to all the negroes to be Soldiers to keep the Country as there is no white men."[78]

As American crewmen placed Ginna's enigmatic letter in the sizable stack bound for North America, residents of Charleston and other places were reporting rumblings of slave unrest. In the South Carolina port city where pro-French residents celebrated Bastille Day with processions and toasts; where Citizen Genet arrived from France to rally support for the Revolution only weeks before the landing of the first refugees from Cap Français; and where French privateers recruited eager North American sailors to cruise against the British, whites began to detect signs of an imminent slave uprising as early as the fall of 1793. In addition to the many other public manifestations of French politics in Charleston, the same printed material which messengers carried from Cap Français across the border to the black troops in Spanish Hispaniola apparently arrived on the mainland. According to one French observer in October, "many copies" of Sonthonax's "proclamation of general liberty" circulated in the city. At the same time newspapers reported that Charleston's slaves had become "very insolent" and that "the St. Domingo Negroes have sown those seeds of revolt." By June 1794, when first word of the abolition decree of the French Convention arrived in Charleston, whites acted quickly to prevent this news from once again elevating the spirits of Charleston slaves. A meeting of 11 June considered the screening of all incoming vessels and other measures "to prevent any evil consequences from that diabolical decree."[79]

A series of fires in June 1796 raised questions among white Charlestonians, some of whom suspected "French Negroes" who

78   Ginna [?] to "Miss Polly Morgan at Mrs. Russel's Widow, No. 5 White point, Charleston," 28 August 1793, in papers of *Fox* (1793), JHCVA Papers, JA.

79   *Journal des Révolutions de la partie française de Saint-Domingue*, 28 octobre 1793; *New York Journal and Patriotic Register*, 16 October 1793, quoted in Treudley, "United States and Santo Domingo," p. 124; Nathaniel Russell to Ralph Izard, 6 June 1794, quoted in Ulrich B. Phillips, "The South Carolina Federalists, II," *American Historical Review* 14 (July 1909), p. 735; Terry, "Impact of the French Revolution," p. 80.

"intended to make a St. Domingo business of it." The following year, the example of Saint-Domingue and the presence of refugees directly influenced a plot to burn Charleston which "originated among the French Negroes" of the city. Authorities tried five French-speaking blacks for their part in the conspiracy, accusing them of intending "to act here as they had formerly done at St. Domingo." The court sentenced three of the conspirators to death by hanging and the two others to transportation, and local whites privately expressed relief that the plot was detected and "completely crushed" before "a single Negro of our Country" had become involved.[80]

Farther north, the mass evacuation of Saint-Domingue in 1793 brought similar tension to coastal areas of Virginia. Two Richmond slaves were overheard in July 1793 plotting to "kill the white people soon in this place" as had the blacks "in the French Island." In Goochland County, whites sensed a new tension in the air, "particularly since the arrival of the French."[81]

Whites in Portsmouth, who reported "many hundreds French negroes landed in this Town" as the second anniversary of the night of 22 August approached, feared for their safety because many of the French slaves were said to "belong to the insurrection in Hispaniola." In October, officials in the area discovered plans for an interracial insurrection in which conspirators intended to burn the French ships in Portsmouth and Norfolk. Given the prevalent rumor along the east coast that the Convention had freed all French slaves, this plot may reflect hidden layers of protest.[82] At the same time, Petersburg officials warned of the dangers of a possible uprising after a grand jury investigation of the "Disorderly Meetings of Negroes in the Streets on Sundays and their Nocturnal meetings and unlawful Night

---

80 New York *Minerva*, 16 July 1796, quoted in Terry, "Impact of the French Revolution," p. 102; Edward Rutledge to John Rutledge, Jr., 21 November 1797, John Rutledge Papers, Duke University Library; J. Alison to Jacob Read, 5 December 1797, Jacob Read Papers, Duke University Library; Lisle A. Rose, "A Communication," *William and Mary Quarterly*, 3rd ser., 26 (January 1969), pp. 162–4.

81 Deposition of John Randolph, 21 July 1793, E. Langhorn to Governor, 3 August 1793, *CVSP*, VI, pp. 452–3, 470.

82 Willis Wilson to Governor, 21 August 1793, *CVSP*, VI, p. 490; Thomas Newton to Governor, 1 October 1793, *CVSP*, VI, pp. 571–2.

Walkings." Slaves in Powhatan County engaged in the same kind of activity, stealing away to the woods at night to meet in an abandoned schoolhouse.[83]

In subsequent years, whites in Virginia continued to link slave unrest with the presence of refugees from Saint-Domingue. In 1795, Norfolk mayor Thomas Newton detected "the squint of freedom" in the eyes of some of the French Negroes whom, despite the Convention's abolition decree, United States law considered slaves. Officials once again considered a mass deportation.[84] The specter of Haiti appeared once again in 1800, when a group of conspirators led by Gabriel Prosser hatched plans for a rebellion of slaves in Richmond. But a severe rainstorm and flooding took out bridges and made roads impassable on the eve of the insurrection, and Gabriel and fellow rebels were executed after a trial whose details remain a secret to this day. An account in a Richmond newspaper, "deterred from a regard for the public safety and for the promotion of justice," stopped short of speculating upon whether Saint-Domingue may have figured in Gabriel's plan, but the author felt free to ask "what could be expected from the unfortunate blacks in our states from the example" of Toussaint Louverture in the French colony?[85]

As the decade of the 1790s drew to a close, blacks continued to apply to their local conditions the ideas of self-determination and antislavery which the Haitian Revolution unleashed. As far north as Massachusetts, the birthplace of Newport Bowers, black mason Prince Hall could proclaim the dawning of a new era "in the French West Indies." All over the Americas, slaves and free blacks shared Hall's fervent hope that recent developments in the French Caribbean finally signaled the long-awaited day when "Ethiopia [would] stretch

---

83   Minute Book, Hustings Court (1791–1797), p. 85, Petersburg Courthouse, Petersburg, Virginia; Robert Mitchell to J. Marshall, 23 September 1793, *CVSP*, VI, p. 547.

84   Quoted in Bogger, "Slave Resistance in Virginia," p. 92.

85   Virginia *Argus* (Richmond), 3 October 1800. For a full account of the Gabriel conspiracy, see Mullin, *Flight and Rebellion*, pp. 140–63. Only weeks before the Gabriel rebellion, President Adams lifted an embargo against trade with Toussaint's government in Saint-Domingue. See Epilogue.

forth her hand from slavery, to freedom and equality" for people of African descent throughout the New World.[86]

The downfall of slavery also appeared imminent to many white observers. Responding to the turmoil of the past decade, Virginian St. George Tucker launched a campaign to colonize Virginia slaves safely to other shores before the inevitable day of reckoning arrived. Tucker urged his readers to recognize that keeping slaves from striking blows for their freedom would only become more difficult as time passed. "We have hitherto placed much reliance on the difficulty of their acting in concert," Tucker observed, but recent events had proved decisively "that the difficulty is not insurmountable." Despite restrictive legal codes and other forms of repression, slaves had managed to maintain "a correspondence which, whether we consider its extent, or duration, is truly astonishing." Because future developments in the Americas would "continually facilitate communication," perhaps the time had arrived to do away gradually with the institution of slavery.[87]

For most white observers throughout the hemisphere, however, isolating the Haitian rebels presented a more workable solution. The revolution in Saint-Domingue and the recent wave of slave rebellions in other territories, they argued, indicated in stark terms the need to circumscribe the masterless Caribbean.

---

86 "Extract from a charge delivered to the African Lodge, June 24th, 1797 … by the Right Worshipful Prince Hall," reprinted in William Cooper Nell, *The Colored Patriots of the American Revolution, with Sketches of Several Distinguished Colored Persons* (Boston, 1855), p. 64.

87 St. George Tucker, *Letter to a Member of the General Assembly of Virginia on the Subject of the late Conspiracy of the Slaves, with a Proposal for their Colonization*, 2nd ed. (Richmond, 1801), pp. 10–11.

Epilogue

Soon after the earliest reports of the revolt in Saint-Domingue reached Jamaica late in 1791, an astute slave from one of the north coast parishes offered a caveat as his associates contemplated mounting a similar uprising in the British island. No matter how well conceived such insurrectionary plans might be, he cautioned, "while the whites were possessed of the communication with the Sea, the Negroes could do nothing."[1] At the turn of the century, the emergence of Saint-Domingue posed the possibility of an autonomous black presence on the sea which seemed impossible only a decade earlier. Toussaint Louverture naturally looked to "communication with the Sea" as a way to consolidate the revolution in the French colony. But the slaveholding powers in the Americas, in an effort to contain the spread of black unrest in the hemisphere, moved decisively to limit Saint-Domingue's contacts with the rest of the Americas by denying the black rebels access to the sea.

When Gabriel began to lay the groundwork for the Richmond conspiracy of 1800, Saint-Domingue stood on the threshold of independence. Under Toussaint's leadership, armies of ex-slaves defeated the Spanish occupation in 1796, and two years later claimed an even greater victory when British forces abandoned their costly five-year attempt to annex the French colony. Upon their evacuation, British commander Thomas Maitland negotiated and signed an unauthorized "secret convention" with Toussaint, promising to cease interfering in the affairs of Saint-Domingue in return for the black leader's promise that he would refrain from exporting revolution to Jamaica.

---

1 "Minutes of the examination of Duke," 11 January 1792, C.O. 137/90, PRO.

In the two years following this treaty, both the British and the Americans wrestled with the thorny diplomatic question of how to deal with Toussaint's regime. Toussaint, on the other hand, made conciliatory overtures to both nations in order to attract the trade which he needed to rebuild the colony after years of war. Spirited debates in London and Philadelphia finally produced a policy which met with the approval of both the British and North American governments. Britain and the United States consented to opening trade with the areas of Saint-Domingue under Toussaint's command and to support the colony's move toward political independence in order to cripple France's empire in the Americas. In May 1799, in another series of secret negotiations, Toussaint agreed to the conditions worked out weeks before by British and American representatives in Philadelphia. Far from aiding Saint-Domingue toward achieving a meaningful independence, however, Toussaint's powerful and worried neighbors would use this settlement to negate his ability to act with any degree of autonomy in regional affairs.[2]

In 1798 and 1799, while the Americans and the British busily debated Saint-Domingue's future, masterless people from Saint-Domingue appeared in ports from Philadelphia to Venezuela, bringing revolutionary ideas with them. The already heated deliberations of the Congress of the United States over the Alien and Sedition Acts, measures designed to exclude rebellious foreigners from the territory of the new nation and to suppress internal dissent, took on added urgency in June 1798. Word reached the floor of the House of a "dangerous mutiny" brewing among 250 to 300 blacks aboard French ships from Saint-Domingue anchored in the Delaware River just a short distance from Philadelphia. Military officials observed the crew of one "sloop of war manned only with negroes ... plying round all the other vessels which have negroes on board" in an apparent effort to land in defiance

---

2   For fuller treatments of the immensely complicated diplomacy during this period, see Logan, *Diplomatic Relations of the United States with Haiti*, pp. 64–111; Alexander DeConde, *The Quasi-War: The Politics and Diplomacy of the Undeclared War with France, 1797–1801* (New York, 1966), pp. 130–41; and Bradford Perkins, *The First Rapprochement: England and the United States, 1795–1805* (Philadelphia, 1955), pp. 106–11.

of regulations confining them to their vessels.[3] In May 1799, inter-racial crews from Saint-Domingue brought three French vessels into the port of Maracaibo on the Venezuelan coast under false pretenses and attempted to ignite a local rebellion against Spanish authority.[4] Later that year, the longstanding fears of white Jamaicans that the rebels in Saint-Domingue would export their revolution "by the help of the magick word Liberty" were almost realized. In December 1799, British officials executed Isaac Sasportas, a Jewish merchant from Saint-Domingue and partisan of the revolutions in France and the Caribbean, after finding him guilty of infiltrating the island in order to rally black support for an invasion from Saint-Domingue. Sasportas's instructions provided striking evidence of the potentially subversive nature of unregulated commerce: he arrived in Jamaica in the company of Spanish contrabandists from Santiago de Cuba; "frequented public Houses" in order to test "public opinion concerning [French] political views"; and met with maroon leaders.[5]

Observers critical of the apparent rapprochement with Toussaint reasoned that licensing ships to trade with Saint-Domingue would only make such episodes more frequent and add to the problem of slave control. "We may expect therefore black crews, and supercargoes and missionaries thence into the southern states," wrote Thomas Jefferson after President Adams lifted the embargo on trade with Saint-Domingue in 1799. "If this combustion can be introduced among us

---

3   United States, Congress, *The Debates and Proceedings of the United States Congress (Annals of Congress)*, 42 vols. (Washington, 1834–1856), 5th Congress (1797–1799), vol. II, col. 2057; Lewis Toussard to Secretary of War, 28 June 1798, reprinted in United States, Office of Naval Records and Library, *Naval Documents Related to the Quasi-War between the United States and France*, 7 vols. (Washington, 1935–1938), I, p. 149 (hereinafter *Quasi-War Documents*).

4   Manuel de Guevara to Antonio Cornel, Caracas, 31 August 1800, AGI, Caracas, leg. 97.

5   Parker to Spencer, 8 December 1799, in Corbett and Richmond, eds., *First Lord of the Admiralty*, III, pp. 282–3; Antoine Chaulatte to Minister of the Marine (translation), [1800], C.O. 137/105, PRO; John Wigglesworth to Duke of Portland, 26 December 1799, War Office Records, Class 1/Vol. 74, PRO (hereinafter W.O. 1/74, PRO); "Dispositions à suivre pour preparer la descente et s'emparer de l'Isle de la Jamaïque," n.d., C.O. 137/103, PRO.

under any veil whatever, we have to fear it." Echoing Jefferson, British admiral Hyde Parker, commander on the Jamaica naval station, registered "strong objections ... against this coloured communication." The Jamaica Assembly requested that colonial policymakers reconsider the pact with Toussaint since it would be "next to impossible" either to keep "improper and dangerous characters" from traveling between Jamaica and Saint-Domingue on trading vessels or to "withhold from our slaves, the knowledge of an authorized intercourse existing between our government, and rebellious slaves of the very worst description."[6]

Unable to dissuade their governments from cultivating commercial and diplomatic relations with the rebellious French colony, local officials attempted to ready themselves by resorting to familiar practices. In Jamaica, for instance, the Assembly passed strict licensing requirements for merchants and captains who chose to enter the trade with Toussaint. These regulations compelled captains to sign an agreement that they would not employ French sailors "or negroes, nor people of colour denominated mulattoes" and to file depositions with the customs immediately upon their return from Saint-Domingue, "lest Foreigners should be introduced in these ships under the character of Sailors." As a further safeguard against unauthorized communication, Jamaica's laws governing the trade between the British and French islands obliged the Board of Police to inspect and clear all letters traveling aboard British ships in either direction.[7]

The secret articles of the May 1799 convention with Toussaint, however, contained more far-reaching and effective measures geared toward the same ends. Replying to critics of the treaty, the British

---

6   Thomas Jefferson to James Madison, 12 February 1799, reprinted in Paul Leicester Ford, ed., *The Writings of Thomas Jefferson*, 10 vols. (New York, 1892–99), VII, p. 349; Hyde Parker to Lord Spencer, 19 May 1799, reprinted in Julian S. Corbett and H. W. Richmond, eds., *Private Papers of George, Second Earl Spencer, First Lord of the Admiralty, 1794–1801*, 4 vols. (London, 1913–24), III, pp. 275–6; Jamaica Assembly, *Report from the Committee Appointed to Inquire into the State of the Colony* (1800), p. 15.

7   Jamaica Assembly, *Report from the Committee to Inquire into the State of the Colony* (1800), p. 48; Balcarres to Portland, Maitland to Balcarres, 4 June 1799, C.O. 137/102, PRO.

Secretary of State countered that the agreement furnished "the best security that can be obtained, against any communication between the Negroes of that Island" and those in other territories.[8] Private official correspondence reveals that Anglo-American policy toward Saint-Domingue aimed specifically at controlling black communication networks. In sharp contrast to their disagreement over a host of current diplomatic issues, Britain and its former colonies found "a common interest in preventing the dissemination of dangerous principles among the slaves of their respective countries," and agreed that "a principal danger to be apprehended from the liberty of the Negroes in St. Domingo" consisted in "the eventual increase of their navigation." British Minister to the United States Robert Liston, who attended the meetings in Philadelphia between officials of his government and their counterparts from the United States and helped to draft the treaty, summarized the deliberations, declaring that the British and the North Americans would work together "to put an end in toto, or as nearly as possible, to all maritime operations or exertion of any kind in the island of St. Domingo."[9]

If Toussaint won the war against the British in 1798, he clearly lost the peace. To the delight of his former enemies, he granted British and North American ships a shared monopoly on Saint-Domingue's foreign trade, in effect rendering the colony "dependent upon us wholly for their daily food, as well as the other necessaries of Life."[10] Although local vessels would retain control of some of the coasting trade between ports, the regulations of the treaty imposed "severe restrictions" upon the operation of these small boats as well as Toussaint's fledgling fleet of armed "ships of the state." These restrictions limited tonnage and size of crews, and, finally, prohibited any local vessel from sailing outside a radius of five leagues, or fifteen miles, of the coast. Boats which violated these terms were subject to seizure.[11]

---

8 Portland to Balcarres, 17 June 1799, C.O. 137/101, PRO.

9 "Articles" of Thomas Pickering regarding trade with Saint-Domingue, in Adams, ed., *Works of John Adams*, VIII, 639n.; Robert Liston to Edward Robinson, 4 November 1800, C.O. 137/105, PRO.

10 Portland to Balcarres, 17 January 1799, C.O. 137/101, PRO.

11 Thomas Maitland to Hyde Parker, 31 May 1799, C.O. 137/102, PRO; Edward Stevens to Christopher R. Perry, 11 October 1799, *Quasi-War Documents*, IV, pp. 279–80.

To Toussaint's dismay, British cruisers patrolling the waters off Saint-Domingue strictly enforced these limits on maritime activity. Naturally, British commanders paid the closest attention to the armed vessels under Toussaint's command. According to one British report, in December 1799 the black general's "force by sea" consisted of thirteen ships manned "chiefly with negroes" and close to 700 sailors.[12] If this fleet appeared modest by British standards, the Royal Navy nevertheless identified these ships and their black crews as potentially troublesome, and soon accused them of violating the stipulations of the convention. Sometime late in 1799, British officials reported the seizure of "a small fleet of war" under Toussaint's orders headed from Port Républicain (formerly Port-au-Prince) around to Jacmel on the southern shore. Alleging that the ships had strayed outside the fifteen-mile limit and had drifted dangerously close to eastern Jamaica, British warships forced these four vessels with more than 400 crewmen aboard into Port Royal as prizes. By February 1800 British ships succeeded in taking off the sea "between five and six hundred Sea-faring Men," who languished in overcrowded Jamaica jails as prisoners of war. Maintaining that these men would sign aboard privateers immediately upon their release and then attack Jamaica's shipping, Admiral Parker refused requests from both Toussaint and Governor Balcarres to have these sailors returned to the French colony.[13]

Parker staunchly opposed the treaty with Toussaint, and under his command, many British vessels zealously overstepped the boundaries of their authority. Not only did they intercept armed ships under dubious pretexts, but they harassed and seized smaller boats engaged in the coasting trade. Despite Toussaint's repeated pleas that "my ships be respected," the cruisers of the Royal Navy frequently preyed on droggers, forcing them ashore and, in some cases, making prizes of them.[14]

---

12   "List of General Toussaint's force by sea," [1 December 1799], *Quasi-War Documents*, IV, pp. 468–9.

13   Wigglesworth to Portland, 20 December 1799, W.O. 1/74, PRO; Henry Shirley to Edward Shirley, 21 May 1800, C.O. 137/104, PRO; Parker to Balcarres, 6 February 1800, C.O. 137/105, PRO.

14   "Extract of a Letter from Gen. Toussaint to Edw. Robinson dated 26 Fructidor an 8," Edward Corbet to Balcarres, 31 March 1801, C.O. 137/105, PRO.

Finally, the British and the other powers buttressed the effort to contain the black rebels in Saint-Domingue by reacting quickly to snuff out any sign of independent maritime initiatives from within the French colony. In Cuba in 1799 as in Jamaica the following year, officials blocked the sale of sizable schooners to envoys who had come from Saint-Domingue for the purpose of acquiring ships. Even the discovery of a small quantity of sail canvas hidden among a cargo of goods smuggled aboard a North American vessel indicated to British merchants trading in Saint-Domingue that Toussaint was surreptitiously planning some adventure at sea.[15]

The policy of containment initiated and carried out in the uncertain years between 1798 and 1800 succeeded in isolating Saint-Domingue from its neighbors, thwarting Toussaint's dream of rebuilding the colony after a decade of war and joining the family of nations on an equal basis. Within Saint-Domingue, these defeats seriously weakened Toussaint's base of support and ultimately spelled the downfall of his authority. In 1802 an envoy of Napoleon captured the black leader and banished him to prison in France as part of the new metropolitan government's attempt to re-establish slavery in the colonies.

Subsequent events, however, vindicated the faith of British poet William Wordsworth and Afro-American mason Prince Hall. As Wordsworth predicted in 1803 upon hearing of Toussaint's imminent death, "not a breathing of the common wind" has forgotten Toussaint; neither did his demise reverse the momentum of the revolution in Saint-Domingue. French soldiers, ravaged by yellow fever and constantly reminded of their own revolutionary heritage by the resistance of black troops, proved no match for ex-slaves fighting to preserve the freedom which had cost them so much. On 1 January 1804, Jean-Jacques Dessalines declared Haiti the second independent republic in the New World. Following independence, Haitians continued to support the cause of black liberation. The earliest issues of the *Gazette officielle de l'état de Hayti*, first published in 1807, commemorated the recent abolition of the British slave trade with a serialized account of

---

15   Marqués de Someruelos to Mariano Luis de Urquijo, La Habana, 6 August 1799, AGI, Estado, leg. 2, doc. 11; H. Shirley to E. Shirley, 21 May 1800, C.O. 137/104, PRO; Hugh Cathcart to Balcarres, 16 September 1799, C.O. 137/102, PRO.

the entire story, highlighting the role of William Wilberforce and other prominent abolitionists.[16] Residents of the black republic also maintained communication with blacks in other parts of the hemisphere. Despite the host of economic and political problems which plagued the new nation born of a revolution of slaves, Haitians made signal contributions to the movement for political liberty in Latin America.

As early as 1805, one year after Haitian independence, officials in Brazil prohibited blacks in the militia of Rio de Janeiro from displaying portraits of Dessalines.[17] After 1804, Haiti replaced Cuba as the focus of the complaints of British officials about slaves deserting Jamaica. One runaway slave who returned to the British island in 1818 testified that he had seen "from thirty to forty" runaways from Jamaica during his stay there, and he explained that sailors from Haiti frequently encouraged and aided escaping slaves. Some of these sailors may have been refugees from Jamaica or other places themselves. In June 1818, four black Jamaican sailors found themselves stranded in London after their discharge from the navy and applied to the Committee for the Relief of Destitute Seamen for aid in finding a way to return to the island. Two of them, however, looked forward to arriving home only because "it would facilitate their passage to St. Domingo," where they hoped to "secure work on a drogger or coasting vessel."[18] Occasionally, officials even discovered Haitians engaged in active organizing in the streets of Jamaica. In 1817, the Assembly accused one Thomas Strafford, a resident of Haiti, of having "circulated printed papers here of a most mischievous tendency," citing as evidence a pamphlet entitled "Reflections on Blacks and Whites."[19]

During the Spanish-American independence movements, Haitian leaders offered asylum to Simón Bolívar and other revolutionaries. In 1817, Bolívar outfitted vessels at Cayes with crews "of different

16 *Gazette officielle de l'état de Hayti* (Port-au-Prince), 7, 14 mai 1807, copies in British Library, London.

17 Luiz R. B. Mott, "A revolução dos negros do Haiti e o Brasil," *Mensario do Arquivo Nacional* (Rio de Janeiro) 13 (1982), p. 5.

18 George Hibbert to Lord Bathurst, [April 1818], J. Erokson to Henry Gaulburn, 17 June 1818, C.O. 137/146, PRO; Patterson, *Sociology of Slavery*, p. 263.

19 Jamaica Assembly, Sessional Papers, 28 November 1817, C.O. 140/100, PRO.

Nations and Colours" to cruise "against the Enemies of Venezuela";
many other ships sailing under the flag of Venezuela were actually
"owned and operated by natives of Hayti." During the same decade,
Spanish officials reported that black citizens of Haiti openly spoke out
in favor of independence as far away as Mexico. Spanish ships seized
copies of the Haitian newspaper *Le Télégraphe* on ships headed for
Spanish-American ports; even the title of the paper draws upon the
imagery of long-distance communication.[20]

Throughout the nineteenth and into the twentieth century, Afro-
North Americans have derived inspiration from the example of
Haitian freedom and maintained both direct and indirect contact with
Haiti. Charlestonian Denmark Vesey, who traveled to the Caribbean
as a cabin boy many times during his youth and actually spent some of
those years as a resident of Saint-Domingue, organized a conspiracy
of slaves and free blacks in 1822 at least partly by using Haiti as a reference point. Vesey and his lieutenants followed events in the new black
nation, passing newspaper articles from hand to hand. At Vesey's trial,
one co-conspirator testified that he "had the habit of reading to me
all the passages in the newspapers that related to Santo Domingo."
Claiming to have corresponded through black cooks who worked the
vessels trading between Charleston and Haiti, Vesey promised his followers that the Haitians would come to their aid if only they would
strike the initial blow for their freedom.[21] The 1820s also witnessed
the first wave of emigration of free blacks from the United States to
Haiti, and blacks continued to migrate to the black republic long after
the end of slavery.[22]

20   Examination of Antoine Louis Pellerin, 23 May 1817, C.O. 137/144, PRO;
J. Fray to John Bennett, Jr., 21 November 1816, C.O. 137/145, PRO; "Papeles que
remite desde la bahía de Santo Domingo el Comandante del bergantín Perignon," 12
March 1817, AGI, Estado, leg. 4, doc. 13. Eleazar Córdova-Bello, *La independencia
de Haití y su influencia en Hispanoamérica* (Caracas, 1964), pp. 115–70 summarizes
the role of Haiti in Latin American independence.
21   John Lofton, *Insurrection in South Carolina: The Turbulent World of Denmark
Vesey* (Yellow Springs, Oh., 1964), pp. 5–26, 73; *The Trial Record of Denmark Vesey*
(Boston, 1970), pp. 28, 42, 68, 70–1, 88, 93, 117; confessions of Bacchus and John,
n.d., Hammet Papers.
22   Floyd J. Miller, *The Search for a Black Nationality: Black Emigration and*

Nineteenth-century Afro-North American historians like ex-slave William Wells Brown characterized the revolution in Saint-Domingue as the pivotal event in the history of Afro-Americans. In the 1850s Brown delivered lectures on the subject, and his research on Toussaint Louverture and the history of Haiti took him into the archives of London and Paris. Up to the present day, Toussaint and the Haitian Revolution continue to occupy a central place in the cultural memory of blacks in North America. A century after Brown published his popular lecture on the revolution, Ntozake Shange discovered Toussaint as a child growing up in the Midwest in the 1950s, and this incident provides one of the memorable sketches in her recent work.[23]

Colonization, 1787–1863 (Urbana, Chicago, and London, 1975), pp. 74–82, 232–49.

23   William Wells Brown, *St. Domingo: Its Revolutions and its Patriots* (Boston, 1855); ibid., *The Rising Son; or, The Antecedents and Advancement of the Colored Race* (Boston, 1874), pp. 140–242; Ntozake Shange, *for colored girls who have considered suicide/when the rainbow is enuf* (New York, 1977), pp. 25–30.

Bibliography

Primary Sources

Manuscripts

Archivo General de Indias, Sevilla, Spain.

    Sección de Gobierno, Audiencia de Caracas, legajos 15, 94–97, 113–115, 153, 168, 180, 426, 472, 503, 505, 507, 514, 907.

    Sección de Gobierno, Audiencia de México, legajos 3024, 3025.

    Sección de Gobierno, Audiencia de Santo Domingo, legajos 953–7, 1027, 1028, 1031, 1032, 1110, 1253–6, 1259–64.

    Sección de Indiferente General, legajos 802, 1595, 2787, 2822.

    Sección de Estado, legajos 2, 4, 11, 13, 14, 58, 65.

    Papeles procedentes de la isla de Cuba, legajos 1434, 1435, 1439, 1446, 1460, 1465, 1468, 1469, 1474, 1486, 1488–90, 1499-A, 1508-A, 1526, 1528.

    Pasquines y Loas, 4.

John Carter Brown Library, Providence, Rhode Island.

    Révolutions de Saint-Domingue Collection.

Duke University Library, Durham, North Carolina.

    Bedinger-Dandridge Family Papers.

    Stephen Fuller Papers.

    William and Benjamin Hammet Papers.

    James Iredell Papers.

    Jacob Read Papers.

    James Rogers Papers.

    John Rutledge Papers.

    Joseph Villars Dubreuil Papers.

    William Wilberforce Papers.

Jamaica Archives, Spanish Town, Jamaica.
Records of the Jamaica High Court of Vice-Admiralty, 1793–1799.
National Library of Jamaica (Institute of Jamaica), Kingston, Jamaica.
MS 368, 1731.
Petersburg Courthouse, Petersburg, Virginia.
Minute Book, Hustings Court (1791–1797).
Public Record Office, London, England.
Admiralty Records, 1/244, 245.
Colonial Office Records, 71/14–20; 137/25, 87–91, 95, 96, 98, 101–5, 144, 145; 140/103.
Foreign Office Records, 4/11.
War Office Records, 1/74.
University of Virginia Library, Charlottesville, Virginia.
West Indian Travel Journal of Robert Fisher, 1800–1801 (typescript).
West India Committee Archives. Institute of Commonwealth Studies, London. England.
Minutes of the West India Planters and Merchants (microfilm, 17 reels), M–915.

Printed Primary Sources

Adams, Charles Francis, ed. *The Works of John Adams*. 10 vols. Boston: Little, Brown, and Co., 1850–56.
Burdon, Sir John Alder, ed. *Archives of British Honduras*. 3 vols. London: Sifton, Praed, & Co., Ltd., 1931–35.
Candy, Thomas D., ed. *A Digest of the Laws of the United States and the State of South Carolina, now of Force, … for the Government of Slaves and Free Persons of Color*. Charleston: A. E. Miller, 1830.
Commerce of Rhode Island, 1726–1800. 2 vols. Boston: Massachusetts Historical Society, 1915.
Corbett, Julian S. and Richmond, H. W., eds. *Private Papers of George, Second Earl Spencer, First Lord of the Admiralty, 1794–1801*. 4 vols. London: Navy Records Society, 1913–24.
Corre, A. *Les papiers du Général A.-N. de la Salle (Saint-Domingue 1792–3)*. Quimper: Imprimerie Ch. Cotonnec, 1897.
Debrett, John, ed. *The Parliamentary Register, or History of the*

Proceedings and Debates of the House of Commons. 45 vols. London: Printed for J. Debrett, 1781–96.

Digest to the Laws of the State of Georgia, from its Settlement as a British Province, in 1755, to the Session of the General Assembly in 1800, Inclusive. Savannah: n.p., 1802.

Donnan, Elizabeth, ed. *Documents Illustrative of the History of the Slave Trade to America*. 4 vols. Washington: Carnegie Institution of Washington, 1930–35.

Ford, Paul Leicester, ed. *The Writings of Thomas Jefferson*. 10 vols. New York: G. P. Putnam's Sons, 1892–99.

Franco, José Luciano, ed. *Documentos para la historia de Haiti en el Archive Nacional*. La Habana: Archivo Nacional de Cuba, 1954.

Great Britain. Board of Trade. *Report of the Lords of the Committee of Council appointed for the consideration of all matters relating to trade and foreign Plantations*. 6 pts. London: n.p., [1789].

Hoare, Prince, ed. *Memoirs of Granville Sharp. Esq., Composed from own Manuscripts and other Authentic Documents in the Possession of his Family and of the African Institution*. London: Printed for Henry Colburn, 1820.

Iredell, James, ed. *Laws of the State of North-Carolina*. Edenton: Hodge & Wills, 1791.

Jamaica Assembly. *Further Proceeding of the Honourable House of Assembly of Jamaica, Relative to a Bill Introduced into the House of Commons, for Effectually Preventing the Unlawful Importation of Slaves, and Holding Free Persons in Slavery, in the British Colonies*. London: Printed for J. M. Richardson and J. Ridgeway, 1816.

——. *Journals of the Assembly of Jamaica*. 14 vols. Jamaica: A. Aikman and John Lunan, 1811–29.

——. *The New Act of Assembly of the Island of Jamaica. Commonly Called. The New Consolidated Act, which was passed by the Assembly on the 6th of November—by the Council on the 5th Day of December—and by the Lieutenant Governor on the 6th Day of December 1788; Being the Present Code Noir of that Island*. London: Printed for B. White and Son, J. Sewell, R. Faulder, J. Debrett, and J. Stockdale, 1789.

——. *The Proceedings of the Governor and Assembly of Jamaica, in*

Regard to the Maroon Negroes; Published by Order of the Assembly. London: John Stockdale, 1796.

———. *Proceedings of the Honourable House of Assembly of Jamaica, on the Sugar and Slave-Trade. In a Session which Began the 23d of October. 1792.* London: Stephen Fuller, 1793.

———. *Report from the Committee of the Honourable House of Assembly, Appointed to Inquire into the State of the Colony, as to Trade. Navigation, and Culture. Ac. Since the Report made to the House, on the 23d of November, 1792.* St. Jago de la Vega: Alexander Aikman, 1800.

Jameson, John Franklin, ed. *Privateering and Piracy in the Colonial Period; Illustrative Documents.* New York: Macmillan, 1923.

King, Charles R., ed. *The Life and Correspondence of Rufus King; Comprising His Letters, Private and Official. His Public Documents, and His Speeches.* 6 vols. New York: G. P. Putnam's Sons, 1894–1900.

Konetzke, Richard. *Colección de documentos para la historia de la formación social de Hispanoamérica.* 3 vols. Madrid: Consejo Superior de Investigaciones Científicas, 1953–62.

Memoir of the Life, Writings, and Correspondence of James Currie. 2 vols. London: Longman, Rees, Orme, Brown, and Green, 1831.

Palmer, William P. and McRae, Sherwin, eds. *Calendar of Virginia State Papers and Other Manuscripts. Preserved in the Capitol at Richmond.* 11 vols. Richmond: James K. Goode, Printer, 1875–93.

La Revolution française et l'abolition de l'esclavage; Textes et documents. 12 tomes. Paris: Éditions d'histoire sociale, [1968].

Robertson, James Alexander, ed. *Louisiana under the Rule of Spain, France, and the United States, 1785–1807.* 2 vols. Cleveland: Arthur H. Clark Co., 1911.

The Trial Record of Denmark Vesey. Boston: Beacon Press, 1970.

United States. Congress. *American State Papers: Documents, Legislative and Executive, of the Congress of the United States, from the First Session of the First to the Second Session of the Tenth Congress, Inclusive. 1789–1809.* 2 vols. Washington: Gales and Seaton, 1834.

———. *The Debates and Proceedings in the Congress of the United States (Annals of Congress), First to Eighteenth Congress.* 42 vols. Washington: Gales and Seaton, 1834–56.

——. Office of Naval Records and Library. *Naval Documents Related to the Quasi-War between the United States and France.* 7 vols. Washington: Government Printing Office, 1935–38.

Whitaker, Arthur Preston, ed. *Documents Relating to the Commercial Policy of Spain in the Floridas with Incidental Reference to Louisiana.* Deland, Fl.: Florida State Historical Society, 1931.

Williams, Eric, ed. *Documents on British West Indian History, 1807–1833.* Port-of-Spain: Trinidad Publishing Co., 1952.

Reports of Travelers and Contemporaries

Atwood, Thomas. *History of the Island of Dominica.* London: Printed for J. Johnson, 1791.

Beckford, William. *A Descriptive Account of the Island of Jamaica.* 2 vols. London: Printed for T. and J. Egerton, 1790.

Brissot de Warville, J. P. *New Travels in the United States of America, 1788.* Translated by Mara Soceany Vamos and Durand Echeverria. Edited by Durand Echeverria. Cambridge: Harvard University Press, 1964.

[Carteau, Félix.] *Soirées bermudiennes, ou entretiens sur les événemens qui ont opéré la ruine de la partie française de l'isle Saint-Domingue.* Bordeaux: Pellier-Lawalle, 1802.

Chalmers, Colonel. *Remarks on the Late War in St. Domingo, with Observations on the Relative Situation of Jamaica, and Other Interesting Subjects.* London: Nichols and Son, 1803.

Clarkson, Thomas. *An Essay on the Impolicy of the Slave Trade, In Two Parts.* London: J. Phillips, 1788.

——. *The History of the Rise. Progress, and Accomplishment of the Abolition of the African Slave-Trade by the British Parliament.* 2 vols. London: Longman, Hurst, Rees, and Orme, 1808.

Considerations on the Present Crisis of Affairs, as it respects the West-India Colonies, And the probable Effects of the French Decree for Emancipating the Negroes. Pointing out a Remedy for Preventing the Calamitous Consequences in the British Islands. London: T. Gillet, 1795.

Cugoano, Ottobah. *Thoughts and Sentiments on the Evil and Wicked Traffic of the Slavery and Commerce of the Human Species.* Humbly

Submitted to the Inhabitants of Great Britain. London: n.p., 1787.

Dallas, R. C. *The History of the Maroons, from their Origin to the Establishment of their Chief Tribe at Sierra Leone.* 2 vols. London: A. Strahan, 1803.

Ducoeurjoly, S. J. *Manuel des habitans de Saint-Domingue.* 2 tomes. Paris: Lenoir, 1802.

Edwards, Bryan. *The History, Civil and Commercial, of the British Colonies in the West Indies.* 4th ed. 3 vols. London: John Stockdale, 1807.

[Equiano, Olaudah.] *The Life of Olaudah Equiano, or Gustavus Vassa the African. Written by Himself.* London: Isaac Knapp, 1837; reprint ed., New York: Negro Universities Press, 1969.

[Falconbridge, Anna Maria.] *Narrative of Two Voyages to the River Sierra Leone. During the Years 1791–1793. Performed by A. M. Falconbridge.* 2nd ed. London: L. I. Higham, 1802.

Hilliard d'Auberteuil, Michel René. *Considérations sur l'état présent de la colonie française de Saint-Domingue.* 2 tomes. Paris: Grangé, 1776.

Humboldt, Alexander von. *Ensayo politico sobre la isla de Cuba.* La Habana: Publicaciones del Archivo Nacional de Cuba, 1960.

——. *The Island of Cuba.* Translated by J. S. Thrasher. New York: Derby & Jackson, 1856.

——. *Personal Narrative of Travels to the Equinoctial Regions of America, during the Years 1799–1804.* Translated and edited by Thomasina Ross. 3 vols. London: G. Bell & Sons, 1831.

Kelly, James. *Voyage to Jamaica, and Seventeen Years' Residence in that Island: Chiefly Written with a View to Exibit Negro Life and Habits.* 2nd ed. Belfast: J. Wilson, 1838.

Lewis, Matthew Gregory. *Journal of a Residence among the Negroes in the West Indies.* London: John Murray, 1845.

Moreau de Saint-Méry, M. L. E. *Description topographique, physique, civile, politique et historique de la partie française de l'isle Saint-Domingue.* Nouvelle édition. 3 tomes. Paris: Société Française d'Histoire d'Outre-Mer, 1958.

Nation, Robert. *A Letter to a Member of Parliament: proposing a Plan of Regulations for the Better and More Compleat Manning the Navy.* London: Printed for the Author, 1788.

Perkins, Samuel G. *Reminiscences of the Insurrection in St. Domingo.* Cambridge, Mass.: John Wilson and Son, 1886.

Pinckard, George. *Notes on the West Indies.* 2 vols. London: Baldwin, Cradock, and Jay, 1816.

"Queries Respecting the Slavery and Emancipation of Negroes in Massachusetts, Proposed by the Hon. Judge Tucker of Virginia, and Answered by the Rev. Dr. Belknap. Williamsburg, Virginia, January 24, 1795." *Collections of the Massachusetts Historical Society,* 1st ser. (1795).

Thomas, E. S. *Reminiscences of the Last Sixty-Five Years, Commencing with the Battle of Lexington.* 2 vols. Hartford: Case, Tiffany, and Burnham, 1840.

Tucker, St. George. *Letter to a Member of the General Assembly of Virginia on the Subject of the late Conspiracy of the Slaves, with a Proposal for their Colonization.* 2nd ed. Richmond: H. Pace, 1801.

Valous, Marquis de. *Avec les "rouges" aux Iles du Vent: Souvenirs du Chevalier de Valous.* Paris: Calmann-Lévy, 1930.

Walton, William, Jr. *Present State of the Spanish Colonies: including a Particular Report of Hispañola, or the Spanish Part of Santo Domingo.* 2 vols. London: Longman, Hurst, Rees, Orme, and Brown, 1810.

Newspapers

Affiches américaines (Port-au-Prince), 1790.

Affiches américaines (Supplément) (Cap Français), 1790.

The American Star, or, Historical, Political, and Moral Journal (Philadelphia), 1793–94.

L'Ami de la Liberté, l'Enemi de la Licence (Port of Spain), 1791.

Barbados Gazette (Bridgetown), 1788.

The Charibbean Register, or Ancient and Original Dominica Gazette (Roseau), 1791.

Cornwall Chronicle and Jamaica General Advertiser (Montego Bay), 1791.

Courrier de la France et des colonies (Philadelphia), 1795.

Daily Intelligencer (Baltimore), 1793.

Gallagher's Weekly Journal Extraordinary (Roseau, Dominica), 1790.

Gazette Nationale ou le Moniteur Universel (Paris), 1790.

Gazette officielle de l'état de Hayti (Port-au-Prince), 1807.

Independent Chronicle (Boston), 1793.

Journal des Révolutions de la partie française de Saint-Domingue (Philadelphia), 1793–94.

Kingston Daily Advertiser (Kingston), 1791.

Morning Chronicle (London), 1792.

Nouvelles diverses (Port-au-Prince), 1790.

Royal Gazette (Kingston), 1787, 1791–93.

St. George's Chronicle and New Grenada Gazette (St. George's, Grenada), 1790.

Savanna-la-Mar Gazette (Savanna-la-Mar, Jamaica), 1788.

Virginia Argus (Richmond), 1800.

Secondary Sources

Books and Articles Published before 1900

[Aspinall, James]. *Liverpool a Few Years Since, by an Old Stager.* 2nd ed. Liverpool: A. Holden, 1869.

Barbé-Marois, François. *The History of Louisiana. Particularly of the Cession of that Colony to the United States of America: with an Introductory Essay on the Constitution and Government of the United States.* Translator anonymous. Philadelphia: Carey and Lea, 1830.

Bréard, Charles. *Notes sur Saint-Domingue, tirées des papiers d'un armateur du Havre. 1780–1802.* Rouen: Imprimerie de Espérance Cagniard, 1893.

Bridges, George Wilson. *The Annals of Jamaica.* 2 vols. London: John Murray, 1828.

Brooke, Richard. *Liverpool as it was during the last Quarter of the Eighteenth Century. 1775 to 1800.* Liverpool: J. Mawdsley and Son; London: J. R. Smith, 1853.

Brown, William Wells. *The Rising Son: or, the Antecedents and Advancement of the Colored Race.* Boston: A. G. Brown & Co., 1874.

——. *St. Domingo: Its Revolutions and its Patriots.* Boston: Bela Marsh, 1855.

Deschamps, Léon. *Les colonies pendant la Révolution, la Constituante et la réforme coloniale*. Paris: Perrin et Cie., 1898.

DuBois, W. E. B. *The Philadelphia Negro; A Social Study*. Philadelphia: Published for the University of Pennsylvania, 1899.

Gardner, W. J. *A History of Jamaica, from its Discovery by Christopher Columbus to the Year 1872*. Reprint, new ed. Frank Cass & Co., Ltd., 1971.

Gayarré, Charles. *History of Louisiana*. 4 vols. New Orleans: A. Honiker, 1885.

Higginson, Thomas Wentworth. *Travellers and Outlaws: Episodes in American History*. Boston: Lee and Shepard, 1889.

Hill, Robert T. *Cuba and Porto Rico, with the other Islands of the West Indies*. New York: Century, 1899.

Joseph, E. L. *History of Trinidad*. Trinidad: Henry James Mills; London: A. K. Newman and Co.; Glasgow: F. Orr and Sons, 1838.

Peytraud, Lucien. *L'esclavage aux Antilles françaises avant 1789. d'après des documents inédits des archives coloniales*. Paris: Hachette, 1897.

Picton, J. A. *Memorials of Liverpool Historical and Topographical, Including a History of the Dock Estate*. 2 vols. London and Liverpool: Longmans, Green, & Co.; Liverpool: Walmsley, 1875.

Sagra, Ramon de la. *Histoire physique et politique de l'isle de Cuba*. 2 tomes. Paris: A. Bertrand, 1844.

Steward, T. G. *How the Black St. Domingo Legion Saved the Patriot Army in the Siege of Savannah. 1779*. Washington: The American Negro Academy, 1899.

Valdés, Antonio J. *Historia de la isla de Cuba y en especial de la Habana*. La Habana: Comisión Nacional Cubana del UNESCO, 1964.

Williams, Gomer. *History of the Liverpool Privateers and Letters of Marque, with an Account of the Liverpool Slave Trade*. London: W. Heinemann; Liverpool: E. Howell, 1897.

Books and Articles Published since 1900

Abrahams, Roger D. *Deep the Water. Shallow the Shore: Three Essays on Shantying in the West Indies*. Austin and London: The University of Texas Press, 1974.

Acosta Saignes, Miguel. *La trata de esclavos en Venezuela*. Caracas:

Centro de Estudios Históricos, 1961.

Aimes, Hubert Hillary Suffern. *A History of Slavery in Cuba, 1511 to 1868*. New York and London: G. P. Putnam's Sons, 1907.

Anstey, Roger. *The Atlantic Slave Trade and British Abolition 1760–1810*. London and Basingstoke: Macmillan, 1975.

Aptheker, Herbert. *American Negro Slave Revolts*. New ed. New York: International Publishers, 1974.

Arcaya, Pedro M. *Insurrección de negros de la Serranía de Coro*. Caracas: Instituto Panamericano de Geografía e Historia, 1949.

Arcaya U., Pedro M. *El cabildo de Caracas*. [Caracas: Comisión de Cultura del Cuatricentenario de Caracas, 1965].

Armytage, Frances. *The Free Port System in the British West Indies; A Study in Commercial Policy, 1766–1822*. London, New York, and Toronto: Longmans, Green, and Company, 1953.

Aspinall, Arthur. "The Reporting and Publishing of the House of Commons' Debates 1771–1834." In *Essays Presented to Sir Lewis Namier*, pp. 227–57. Edited by Richard Pares and A. J. P. Taylor. London: St. Martin's Press, 1956.

Baralt, Guillermo A. *Esclavos rebeldes: Conspiraciones y sublevaciones de esclavos en Puerto Rico (1795–1873)*. Río Piedras: Ediciones Huracán, 1981.

Baur, John. "International Repercussions of the Haitian Revolution." *The Americas* 26 (June 1970): 394–418.

Beeman, Richard R. *The Old Dominion and the New Nation, 1788–1801*. Lexington: University Press of Kentucky, 1972.

Begouën-Démeaux, Maurice. *Memorial d'une famille du Havre: Stanislas Foäche (1737–1806)*. Paris: Larose, 1951.

Besson, Maurice. "La police des noirs sous Louis XVI en France." *Revue de l'histoire des colonies françaises* 21 (juillet–août 1928): 433–46.

Blume, Helmut. *The Caribbean Islands*. Translated by Johannes Maczewski and Ann Norton. London: Longman, 1974.

Bogger, Tommy L. "Slave Resistance in Virginia during the Haitian Revolution." *Journal of Ethnic Studies* 5 (April 1978): 86–100.

Boyd, Thomas. *Light-horse Harry Lee*. New York and London: Charles Scribner's Sons, 1931.

Brathwaite, Edward. *The Development of Creole Society in Jamaica 1770–1820*. London: Oxford University Press, 1971.

Brutus, Edner. *Révolution dans Saint-Domingue*. 2 tomes. [Belgium]: n.p., n.d.

Buckley, Roger Norman. *Slaves in Red Coats: The British West India Regiments, 1795–1815*. New Haven and London: Yale University Press, 1979.

Burns, Sir Alan. *History of the British West Indies*. London: George Allen & Unwin, 1954.

Burson, Caroline Maude. *The Stewardship of Don Esteban Miró, 1782–1792*. New Orleans: American Printing Co., 1940.

Callahan, William J., Jr. "La propaganda, la sedición y la Revolución Francesa en la Capitanía General de Venezuela (1789–1796)." *Boletín histórico* (Caracas) 14 (mayo de 1967): 177–205.

Carroll, Joseph Cephas. *Slave Insurrections in the United States, 1800–1865*. Boston: Chapman & Grimes, 1938.

Childs, Frances S. *French Refugee Life in the United States, 1790–1800: An American Chapter of the French Revolution*. Baltimore: The Johns Hopkins University Press, 1940.

Christelow, Allan. "Contraband Trade between Jamaica and the Spanish Main, and the Free Port Act of 1766." *Hispanic American Historical Review* 22 (May 1942): 309–43.

Clarke, Colin G. *Kingston, Jamaica: Urban Development and Social Change, 1692–1962*. Berkeley, Los Angeles, and London: University of California Press, 1975.

Coatsworth, John H. "American Trade with European Colonies in the Caribbean and South America, 1790–1812." *William and Mary Quarterly*, 3rd ser., 24 (April 1967): 243–66.

Córdova-Bello, Eleazar. *La independencia de Haiti y su influencia en Hispanoamérica*. Caracas: Instituto Panamericano de Geografía e Historia, 1964.

Coupland, Reginald. *The British Anti-Slavery Movement*. London: Frank Cass & Co., 1964.

Cox, Edward L. *Free Coloreds in the Slave Societies of St. Kitts and Grenada. 1763–1833*. Knoxville: University of Tennessee Press, 1984.

Craton, Michael. *Testing the Chains: Resistance to Slavery in the British West Indies.* Ithaca and London: Cornell University Press, 1982.

Curtin, Philip D. *The Atlantic Slave Trade: A Census.* Madison, Milwaukee, and London: University of Wisconsin Press, 1969.

Davis, David Brion. *The Problem of Slavery in the Age of Revolution. 1770–1823.* Ithaca and London: Cornell University Press, 1975.

Debien, Gabriel. "Les colons de Saint-Domingue refugies à Cuba (1793–1815)." *Revista de Indias* 13 (octubre–diciembre de 1953): 559–605.

——. "Les colons de Saint-Domingue refugies à Cuba (1793–1815) (Conclusión)." *Revista de Indias* 14 (enero–junio de 1954): 11–36.

——. *Études antillaises (XVIIIe siècle).* Paris: Librairie Armand Colin, 1956.

——. "Gens de couleur libres et colons de Saint-Domingue devant la Constituante (1789–mars 1790)." *Revue d'histoire de l'Amérique française* 4 (décembre 1950): 393–426.

——. "Le marronage aux Antilles françaises au XVIIIe siècle." *Caribbean Studies* 6 (October 1966): 3–41.

——. "Les marrons de Saint-Domingue en 1764." *Jamaican Historical Review* 6 (1966): 9–20.

——. *Plantations et esclaves à Saint-Domingue.* Dakar: Publications de la Section d'Histoire, 1962.

DeConde, Alexander. *The Quasi-War: The Politics and Diplomacy of the Undeclared War with France, 1797–1801.* New York: Charles Scribner's Sons, 1966.

Deerr, Noel. *The History of Sugar.* 2 vols. London: Chapman and Hall, 1949–50.

Din, Gilbert C. "Proposals and Plans for Colonization in Spanish Louisiana, 1787–1790." *Louisiana History* 11 (Summer 1970): 197–213.

Domínguez, Jorge I. *Insurrection or Loyalty; The Breakdown of the Spanish American Empire.* Cambridge, Mass. and London: Harvard University Press, 1980.

Dunn, Richard S. *Sugar and Slaves: The Rise of the Planter Class in the English West Indies, 1624–1713.* Chapel Hill: University of North Carolina Press, 1972.

Elliott, Marianne. *Partners in Revolution: The United Irishmen and*

France. New Haven and London: Yale University Press, 1982.

Farmer, Henry George. *Military Music.* London: Parrish, 1950.

Fisher, Ruth Aima. "Manuscript Materials Bearing on the Negro in British Archives." *Journal of Negro History* 27 (January 1942): 83–93.

Foner, Eric. *Politics and Ideology in the Age of the Civil War.* Oxford, New York, Toronto, and Melbourne: Oxford University Press, 1980.

Fordham, Monroe. "Nineteenth-Century Black Thought in the United States: Some Influences of the Santo Domingo Revolution." *Journal of Black Studies* 6 (December 1975): 115–126.

Fouchard, Jean. *Les marrons de la liberté.* Paris: Éditions de l'École, 1972.

——. *Les marrons du syllabaire.* Port-au-Prince: H. Deschamps, 1953.

——. et Debien, Gabriel. "Aspects de l'esclavage aux Antilles françaises: le petit marronage à Saint-Domingue autour du Cap (1790–1791)." *Cahiers des Amériques Latines: série "Sciences de l'homme"* 3 (janvier–juin 1969): 31–67.

Franco, José Luciano. "La conspiración de Morales." In *Ensayos históricos,* pp. 95–100. La Habana: Editorial de Ciencias Sociales, 1974.

——. *Las minas de Santiago del Prado y la rebelión de los cobreros, 1530–1800.* La Habana: Editorial de Ciencias Sociales, 1975.

Furness, A. E. "The Maroon War of 1795." *Jamaican Historical Review* 5 (November 1965): 30–49.

García Chuecos, Hector. "Una insurrección de negros en los dias de la colonia." *Revista de historia de América* 29 (junio de 1950): 67–76.

Garrett, Mitchell Bennett. *The French Colonial Question, 1789–1791.* Ann Arbor: George Wahr, 1916.

Gaspar, David Barry. "A Dangerous Spirit of Liberty: Slave Rebellion in the West Indies during the 1730s." *Cimarrons* 1 (1981): 79–91.

Geggus, David Patrick. "From His Most Catholic Majesty to the Godless *République:* The *"Volte-Face"* of Toussaint Louverture and the Ending of Slavery in Saint-Domingue." *Revue française d'histoire d'Outre-Mer* 65 (1978): 481–99.

——. "Jamaica and the Saint Domingue Slave Revolt, 1791–1793." *The Americas* 38 (October 1981): 219–33.

——. *Slavery, War, and Revolution: The British Occupation of Saint Domingue 1793–1798.* London: Oxford University Press, 1982.

Genovese, Eugene D. *From Rebellion to Revolution: Afro-American Slave Revolts in the Making of the Modern World.* Baton Rouge and London: Louisiana State University Press, 1979.

George, Carol V. R. *Segregated Sabbaths: Richard Allen and the Emergence of Independent Black Churches, 1760–1840.* New York: Oxford University Press, 1973.

Gershoy, Leo. *The French Revolution and Napoleon.* New York: Appleton-Century-Crofts, 1964.

Gipson, Lawrence Henry. *The British Empire before the American Revolution.* 15 vols. New York: Alfred A. Knopf, 1966–70.

Goslinga, Cornelis Christiaan. *Emancipatie en emancipator: de geschiedenis van de slavernij op de Benedenwindse eilanden en van het werk der bevrijding.* Assen: Van Gorcum & Comp., [1956].

——. *A Short History of the Netherlands Antilles and Surinam.* The Hague, Boston, and London: Martinus Nijhoff, 1979.

Goveia, Elsa. *Slave Society in the British Leeward Islands at the End of the Eighteenth Century.* New Haven: Yale University Press, 1965.

Greene, Lorenzo Johnston. *The Negro in Colonial New England.* New York: Columbia University Press, 1942.

Guerra y Sánchez, Ramiro. *Sugar and Society in the Caribbean: An Economic History of Cuban Agriculture.* New Haven and London: Yale University Press, 1964.

Haring, Clarence H. *The Buccaneers in the West Indies in the XVII Century.* London: Methuen & Co., 1910.

Harris, Sheldon H. *Paul Cuffe: Black America and the African Return.* New York: Simon and Schuster, 1972.

Hartridge, Walter Charlton. "The Refugees from the Island of St. Domingo in Maryland." *Maryland Historical Magazine* 38 (June 1943): 103–22.

Heuman, Gad J. *Between Black and White: Race, Politics, and the Free Coloreds in Jamaica, 1792–1865.* Westport: Greenwood Press, 1981.

Hill, Christopher. "Radical Pirates?" In *The Origins of Anglo-American Radicalism,* pp. 17–32. Edited by Margaret Jacob and James Jacob. London, Boston, and Sydney: George Allen & Unwin, 1984.

———. *The World Turned Upside Down: Radical Ideas during the English Revolution*. London: Maurice Temple Smith Ltd., 1972.

Holmes, Jack D. L. "The Abortive Slave Revolt at Pointe Coupée, Louisiana, 1795." *Louisiana History* 11 (Fall 1970): 341–62.

———. *Honor and Fidelity: The Louisiana Infantry Regiment and the Louisiana Militia Companies, 1766–1821*. Birmingham, Al.: By the Author, 1965.

Jackson, Melvin H. *Privateers in Charleston, 1793–1796: An Account of a French Palatinate in South Carolina*. Washington: Smithsonian Institution Press, 1969.

James, C. L. R. *The Black Jacobins: Toussaint L'Ouverture and the San Domingo Revolution*. 2nd ed., rev. New York: Vintage, 1963.

———. *Mariners, Renegades, and Castaways: The Story of Herman Melville and the World We Live In*. New York: By the Author, 1953.

Katzin, Margaret Fisher. "The Jamaican Country Higgler." *Social and Economic Studies* 8 (December 1959): 421–35.

King, James Ferguson. "Evolution of the Free Slave Trade Principle in Spanish Colonial Administration." *Hispanic American Historical Review* 22 (February 1942): 34–56.

Kiple, Kenneth F. *Blacks in Colonial Cuba, 1774–1899*. Gainesville: University of Florida Press, 1976.

Klein, Herbert S. *The Middle Passage: Comparative Studies in the Atlantic Slave Trade*. Princeton: Princeton University Press, 1978.

Kuethe, Allan J. "The Status of the Free *Pardo* in the Disciplined Militia of New Granada." *Journal of Negro History* 56 (April 1971): 105–17.

Lachance, Paul F. "The Politics of Fear: French Louisianans and the Slave Trade, 1786–1809." *Plantation Society in the Americas* 1 (June 1979): 162–97.

Landers, Jane. "Spanish Sanctuary: Fugitives in Florida, 1687–1790." *Florida Historical Quarterly* 62 (January 1984): 296–313.

Leal, Ildefonso. "La aristocracia criolla venezolana y el Código Negrero de 1789." *Revista de historia* (Caracas) 6 (febrero de 1961): 61–81.

Lee, Everett S. and Lalli, Michael. "Population." In *The Growth of the Seaport Cities, 1790–1825*, pp. 25–37. Edited by David T. Gilchrist. Charlottesville: University Press of Virginia, 1967.

Lefebvre, Georges. *The Great Fear of 1789: Rural Panic in Revolutionary France.* Translated by Joan White. New York: Vintage, 1973.

Lémery, Henry. *La Révolution française à la Martinique.* Paris: Larose, 1936.

Lemisch, Jesse. "Jack Tar in the Streets: Merchant Seamen in the Politics of Revolutionary America." *William and Mary Quarterly,* 3rd ser., 25 (July 1968): 371–407.

Léon, Pierre. *Marchands et spéculateurs dans le monde antillais du XVIIIe siècle; les Dolle et les Raby.* Paris: Société d'édition "Les Belles Lettres," 1963.

Liljegren, Ernest R. "Jacobinism in Spanish Louisiana, 1792–1797." *Louisiana Historical Quarterly* 22 (January 1939): 47–97.

Linebaugh, Peter. "What If C. L. R. James Had Met E. P. Thompson in 1792?" *Urgent Tasks* 12 (Summer 1981): 108–10.

Link, Eugene Perry. *Democratic-Republican Societies, 1790–1800.* Morningside Heights, N.Y.: Columbia University Press, 1942.

Lofton, John. *Insurrection in South Carolina: The Turbulent World of Denmark Vesey.* Yellow Springs, Oh.: Antioch Press, 1964.

Logan, Rayford W. *The Diplomatic Relations of the United States with Haiti, 1776–1891.* Chapel Hill: University of North Carolina Press, 1941.

Lowenthal, David. *West Indian Societies.* London, New York, and Toronto: Oxford University Press, 1972.

Lynch, John. *Spanish Colonial Administration, 1782–1810: The Intendant System in the Viceroyalty of Río de la Plata.* London: University of London Press, 1958.

McCloy, Shelby T. *The Negro in France.* Lexington: University Press of Kentucky, 1960.

McConnell, Roland C. *Negro Troops of Antebellum Louisiana: A History of the Battalion of Free Men of Color.* Baton Rouge: Louisiana State University Press, 1968.

MacInnes, Charles Malcolm. "Bristol and the Slave Trade." In *Bristol in the Eighteenth Century,* pp. 161–84. Edited by Patrick McGrath. Bristol: David and Charles, 1972.

——. *A Gateway of Empire.* London: Arrowsmith, 1939.

Manigat, Leslie. "The Relationship between Marronage and Slave

Revolts and Revolution in St-Domingue-Haiti." In *Comparative Perspectives on Slavery in New World Plantation Societies*, pp. 420–38. Edited by Vera Rubin and Arthur Tuden. New York: New York Academy of Sciences, 1977.

Metcalf, George. *Royal Government and Political Conflict in Jamaica. 1729–1783*. London: Longmans, 1965.

Miller, Floyd J. *The Search for a Black Nationality: Black Emigration and Colonization, 1787–1863*. Urbana, Chicago, and London: University of Illinois Press, 1975.

Mintz, Sidney, and Hall, Douglas. "The Origins of the Jamaican Internal Marketing System." *Yale University Publications in Anthropology* No. 57, 1960.

Montague, Ludwell Lee. *Haiti and the United States, 1714–1938*. Durham: Duke University Press, 1940.

Moreno Fraginals, Manuel. *The Sugarmill: The Socioeconomic Complex of Sugar in Cuba 1760–1860*. Translated by Cedric Belfrage. New York and London: Monthly Review Press, 1976.

Mörner, Magnus. *Race Mixture in the History of Latin America*. Boston: Little, Brown and Co., 1967.

Mott, Luiz R. B. "A revolução dos negros do Haiti e o Brasil." *Mensario do Arquivo Nacional* (Rio de Janeiro) 13 (1982): 3–10.

Mullin, Gerald W. *Flight and Rebellion: Slave Resistance in Eighteenth-Century Virginia*. New York: Oxford University Press, 1972.

Nash, Gary B. *The Urban Crucible: Social Change, Political Consciousness, and the Origins of the American Revolution*. Cambridge and London: Harvard University Press, 1979.

Nelson, George H. "Contraband Trade under the Asiento." *American Historical Review* 51 (October 1945): 55–67.

Nicholls, David. *From Dessalines to Duvalier: Race, Colour, and National Independence in Haiti*. Cambridge: Cambridge University Press, 1979.

Ott, Thomas O. *The Haitian Revolution, 1789–1804*. Knoxville: University of Tennessee Press, 1973.

Packwood, Cyril Outerbridge. Chained on the Rock: Slavery in Bermuda. New York: Eliseo Torres; Bermuda: Baxter's Ltd., 1975.

Pares, Richard. "The Manning of the Navy in the West Indies,

1702–63." *Transactions of the Royal Historical Society*, 4th ser., 20 (1937): 31–60.

——. *Merchants and Planters.* Cambridge: Cambridge University Press, 1960.

——. *Yankees and Creoles: The Trade between North America and the West Indies before the American Revolution.* Cambridge: Harvard University Press, 1956.

Patterson, Orlando. *The Sociology of Slavery: An Analysis of the Origins. Development, and Structure of Negro Slave Society in Jamaica.* Rutherford, Madison, and Teaneck: Farleigh Dickinson University Press, 1967.

Perkins, Bradford. *The First Rapprochement: England and the United States, 1795–1805.* Philadelphia: University of Pennsylvania Press, 1955.

Phillips, Ulrich B. "The South Carolina Federalists, II." *American Historical Review* 14 (July 1909): 731–43.

Pitman, Frank Wesley. *The Development of the British West Indies, 1700–1763.* New Haven: Yale University Press, 1917.

Price, Richard, ed. *Maroon Societies: Rebel Slave Communities in the Americas.* Baltimore: The Johns Hopkins University Press, 1979.

Quarles, Benjamin. *The Negro in the American Revolution.* Chapel Hill: University of North Carolina Press, 1961.

Ragatz, Lowell Joseph. *The Fall of the Planter Class in the British Caribbean, 1763–1833.* New York and London: Century, 1928.

Reinecke, John E. "Trade Jargons and Creole Dialects as Marginal Languages." *Social Forces* 17 (October 1938): 107–18.

Resnick, Daniel P. "The *Société des Amis des Noirs* and the Abolition of Slavery." *French Historical Studies* 7 (Fall 1972): 558–69.

Roberts, George W. *The Population of Jamaica.* Cambridge: Cambridge University Press, 1957.

Rogers, George C., Jr. *Charleston in the Age of the Pinckneys.* Norman: University of Oklahoma Press, 1969.

Rogers, H. C. B. *The British Army of the Eighteenth Century.* New York: Hippocrene, 1977.

Rose, Lisle A. "A Communication." *William and Mary Quarterly*, 3rd ser., 26 (January 1969): 162–4.

Rose, R. Barrie. "A Liverpool Sailors' Strike in the Eighteenth Century." *Transactions of the Lancashire and Cheshire Antiquarian Society* 68 (1959): 85–92.

Rout, Leslie B. *The African Experience in Spanish America: 1502 to the Present Day.* Cambridge, London, New York, and Melbourne: Cambridge University Press, 1976.

Rydjord, John. *Foreign Interest in the Independence of New Spain: An Introduction to the War for Independence.* Durham: Duke University Press, 1935.

Sánchez-Albornoz, Nicolás. *The Population of Latin America: A History.* Translated by W. A. R. Richardson. Berkeley, Los Angeles, and London: University of California Press, 1974.

Sanz Tapia, Angel. *Los militares emigrados y los prisoneros franceses en Venezuela durante la guerra contra la Revolución: Un aspecto fundamental de la época de la preëmancipación.* Caracas: Instituto Panamericano de Geografía e Historia, 1977.

Shange, Ntozake. *for colored girls who have considered suicide/when the rainbow is enuf.* New York: Macmillan, 1977.

Sheridan, Richard B. "The Jamaica Slave Insurrection Scare of 1776 and the American Revolution." *Journal of Negro History* 61 (July 1976): 290–308.

———. *Sugar and Slavery: An Economic History of the British West Indies.* Baltimore: The Johns Hopkins University Press, 1973.

Siebert, Wilbur H. *The Legacy of the American Revolution to the British West Indies and Bahamas: A Chapter out of the History of the American Loyalists.* Columbus: Ohio State University, 1913.

Sterkx, H. E. *The Free Negro in Ante-Bellum Louisiana.* Rutherford, Madison, and Teaneck: Farleigh Dickinson University Press, 1972.

Stoddard, T. Lothrop. *The French Revolution in San Domingo.* Boston and New York: Houghton Mifflin, 1914.

Tarrade, Jean, *Le commerce colonial de la France à la fin de l'Ancien Régime; l'évolution du régime de l'Exclusif de 1763 à 1789.* 2 tomes. Paris: Presses Universitaires de France, 1972.

TePaske, John J. "The Fugitive Slave: International Rivalry and Spanish Slave Policy, 1687–1764." In *Eighteenth-Century Florida and Its Borderlands*, pp. 1–12. Edited by Samuel Proctor. Gainesville:

University of Florida Press, 1975.

Thésée, Françoise. *Négociants bordelais et colons de Saint-Domingue; "Liaisons d'habitations;" La maison Henry Romberg. Bapst et Cie, 1783–1793*. Paris: Société Française d'Outre-Mer, 1972.

Thompson, E. P. "Patrician Society, Plebeian Culture." *Journal of Social History* 7 (Summer 19/4): 382–405.

——. *The Making of the English Working Class*. New York: Pantheon, 1974.

Todd, Loreto. *Pidgins and Creoles*. London and Boston: Routledge and Kegan Paul, 1974.

Torre Revello, José. "Origen y aplicación del Código Negrero en la América española (1788–1794)." *Boletín del Instituto de Investigaciones Históricas* (Buenos Aires) 15 (julio–septiembre de 1932): 42–50.

Toth, Charles W., ed. *The American Revolution in the West Indies*. Port Washington, N.Y. and London: Kennikat Press, 1975.

Treudley, Mary. "The United States and Santo Domingo, 1789–1866." *Journal of Race Development* 7 (July 1916): 83–145.

——. "The United States and Santo Domingo, 1789–1866." *Journal of Race Development* 7 (October 1916): 220–74.

Trouillot, Hénock. "Les sans-travail, les pacotilleurs et les marchands à Saint-Domingue." *Revue de la société haïtienne d'histoire* 29 (1956): 47–66,

Vassière, Pierre de. *Saint-Domingue: la société et la vie créoles sous l'ancien régime (1629–1789)*. Paris: Librairie Académique, 1909.

Viles, Perry. "The Slaving Interest in the Atlantic Ports, 1763–1792." *French Historical Studies* 7 (Fall 1972): 529–43.

Villiers du Terrage, Marc de. *The Last Years of French Louisiana*. Translated by Hosea Phillips. Edited by Carl A. Brasseaux and Glenn R. Conrad. Lafayette, La.: Center for Louisiana Studies, University of Southwestern Louisiana, 1982.

Viotti da Costa, Emilia. "The Political Emancipation of Brazil." In *From Colony to Nation: Essays on the Independence of Brazil*, pp. 43–88. Edited by A. J. R. Russell-Wood. Baltimore: The Johns Hopkins University Press, 1975.

Walker, James W. St. G. *The Black Loyalists: The Search for a Promised Land in Nova Scotia and Sierra Leone 1783–1870*. London: Longman and Dalhousie University Press, 1976.

Walvin, James. *The Black Presence: A Documentary History of the Negro in England, 1555–1860.* London: Orbach and Chambers, 1971.

——. "The Public Campaign in England Against Slavery." In *The Abolition of the Atlantic Slave Trade*, pp. 63–79. Edited by David Eltis and James Walvin. Madison and London: University of Wisconsin Press, 1981.

Wells, Robert V. *The Population of the British Colonies in America before 1776: A Survey of Census Data.* Princeton: Princeton University Press, 1975,

Winship, George Parker. "French Newspapers in the United States from 1790 to 1800." *Papers of the Bibliographical Society of America* 14 (1920): 82–147.

Wood, Peter H. *Black Majority; Negroes in Colonial South Carolina from 1670 through the Stono Rebellion.* New York: Alfred A. Knopf, 1974.

——. "'Taking Care of Business' in Revolutionary South Carolina: Republicanism and the Slave Society." In *The Southern Experience in the American Revolution*, pp. 268–93. Edited by Jeffrey J. Crow and Larry E. Tise. Chapel Hill: University of North Carolina Press, 1978.

Woodson, Carter G. *The History of the Negro Church.* Washington: Associated Publishers, 1921.

Zilversmit, Arthur. *The First Emancipation: The Abolition of Slavery in the North.* Chicago and London: University of Chicago Press, 1967.

Theses and Dissertations

Fiehrer, Thomas Marc. "The Barón de Carondelet as Agent of Bourbon Reform: A Study of Spanish Colonial Administration in the Years of the French Revolution." Ph.D. dissertation, Tulane University, 1977.

Hunt, Alfred Nathaniel. "The Influence of Haiti on the Antebellum South." Ph.D. dissertation, University of Texas at Austin, 1975.

Terry, George D. "A Study of the Impact of the French Revolution and the Insurrections on Saint-Domingue upon South Carolina: 1790–1805." M.A. thesis, University of South Carolina, 1975.

Index

Jean-Louis, 115
Jemmy, 73
Jeremiah, Thomas, 79n5
Jérémie, 19, 47, 148
Jesús, Diego de, 102
"Jingling Johnies," 35
John (native of Grenada), 127
Johnson, William, 197
Juno, 195

K
Kelly, James, 42, 71
King, Tom, 38
King John, 127
Kingston
 "air of insolence" among blacks
  in, 98
 "Damnation-alley" section of, 36
 French refugees in, 145
 as hub of trade in British orbit,
  16
 insurrection as common
  knowledge in, 142
 Jamaica's free people of color as
  migrating to, 24, 25
 as one capital of Afro-America,
  15
 population of, 15
 runaway slave problem in, 20, 51
 workhouse in, 49, 58, 61, 146,
  149, 196
Kitty (seller of goods around St.
 George), 127

L
labor mobility, 2, 3
La Guaira, 105, 170, 171–2, 174,
 178
La Luzerne, 43, 110, 112
L'Ami de la Liberté. l'Enemi de la

*Licence (The Friend of Liberty, the
 Enemy of License)*, 135–6
"La Pierre" (French mulatto), 126
La Salle, A. N. de, 107–8, 111
Las Casas, Luis de, 159, 162, 163,
 166
Lees, Joseph, 35
Liele, Goerge, 58
Liston, Robert, 206
London Committee, 109
long boats, 66
Louisiana, as sharing several
 characteristics with island colonies
 of eastern Caribbean, 180–8
Louis XVI, 108, 112, 154
Lucea, 18, 154, 156

M
Mackandal, 28, 53
Maitland, Thomas, 202
Mansfield, Lord, 79, 82
Maracaibo, 174, 176, 204
Marco Antonio, 166
Marine Anti-Britannic Society, 140
maroons, 7, 8–9, 11, 12, 13–14, 15,
 18, 28, 53, 204
Martha Brae, 17–18
martial law, 143, 151
Martin, Richard, 65
Martinique, 31, 62, 78, 110, 112,
 114, 120, 130, 131, 132, 133, 134,
 136, 170
masterless blacks and browns, 38,
 145, 166, 196
masterless Caribbean, 7, 22, 76, 201
masterless characters, 74
masterless existence, 2, 59
masterless Frenchmen, 173
masterless French-speaking
 runaways, 128

P

Paine, John, 158, 165, 196
Paine, Tom, 98, 140n52, 155, 156, 157, 159
pamphlets, 90, 108, 156, 160, 164, 182, 209
"Pandora's Box," 34
pardo, 23, 24, 24n45
Parker, Hyde, 205, 207
Parker, Robert, 11
Parry, Governor, 70, 94
peace of 1783, 47, 80
pesos fuertes, 59
Petit-Goave, 52
petits blancs, 30, 31
Pettigrew, Ebenezer, 190
Phebe (seamstress), 27
Philip ("Spanish negro"), 153–4
Phillips, Joseph, 52
Phillips, Williams, 52
pidgin language, 42
Pierrot (ex-slave), 167–8, 195
Pinney, John, 83
pirates, 1, 2, 38, 72
Pitt, William, 84, 85, 87
plantain boats, 68, 69, 70, 73, 74
plantation dissidents, 20, 52
plantation monoculture, 1
planter consolidation, 4
Plymouth, 53
"Police Act" of 1789 (Grenada), 41
popular resistance, 4, 32, 37
Porlier, Antonio, 99–100
Port Antonio, 17, 73
Port-au-Prince, 19, 45, 47, 48, 52, 113, 114, 139, 140, 165, 196, 197. *See also* Port Républicain
Port Républicain, 207
Port Royal, 1, 15, 18, 22, 33, 38, 40, 69, 72, 123, 147, 149, 150, 151, 207

Pousson, Jean, 181–2
Poydras, Julien, 186
privateers, 46, 80, 174, 175, 176, 180, 198, 207
Prosser, Gabriel, 200
Puerto Principe, 17
Puerto Rico, 50, 60, 62, 63, 68, 99, 121, 122
Puncel, Josef Isidro, 34
"pure Republicanism," 140n52

Q

Quakers, 83, 84, 152

R

Raimond, Julien, 109
rebelliousness, in British Caribbean, 8n8
Reed, Samuel, 35
Regan, James, 32
regional trade, 16, 46, 49
religious asylum, 61, 63
renegados, 125
Rigaud, André, 57, 180
Rising Sun, 197
Rogers, James, 142
Royal Gazette, 143, 146, 149
rumors
    about liberation, 119
    influence of on politics, 130
    use of to advance hopes of black emancipation, 78–9, 81
runaway slaves, 1, 3, 4, 7, 8, 9–10, 11, 13, 14, 15, 20–2, 29, 30, 31, 33, 34, 38, 49, 52, 53, 58, 59, 60–7, 68, 70, 72, 73, 74, 75, 76, 78, 81, 89, 112, 115, 125, 126, 127, 128, 131, 132, 146, 148, 164, 166, 167, 169, 171, 177, 193, 209